CONVERSATIONS WITH SETH

Volume Two

CONVERSATIONS WITH SETH
Volume Two

SUSAN M. WATKINS

Illustrations by George Rhoads

Prentice-Hall, Inc., Englewood Cliffs, New Jersey

Conversations With Seth, Volume Two
by Susan M. Watkins

Copyright© 1981 by Susan M. Watkins

All previously unpublished Seth material copyright
© 1981 by Jane Roberts, used by permission.

"Buddha Slumped," "A Tudor Song," "The Green Man," "Caught Up
With," and untitled poem, copyright © 1981 by Dan Stimmerman, used
by permission.

"Repetition of Our Constant Creations," "Rule #1," and two untitled
poems, copyright © 1981 by Barrie Gellis, used by permission.

"Joyful Rain" and "The Inbetweens of Time," copyright© 1981 by Richie
Kendall, used by permission.

"Children of Always," "Somewhere," and "a man i don't know,"
copyright© 1981 by Jane Roberts, used by permission.

Printed in the United States of America
Prentice-Hall International, Inc., London
Prentice-Hall of Australia, Pty. Ltd., Sydney
Prentice-Hall of Canada, Ltd., Toronto
Prentice-Hall of India Private Ltd., New Delhi
Prentice-Hall of Japan, Inc., Tokyo
Prentice-Hall of Southeast Asia Pt. Ltd., Singapore
Whitehall Books Limited, Wellington, New Zealand
10 9 8 7 6 5 4 3 2

Library of Congress Cataloging in Publication Data
Watkins, Susan M
    Conversations with Seth.
    Includes index.
    1. Spirit writings. 2. Spiritualism. 3. Reincarna-
tion. I. Seth. II. Roberts, Jane. III Title.
BF1301.W226   133.9'3   80-17760

ISBN 0-13-172007-4 {V. 1} AACR1

ISBN 0-13-17208-5 {V. 2} {PBK.}

for Sean
who unknowing, Knows

CONTENTS

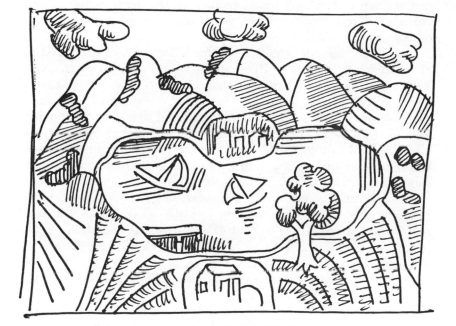

PROLOGUE

More than two years have passed since I began the preparation and work for *Conversations with Seth*. Within that time span, the same old questions that confronted and confounded class have emerged anew, different only in the context of their appearance. Hostages in Iran. Starvation in Cambodia. Wars and revolutions. Energy demands. Three-Mile Island. Pollution. Nuclear weapons. All of humankind's works wrought not wisely but well, it seems, upon the Earth.

And yet, the planet itself, with its natural progression of days and nights and seasons, maintains its harmony around us. Of all the worries and fears expressed in class, none of the worst expectations have panned out—and some of our best hopes still seem hopeful. And in reflecting on the events of the past two years—those events deemed "newsworthy" by the media as well as those daily events too "ordinary" to report—the ideas we encountered in Jane Roberts's ESP class become an even more natural product of our species than any of us, I think, realized at the time; perhaps more "natural" than the wars, crimes, and cruelties we continue to inflict on our fellow creatures.

For me, the roots of this book grew out of the Flood of 1972, when the Chemung River washed through my Elmira, New York, apartment and destroyed nearly every book, every manuscript, every scrap of paper I'd ever written a word on. I remember standing knee-deep in mud in my shattered living room, looking around at the mucky mess of papers and plants and clothes and furniture, and thinking, "Well—a clean sweep!" And strangely, there was something quite reassuring about this sweep (though hardly a clean one) of nature, and in the absolute simplicity of that moment in which I stood, utterly without possessions for the first time in my life; yet alive and well, breathing in the dank mud-stink that represented, after all, the basic stuff of my own physical body. I felt strong and secure: the triumph of survival, perhaps; or a glimpse of the elementary self-awareness that the animals so gracefully possess.

Nearly eight years later, I finished Volume 2 of *Conversations* a few weeks after the eruption of Mount Saint Helens. Driving along the Oregon coast, I saw the dust and ash that coated everything and clogged workings everywhere; I heard terrible stories of people and land lost beneath hot ash and rock. Yet I also saw the remains of logged forests and the pitted, raw, devastated mess left behind by the lumbering process. Angrily, I tried to believe that humankind's environmental disasters might also be part of nature, just as a volcano was, or a flooding river. But I still felt shame for my own kind. Why is it that we barely understand the consciousness we call our own; the body of events we experience even less?

The gouged fields, the ugly stumps, the giant plastic monument to Paul Bunyan—who had, in the story, chopped down whole stateful of trees, apparently without remorse—sped by the car windows, dust and ash swirling up like gritty snow. And then the redwoods loomed up, so incredible to the eye as to become un-real—not part of nature at all. Resting in the presence of those awe-some tree-beings, I began to think how man had indeed created God in his own image; and how desperately we need new gods now—how much we yearn for them, in fact. New gods, with a lower-case "g" and a sense of humor, who would be insulted by groveling and wor-ship; who would not disenfranchise the snake, who would cherish the world without guile. New gods who would *naturally* evoke one's powerful, secure, and forever untamable creaturehood—without shame for its contents and its impulses.

In retrospect, the writing of this book made clear to me how, all without conscious purpose, Jane's ESP class brought to-gether an alliance of people who were ready to make new gods, and who were willing to take off on a daring and irreverent journey through their individual identities to find where these new gods might reside. In doing so, we discovered that each one of us is mirac-ulously and quite naturally set up to take those journeys, with or without philosophies or groups—as Jane and Rob's extraordinary private experience demonstrates. And so I hope that you who read this book will dive within it, and yourselves, with exuberance and sensibility and silliness and desire, as we did. I think that wherever your journey takes you, there are new gods waiting there, with divine patience—and laughter.

Susan M. Watkins
Dundee, New York

"Whenever you think in such. . . Kindergarten terms
as 'ESP,' then you divorce your own natural abilities
from yourself, and those abilities seem dangerous—
they belong to the gods or to the demons. [But] your
cells have precognitive knowledge. They operate
precariously and beautifully in a balance of time, as
you understand it, and help steer your corporeal
course. . ."

Seth in Class,
June 18, 1974

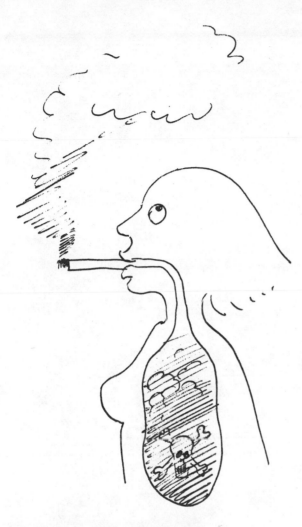

CHAPTER ELEVEN

Health, Healing and How We Walked
Through Each Others' Bones

THE GREEN MAN

When the Green Man
steps out of the woods,
and he beckons,
will you go?
All made of leaves,
his words are slow—
When he beckons,
will you go?

Whispering to branches
in the pale green Spring,
he makes the leaf buds grow
worshiping the sun
in the tall oak trees,
he watches the heron come and go.

(Oh, go, go—
go with the Green man—go!)

While he is fast
on his dark green feet,
and the wind blows freely
in his hair—
lay aside for winter time,
your problems and your cares

(and go, go—
go with the Green Man—go!)

Quick! Before the leaves turn brown,
and the Green Man falls to sleeping
in the ground—
Ripe red wintergreen berries
to be gleaned,
when you go with the Green Man, go.

(place your hands in his hands of green—
place your hands in his hands of green.)

When the Green Man
steps out of the woods,
and he beckons,
Will you go?

—Dan Stimmerman, 1974

She was a pale ghost of a girl, sitting passively on the floor, a bright green paisley scarf tied over her dark red hair; her face so flat, pasty white that I had to force myself not to stare at her in disbelief. She was a visitor in class that October night in 1973, and even though it was nearly 10 P.M., she hadn't said a word, although I'd noticed her talking at length to Jane during break.

Not that anyone could get a word in edgewise anyway, I grumbled to myself. Tonight, the Boys from New York were really at their peak—everybody talking at once, and nobody getting more than a sentence or two in before being interrupted: a boisterous, lively, exasperating bunch, these guys. Usually, the great good fun of it all was worth the hassle—moreover, they'd given class a new kind of stimulus; an untamed, galumphing glee with a healthy dash of irreverence besides. But tonight, the noise and constant jostling to speak were just irritating. Wouldn't anybody shut up long enough to *listen*? Sitting there, my chair jammed among other chairs in the crowded room, I found myself boiling up into a lovely resentment of the whole crew. What had happened to the good old days when class sat quietly around the coffee table and discussed—sometimes with emotion—the possibilities behind Seth's theories?

The pall of cigarette smoke burned my eyes; my nose felt stuffed with wool. I thought of the forty-mile drive that awaited me after class. I thought of leaping out the window for some cool, fresh air, and for home. I thought of standing up in the middle of the room and screaming. At that moment, such thoughts were all quite delicious.

"*Hold it!!*" Jane yelled, and a momentary quiet fell on the group for the first time that evening. Jane grinned at the tangled legs and arms and tee-shirted bodies bunched around the floor of the living room. "Now that," she said, "is golden silence for you."

Immediately, thirty-five voices started talking at once, all of them vying for Jane's attention.

"*HOLD IT!*" Jane yelled again, good-naturedly. Sometimes, back then, I just couldn't understand that part of her. Here I sat, fuming at all this impertinence, while Jane seemed to bask in the racket and chaos. In her way, Jane has complete trust in sheer, untamed romp. But, for me, exuberance was turning into a real pain in the neck—if spontaneity knew its own discipline, then where the hell was it tonight?

"Listen," Jane said, looking around at us, "I think our visitor here has something she wants to say." Jane smiled down at the pale ghost-girl, who by this time had been jiggled and joggled over by the sofa at Will Petrosky's feet.

"Well," the girl said in a voice only shades less pale than her skin, "I've been sitting here listening to you all talk about your dreams and everything, and it's great . . . but, see, I have Hodgkin's Disease."

Nobody said anything, for once, but I was too choked on frustrated resentments to register what the girl was talking about. I didn't even know what Hodgkin's Disease was[1] — so what? I thought. She cast her eyes down in a strange, maidenly gesture, fumbling nervously with the scarf's knot under her chin.

"I read the books," she continued, "and I wanted to come to class, and I've been listening to you, but — "

"Cora," Jane said gently, interrupting the girl. My god, I thought, Jane's catching it too. "Cora," Jane repeated.

Jane Roberts

The girl looked up, confused. "What?" she said. The room waited expectantly.

"Cora," Jane said again. "Your name is Cora. Tell them."

"Tell them?" the girl answered back.

"Tell them that your name is Cora," Jane said, and then she leaned forward toward the girl and repeated, slowly and carefully, "Tell-them-what-your-name-is."

"Oh, sure," the girl said. "Well, yes, my name is Cora, and I've been trying to get it into my head about what you guys are saying about making your own reality and being spontan—"

Twenty voices lurched into gear. "Yep, the old joy-and-vitality bit!" several people yukked. "*YOU!!* Be spontaneous—*now!!*" Richie yelled at Lauren. Cora smiled at the people sitting on the floor with her. She didn't seem perturbed in the least by all the noise.

"Wait a minute," Jane said, removing her glasses. "I think we have a Sumari song for you, Cora—something about the cells and molecules of your body having names. . . . " The room quieted down as Jane slipped into a delicate, lovely Sumari song that gradually built into a ringing crescendo of self-affirmation. The girl had never heard Sumari before, but her pale, angular face almost glowed with rapt attention. The song was punctuated throughout with pantomimed dancing motions as Jane swayed gracefully back and forth in her chair. At several points in the song, Sumari-Jane imitated Cora's own fumblings with her scarf, except that Sumari seemed to be encouraging her to remove it, or to at least be free of it in some way.

The song ended on a long, powerful note, and Jane came almost instantly out of trance. "Um—" she found her glasses and replaced them. "That was Sumari," she explained innocently.

"Oh, yes, it was beautiful," Cora said. "Was that Seth, or what was it? I really liked it."

Class immediately wound up again; several people jumped in with explanations tumbling all over. "Sumari's a family of consciousness," someone said; two or three others yelled a simultaneous explanation of "sounds that are about other levels of perception."

"I get the idea that it had something to do with telling you to acknowledge your own being in some way that you aren't doing," Jane said. "*HOLD IT!*" she shouted above the din of voices. "Let Cora tell her impression."

"I . . . " Cora hesitated, and incredibly, a chorus of voices interrupted her again. By this time, I was seething, ready to leave and slam the door behind me, when Will Petrosky suddenly caught the floor. "You don't have to cover up in here!" he shouted at the girl. "And so you don't need that scarf on either, like Sumari said!" And with that, he bounded forward, reached over, and in an exaggerated version of the Sumari gesture, yanked Cora's scarf from her head.

And with the scarf, horribly, came the red, red wig that Cora had been wearing to cover the poor, pale, utter baldness of her naked skull.

A silence more total than the tomb fell on the class, and Will cringed back on the sofa, his hand still locked in the grabbing gesture, a look of absolute horror on his face; the horror that was enveloping everyone, as it finally got through to us all what the girl had been talking about when she'd said "Hodgkin's Disease."

I was scandalized: this was the ultimate invasion of privacy. But I must admit that I was also wickedly triumphant. There! I thought nastily, that's what you guys get! That'll teach you! Now maybe you'll learn something about manners!

Cora was calmly readjusting her wig and scarf. "Well now, that's one of the things that happens when you're on the drugs they put you on for this," she said easily, as though this violent revelation were nothing to her. "Lately, I've been able to do without some of them, and I've been in a period of remission . . . I read the books, and I think it's helped me some."

Will Petrosky

Complete silence reigned supreme. Petrosky looked as though he wanted to disappear into the Chemung River. Jane looked around, waiting.

"What a lesson for those poor guys," Warren Atkinson recalls with affection. "Will's impulsive brashness brought feedback he did not expect! His face, his devastation, and the startled class are all etched in my memory. Suddenly we saw how near death she was and how she was hiding it while still trying to live."

"I think," Jane said quietly, "this is a good time to take a break."

Break, usually a circus of romping between the bathroom and the kitchen, was subdued, to say the least. Nobody had to yell that break was over, either. And after everyone slumped back in their places, Seth came through almost immediately.

"Now, I have a few words to say to some individuals, and first of all," he said, bending toward Cora, "I bid you my greetings, and I simply point out to you that you identified yourself here as a young lady with a disease. The first words you spoke identified yourself as a person with a disease. Your self-image is too involved in the disease that has a name that has been given it.

"Now hear me!" Seth boomed, his voice roaring out the autumn windows. "You have your own name—assert it in the joy of your being! And if you want to live in vitality and joy, then your name is more important than the name of any group of symptoms, for they have not the kind of reality that you have! And your glowing integrity identifies you here, so then accept the vitality of your being, and speak your own name over and over! For that name is the name given you in this space and in this time, and do not accept instead the name of a disease in which you lose, it seems, identity and strength. Do not quail before vocabulary! Your integrity and your beauty and your strength identify you here, and identify you for all time. Therefore, do not look wan! And forget thoughts of tragedy that are spelled out, and assert the vitality of your being!"

Cora was listening to Seth's words, huge as they were in that humbled room, with the same calm in which she had accepted everything else this evening. As for me, my heart was pounding hard with the strange shock of looking upon a person younger than I was, who was actually dying; someone who had been told that she had *this* much time left to be alive. How could she stand it? How could Seth's words make any difference now? It *was* humbling. And as I began to sort out my earlier feelings of rage, I realized that Will's impulsiveness had opened all our eyes—including Cora's—to an inescapable application of theory: her condition was either a result of her beliefs or else she was the victim of an indiscriminate insanity of impersonal cells. Facing her now, which could you accept?

"Now, if you decide to leave this world, that is your right, and go in joy and vitality," Seth was telling Cora. "But go because you know *you* decide to leave, and not as the victim of a disease that has been given a name. If you decide that you want to live, then live in your full glory and strength, *but make up your mind*, and do not allow yourself to be victimized.

Jane Roberts in trance, speaking as Seth

"If you want to die, then *why* do you want to die? Know the reasons, and go because you have made up your mind, and go with strength and vitality, making your own decisions— but not as a victim, and not in tragedy, and not wan!

"If you decide to live, then tell yourself you want to live and know the reasons, and your body will repair itself in joy and glory," Seth added. "You are *not* a victim!"

With that, those dark, penetrating eyes turned to Petrosky. "The energy in this room is always apparent," Seth continued. "And it is one of the reasons why Ruburt does not tell you to shut up more frequently, even though sometimes such thoughts abound!" I squirmed in my chair, blushing, but Seth went on with his usual dry composure.

"In this room, you have the energy that forms each of your worlds, and that reaches out with its great vitality to touch others. Therefore, as it surges through you, it is inexhaustible; and send it, therefore, to this girl, and let her use it as she wishes. Let her make her own decisions as each of you must make your own decisions. No god made victims—you make victims of yourselves by your beliefs.

"Now, let us see a smile and some apples in those cheeks," Seth said to Cora, reaching out to touch her under her chin. "I have died many times, but never as a victim, and each of you choose the time of your death and the time of your birth. As you trust in the ground of your being, then you will also share in the *joy* of your being and trust yourself—trust that what comes from you is good and adds to the universe. Trust in the integrity of your blood and the molecules. Trust that you are here for a reason."

When Jane came out of trance, she pointed out to Cora that she'd been identifying so strongly with her condition that she hadn't even given her *name* as an introduction, but had instead given the name of a disease. Cora admitted that she did this at other gatherings; in parties, in casual conversation; even in letters. She said she now realized how she'd actually been depending on the symptoms to give her a feeling of importance and strength: she, Cora, victimized by a disease, was bravely fighting it. Pending death, she acknowledged, had literally become her life's blood.

"I think our friend Will here did us a favor," Jane said, and perhaps that's what it was. We'd certainly never had a more direct confrontation with whether we *really* accepted that beliefs created our experience—or if we felt, underneath it all, that this was fascinating theory, but not "real."

For one thing, there is an abundance of "obvious" evidence that the physical body on its own is helpless; that good health is in fragile opposition to the powerful evil of disease; and that the body (like peace) requires constant vigilance against decay. And on the surface of historical evidence alone, it seems crazy not to accept the benefits of medical science—except that, looking at Cora, you had to wonder about the trade-offs of such benefits: diagnosis, treatment, and death, all medically tied up and labeled in a neat package, from which Cora was not likely to escape.

However, the traps inherent in placing all of your trust in an outside authority—medical, spiritual, or otherwise—are not so evident once you've accepted its terms. For Cora, only a newer drug would give her remission. For others, the method might be trickier. Recently I received a letter from a man in California who had attended class once in the early 70's: He'd "heard," he said, that Jane was dying of cancer and asked if I could verify this for him: "I have found it depressing, since if we make our own reality, and Jane has been learning this from the horse's mouth, so to speak, there doesn't seem to be much hope for the rest of us."

I assured him that Jane and Rob are both healthy and happily engrossed in their work,[2] but that relying on Jane's physical perfection as "proof" that you create your own reality was missing the point. "Jane isn't setting herself up as a new goddess on earth," I wrote. "The point is that each of us makes his or her own experience, and if there's something there we don't like, we should examine that reality—not Jane's."

Well, I patted me on the back for that one—yep, catch the guru weed early in the bud, I congratulated myself, forgetting for the moment how many times I'd terrified myself by reading cancer statistics and symptom lists. But not long afterward, I learned that a friend in Elmira had died at age thirty-five, after contending for several years with leukemia—and with a set of beliefs that at first glance might appear to be concentrating on health.

Bill had been a strict vegetarian and organic food advocate for nearly ten years. He balanced his diet carefully, never consumed sugar or alcohol, and maintained an active daily life. On second glance, however, you could see that food in Bill's world was dangerous business—one slip could cause havoc—and filled with potential spiritual disaster. (Eggs, for example, were "too high on the Karmic scale" to eat—a status apparently not granted to the plant kingdom.) Bill and his wife were members of a meditative sect whose guru-type leader demanded denial of the flesh in all of its expressions for the sake of "purity"—they weren't supposed to have sex, for one thing ("We try very hard not to," Bill told me once, sighing for the weakness of his failures). At Bill's request, Jane attempted on several occasions to give him some insight into the origins of his condition: for openers, it was obvious that in Bill's eyes, the body was a literal cancer upon the spirit. And Bill died believing it—because this was what his "master" had decreed.

On the other hand, medical doctors are routinely granted the authority and power over our physical salvation: in Cora's case, she'd been pronounced dead several years before the fact—and she died in the spring of 1975, believing in the diagnosis. And in all of these systems, the self is granted very little authority or power of decision at all.[3]

Certainly, little attention has been given to the ferreting-out of beliefs behind medical conditions; or to why consciousness developed in the particular way it did, forgetting the inner origin of outer events. And so, in this regard, Seth didn't automatically "heal" anyone—nor did he, Jane, or class ever posture that they could. It was placed upon the individual to do this, as Seth's remarks to Cora implied. Health and the body's condition were treated as the result of beliefs; as a reflection of the inner order of logic, springing into physical expression. Help was offered through belief "therapy," Alpha energy, or other methods; but with superb psychological respect, Seth (and Jane) gave people credit for being able to solve their own problems—for being *themselves* healers of physical difficulties, no matter what external system (including medical science) was used.

"What [do] you think about the odor of the Earth and of people—do they smell?" Seth once asked a visitor who'd wondered aloud why he had pains in his nose. "In derogatory terms . . . what portion of you believes that they smell, so that you want to close out half of the odor of that reality? That is all I will say, and it has a scented message!"

The literal and symbolic harmony of circumstance as expressed by Seth was hilariously evident in that kind of remark, as it was when I asked, for example, why a rash had covered my son's body in less than an hour one afternoon, turning him into a mottled, scarlet mess, and then disappearing as suddenly. "For a hint . . . while I will not give you an answer, consider your thoughts about invading armies," Seth replied. "Not of warring nations, now, but of invading armies; and the word *armies* is important, in relationship to what you think of as reincarnational memories [*as related in Chapter 8, Volume 1*]. And that is all I will say, and, as you know, it is far too much!"

Invading armies? Oh, hell, I thought at the time, why isn't it ever anything simple like, "Your son is allergic to the dog," or, "Stop making him eat spinach"? No, it's something about figuring out what "invading armies" means! But once I'd deciphered this hint (insane mass forces attacking the innocent . . . hmmm . . . a process that actually took me several months), I achieved insight into my beliefs about children and disease that were far more "practical" than, say, a ghostly prescription for calamine lotion. The rash never did come back, and I also learned something about the power of suggestion and the interrelationship of beliefs within families.

"I feel that everyone causes their own illnesses for a subconscious purpose and can heal themselves if it 'suits' them at the time." says "Nurse Nadine" Renard. "However—my kids were sick all the time [at the time of class]! We ran to the doctor, but still they were sick, and consequently, I was preoccupied with them most of the time." Because her family considered her the one who supposedly understood both medical and psychic matters, Nadine felt responsible for keeping everyone healthy. One night in class, Nadine explained her family's struggles with a never-ending series of colds, sore throats, and flu. Despite her good intentions, she complained, this situation had left her with a terrible fear of germs—which seemed sensible in the face of things.

"You can get rid of all the illness," Seth advised her, "when you realize that you have the habit of creating and drawing it to you out of fear. What you fear most, you draw to yourself. Instead, you must concentrate upon what you *want*—and do not be so worried! You can learn to concentrate upon what you want and draw that to yourself, and to completely restructure the health habits of your family.

"Now, there are some past-life reasons for your attitudes and also for the profession in which you find yourself, but first of all, you must understand that you can draw health and vitality and strength to yourself and that you are not at the mercy of any poor crawling germ or little flying monsters that come to attack you or your family! I tell you this because there is a connection in your mind; illness becomes to you the symbol of something far different and far more profound. It becomes in your mind the symbol of evil, which attacks you—in your mind—in small ways as small illnesses.

"It often occurs that those who have strong healing abilities focus upon illness and sickness and are obsessed with it," Seth told Nadine. "It is in the same way that many ministers, given to thoughts of good and God, are obsessed with the idea of the devil and evil. You also have strong healing abilities, but these, so far in your personal life, have been latent because of your fear and your obsession in the other direction.

"If you will forgive me, it is somewhat like a woman with very earthy desires . . . who rigorously refuses to use them and dwells instead on thoughts of their evil, holding them back simply because she realizes they are so strong. In your own personal life, you are afraid to use your abilities of healing. You do not understand them, and yet in your profession you are free to use them and you have seen them work."

In a later class, Seth addressed himself again to Nadine, who had asked how she could change her thinking to keep her family well "instead of making them sick."

"Realize that you do not form events alone," Seth told her. "You are involved in a cooperative venture. You are not alone responsible for an event, therefore, in that usually others participate in its creation and for their own reasons.

"Now, the question cannot be answered simply in one evening," Seth continued, "but each living consciousness has its own defense system and its own vitality, and you should trust your own—[but] you do not trust your own. You *do* cooperate together to form the physical reality that you know, telepathically, through ways and means that are unknown to you. You weave these webs of psychic reality that then coalesce into physical reality. You do not weave them alone, necessarily—you weave them together. Your thoughts intertwine with the thoughts of others. You are responsible for your own thoughts.

"You need to learn the power of thought and emotion, but this should fill you with the joy of creativity. Once you realize that your thoughts form reality, then you are no longer slave to events . . . Why do you water your fears like weeds, and insure that they do grow?

"Now, you are involved in healing—it is your interest. But you must also find the peace of your existence in the area where ill health does not exist, or you will indeed be dragged down into that aura. And therefore must you also begin to concentrate instead, and purposely, upon the healthy organisms and not imagine unhealthy ones. You would do better if you completely changed your focus away from health—because to you, health also means poor health!

"You are at a level where opposites seem to exist, though they do not exist." Seth added to the class in general. "Therefore, when you think of good, you think of evil, and when you think of health, you think of disease. It would be better if, when you find such thoughts occurring to you, you change your focus completely into another area. Find the area yourself, but have an area that engages your interest; a place of energy and peace—in which you realize that in your dealings with health and disease, you are dealing with shadows."

Nadine does say that her healing abilities, when freed from the anxieties of her immediate family, have apparently helped others. "I used suggestion on some neighbors with problems," she says. "I just tell 'em good stuff, and the doctors say they're amazed at how well they get over whatever it is."

One neighbor, Nadine says, had been through two cataract operations and was home only a few days when one eye swelled up, became inflamed, and began oozing. "It looked something awful, but I would say things like, 'You look great, Frances,' or something, or sometimes I would gently lay my hands across her face and tell her that her eye was well now." Nadine says. "Once in the middle of all this, Frances called me up and asked me if I could get her some strong pain pills. Well, I only had some Tylenol and that wouldn't give her much relief—I mean, her eye was swollen so you could see the stitches—so I told her the stuff was codeine and boy did she get relief! And her doctor later told me that her eyes healed much better than he'd thought they would.

"Another friend of mine died of cancer some time ago," Nadine says. "I used to go and just hold her hands and give her suggestions of peace, and then she would say she felt better and fall asleep, which was a lot to give her then, I guess."

Sending energy to friends, seeing the beliefs behind another's ills, or listening to Seth's astute psychological assessments were all easy enough to go along with when applied to someone else. But when the illness is your own (or a loved one's) and you're supposed to look around *your* discomfort or fear or immediate physical effects to grasp the root, then that little bit of necessary distance all too often evaporates.

One Monday afternoon in the summer of 1971, within the space of a few hours, a painful, throbbing abscess blossomed in my left ear. At the time, it just seemed like one more thing attached to a string of lousy days. George Rhoads and his wife, visiting my parents and me on their way out West, had delivered long and somewhat merciless health-food lectures on whatever I fed my son; during Sean's checkup that week, the pediatrician had stated flatly that because Sean ate several eggs a week, "He'll drop dead of a heart attack at age fifty and it'll be *your fault*." My divorce from Ned had been final for a month, and I was trying to force myself back into the job market. To complete the picture, the abscess had filled my skull with pain; moreover, I was filled with the fear that I'd end up as I had five years before, when a doctor had sloppily lanced an abscess in the same ear, landing me in the hospital with a meningitis infection.

As I drove to class that Tuesday evening, determined to divert my attention from the earache, every detail of that hospital stay loomed up like nightmare lights: the shots of toothpaste-thick penicillin; the stiff, hot pain in my neck and head; the whirlpool smog of Demerol numbness.

In Jane's apartment, I slumped on the rug by the bathroom door and tried to concentrate on the people around me. Juanita, a recent newcomer, sat on the sofa, a wide, fixed grin on her somewhat care-worn face. Someone spoke to her and she didn't respond. The person sitting beside her on the sofa nudged her. "Hey, John said 'hello'!"

"What?" Juanita said loudly. "I'm sorry, I can't hear you." So—two of us here tonight have ear problems, I mused.

Class started with a discussion of our current experiments with Alpha.* Juanita strained to hear, literally stretching herself half off the sofa. My ear pinged and stabbed; my neck ached. Visions of those hourly shots danced in my head. Given these kinds of troubles, the condition of the entire world looked pretty hopeless to me.

Jane was watching me with an expression of sympathy, combined with something like scientific alertness, a communication we often shared. I grinned at her and shook my head. On the phone that afternoon. I'd told her about the earache and about the earlier experience in 1966, when I'd lost a semester of college and ended a long-standing relationship with a man I'd known since high school. Now five years later, I was newly divorced and facing the need to stand on my own with a young child and no job. In both circumstances, I'd developed the same physical malady. More than coincidence was involved, I knew, but somehow I just plain didn't want to think about it.

"It has something to do with the woman thing," Jane said, out of the blue, still watching me with that rapt alertness.

"It what?" I said. Class noise and chatter screened us into privacy. "The woman thing?"

"Right," Jane said. She waited. I didn't get it

---

* See Appendix 1, Volume 1, of *Conversations*.

"Hey, people," Jane called out to the class, "let's do some Alpha on Sue and Juanita." She told them briefly what our troubles were; Juanita, it seemed, had a chronic blockage of the ear canal that was gradually destroying her hearing.

But before class could begin the Alpha attempt, Jane's glasses were whipped off and Seth's old familiar "Now!" cut through all conversation.

"Both of you have this thing about noise!" Seth said—very noisily!—addressing Juanita and me. "I will speak to you both at once, therefore.

"The world is not as tumultuous as you imagine it to be, and you can hold your own within it," Seth told Juanita. "You can indeed! You can clear your own ears and your own vision [*Juanita also wore very thick glasses*]. All you have to do is realize that within yourself is the ability to face each day as you come to it. You are trying too hard now. You must relax and trust the inner self to see and to hear. The early troubles that helped trigger your difficulty you can now, as an adult, overcome by realizing that the inner self has its own knowledge and its own ways. You *can* hear me, and I will see to it that you do!

"Imagine yourself answering questions that have been put to you," Seth continued to Juanita. "You need not imagine that you are hearing clearly. If you imagine that you are answering the questions, then it will be taken for granted that you have heard them correctly. When you try too hard to hear or see, you hear and see less. Relax and let this be taken care of for you. Now, you do not trust the inner self to do these things, and you must learn to accept the inner ancient wisdom that is your own!"

I gulped. Me next! I flinched; my ear crackled jabs of pain. Seth turned to me, regarding me with what I hoped was only my interpretation of severity.

"And *you* must learn that love is noisy and can be a bother and can get in the way, and you must learn not to deny the validity of your own feelings in those directions where you are now tending to hide them from yourself," Seth said evenly. "Much later I will see that Ruburt tells you about it specifically. For now I will simply tell you that the earlier incident of which you spoke to Ruburt [*the earache I'd had in 1966*] *is* connected with this one. You know that it is, but you must think of what noise represents to you and what it is that you do not want to hear and why at this particular time you do not want to hear it."

Illogically, I remembered George Rhoads registering stern disapproval of Sean's Cheerios breakfast, while Sean had banged happily away on his high-chair tray with a spoon—a noise unequaled for sheer nerve-destroying capability. "Then it's related to Sean?" I asked.

"It is connected with Sean, but it also has deeper roots," Seth answered. "I will see that Ruburt tells it to you. This also has to do, however, with the fear of exterior stimuli and the basic fear that it will sweep you away, destroy your person. You have, now, security, and these thoughts and feelings are highly erroneous. You have physical senses for a reason. They are to help you, not to hinder you. When you refuse to use them for whatever reason, you lessen your own abilities and your own effectiveness, as you know; but this is not ever thrust upon you. This is a method of learning and as you learn, you will solve the problem." Seth then addressed the group, pointing out that "each of you in your own way hides certain groupings of feelings from yourselves, so I am not necessarily directing this specifically at our friend here [me], except that she has the trouble with the ear this evening."

Finished, Seth disappeared through his dimensional doorway. I told Jane what he'd said.

"Sure," she replied, puffing on the Pall Mall that had been smoldering patiently in the ashtray, "it's a thing you have about noise, and . . ." Her eyes widened. "Food!"

Food??

"Sure, food—I get it," Jane continued, speaking rapidly. "Food represents not only nourishment to you, but it's a symbol of your femaleness, see? The whole thing started this time when George and his wife and the doctor all got after you about how you're feeding Sean. You didn't want to hear it! Besides," she added, a bit conspiratorily, "*sex* and noise are connected in your mind—loud noise and violence and sex; you feel they could utterly shatter you, so you also eat too much to build up a protection against all of it, so you'll be left alone, from the whole works."

It made gorgeous sense, but . . . I jotted down some notes, and evaded it. Class did a *MU* chant for Juanita and me,[4] and that night I went home feeling a little better. But the next morning, my ear was just as painful, and eventually I did end up in the hospital again, although this time no widespread infection ensued. I didn't face up to the beliefs Seth and Jane's remarks implied for many years, however,—and in the meantime, I would deal with their manifestation in numerous forms, and not just as physical symptoms.

Class did try some healing experiments on itself, of course, as part of our exploration of the unplumbed properties of imagination and consciousness. In the early 1970's, Alpha biofeedback was emerging as an accepted method of regulating some of the "involuntary" body functions. Alpha, one of the officially labeled brain waves, involves a relaxed awareness, and is not as intense a state as the "normal" Beta level—or even a light trance. After a few inconclusive jousts with an Alpha lamp (which was supposed to change colors to the individual eye as you switched brain wave levels), Jane suggested that we forget the lamp and try to see what subjective information might be available in the Alpha state.

To go into Alpha, we'd usually imagine ourselves doing something inspiring, like painting or writing, or listening to music; then we'd "hold" that feeling. Some would instead imagine a tiny self standing off to one side of our heads (Jane's favorite method), or we'd concentrate on one of Rob's many paintings. At first, it was hard not to go *deeper* than Alpha; but after a few weeks of practice, most of us were pretty adept at switching to that state whenever something unusual happened in class: it was like seeing an event from many sides at once, since you never lost track of "normal" perceptions—you added to them.

The experiment that class did most often in Alpha—aside from altered-perception "journeys"—was to direct our collective awareness toward a volunteer and mentally rummage through his or her body, accepting any images we perceived in a lighthearted spirit of playful investigation. Anything that we "saw" that didn't "look right" was to be fixed up according to our own mental imagery. Class members would spend four or five minutes at this and then come out of Alpha and write down what we'd perceived. The volunteer would then describe his reactions during the experiment, and we'd read our "findings." (To supplement it all, we'd send the person energy during the week.) It was great fun to see if members' Alpha perceptions would coincide—and they often did.

After tripping imaginatively through Joel Hess, for instance, several of us made independent notes on seeing "inflamed muscles" around his spine and lower back. "I imagined that I had a miniature fire hose in my hands," Sally Benson said. "I made it spray some kind of soothing salve all over the place, and I made it work, too!"

Joel admitted that he'd strained his back that week, although for years it had ached chronically anyway. "I'd tell you all that it feels better tonight than it has in a long time," Joel said humorously, "but you'd probably all put it down as suggestion." Similarly, after trying out Alpha on another student, several members reported that they'd seen Jeanette's stomach as "a forest of animals, prowling around and hunting one another." Some of us imagined tiny versions of ourselves chasing the predators out; others tried petting the animals and creating a miniature *Peaceable Kingdom* out of Jeanette's insides. Jeanette later said that for several weeks she'd been nervous and "tied up in knots," and that her stomach was often upset.

One class visitor swung into this Alpha experiment with great revealing gusto. "I imagined myself going in your left lung," the woman told Jane enthusiastically, "and I found myself in a great big coal bin. It was really filthy dirty in there—yukk! So I started washing the walls with this giant squeegee and I opened the windows to let all the poison smoke out . . ."

'Uh—wait a minute," Jane said mildly. "Before you get too carried away with those suggestions, maybe you ought to examine your beliefs about my smoking."

"Beliefs?" the woman wailed. "What do beliefs have to do with it? I mean, everybody knows smoking is bad for you, and you of all people should know that it's bad, since you're . . ." the woman hesitated.

"Yes?" Jane baited. "I'm what?"

"Uh, well," the woman confessed, "you're speaking for *Seth*, after all, and involved in your spiritual work, and smoking is so *un*spiritual, and doesn't Seth tell you to stop it?"

Jane sighed. "Actually, he'd love it if I took up cigars," she said. "But to hell with that! Besides, I have great lungs!" And Jane bellowed a huge, drawn-out "*MUUUUUU!*" to prove it.

Class didn't interpret its Alpha healing experiments in such a literal sense, but neither did we see them as being strictly symbolic or "imaginary," in usual terms. Also, Alpha exercises were not used as a replacement, necessarily, for medical advice. They *were* used as a means to uncover the inner reasons for physical events (in this case, physical symptoms).

"I learned to *believe* in health," Arnold Pearson simply states, referring to his happy retirement years after class had ended. Mary Strand, a nurse, says that she taught her children to believe in health also, "and in their power to heal themselves. We've managed to avoid medication and doctors for several years, [although] old gods and beliefs still threaten me in times of trial." I'm sure the old gods threaten anyone who starts to bridge the gap between the selfhood that's been taught to us through centuries of human experience and the kind of selfhood as revealed, if only partly, in Jane's class. To understand private and mass reality as creations of the self is a radical departure, and few, if any, social frameworks exist that allow a balanced expedition into the worlds of circumstance.

NOTES FOR CHAPTER ELEVEN

1. According to a 1953 edition of *Stedman's Shorter Medical Dictionary*, Follett Publishing Co., New York, N.Y., Hodgkin's Disease is a "malignant inflammatory enlargement of the lymph nodes, accompanied by enlargement of the spleen and often of the liver and kidneys, affecting the blood vessels."

2. Jane *is* working out some physical problems, which involve stiffness in some of her joints. She's been unraveling the beliefs behind these symptoms for several years; mention is made of some of these beliefs in *Psychic Politics*, in Vols. 1 and 2 of *The "Unknown" Reality*, and in *The God of Jane: A Psychic Manifesto* (1981). But the "rumor" mentioned in the man's letter is just one of many about Jane that apparently circulate among people she and Rob have never met. It's come back to her in one way or another that she's dead or dying, an alcoholic, confined to a mental institution, or living in a house surrounded by a ten-foot electrified fence and a pack of guard dogs! "The only one that really got me *mad*," Jane says, "is when I heard the rumor that I'd repudiated Seth and become a Born-Again Christian!!"

3. Places now exist, however, where the self is granted its rightful power of choice and creativity in health matters. Carl Simonton, M.D., whose medical center in Fort Worth, Texas, treats cancer patients with belief therapy, positive-image training, and other Sethian techniques for helping people "think their way to survival." Those interested can contact Dr. Simonton by writing to J. P. Tarcher, 9110 Sunset Blvd., Los Angeles, CA 90069, for a copy of his book, *Getting Well Again*, or by ordering the book in any bookstore. You can also call the Simonton treatment center in Fort Worth.

Another recent book along these lines is *Anatomy of an Illness As Perceived by the Patient*, by former *Saturday Review* publisher Norman Cousins (Norton, 1979), in which Cousins refuses to play the role of a medical "victim."

4. The "Mu" chant, like its sister "Om," are both word-sounds used by meditative sects and groups for a number of reasons, one of them being to utilize sound and energy to maintain light trance states. Class used "Mu" to send energy, or sometimes just for fun—but whenever we held a "Mu" contest to see who could keep this word going the longest, Jane always won!

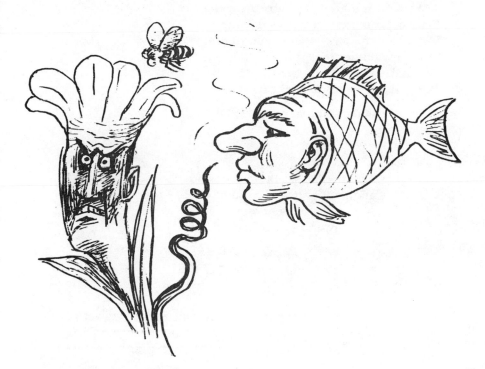

CHAPTER TWELVE

The War of the Idiot Flowers: In
Which Dream Fish, Spontaneity, and
the Draft Are Kicked Around

Consorting with the forms of the dead,
these spirits take you by the hand
and walk you from your bed.
—Where may we be headed?—
The world is a ghost to your dreaming,
Your dreams seem as ghosts to your world.
We take our worlds and we mix them;
into one another they spill.
We make a real hand ghostly—
We make a ghost's hands real.

—*Dan Stimmerman, 1979*

The pacifist sat upon the road
and gently stroked a quiet toad.
A stranger came intent to hit
but slipped upon a load of shit.

—*Barrie Gellis, 1974*

"The gods did not conceive the universe
in sorrow; this earth did not come from
a tear. You have formed your own tears."

—*Seth in class,*
March 1972

Outside those bay windows, the late 60's and early 70's marched on, the world boiling over, it seemed, in violence and social revolution. Riots ripped through the inner cities. Self-proclaimed prophets blew up buildings in the name of peace. The war in Vietnam raged on and on. Peaceful solutions were condemned by some as too slow a path to justice; scorned by others as naive. How could you put down your guns in a world full of weapons?

The Vietnam war and all its subsidiary questions of violence, aggression, patriotism, and dissent reached its tentacles down into Jane's class in those years as the men—and women—faced the very real possibility of personal involvement. Events around us often served to square us off on matters of philosophy: Was violence ever justified? If a ghetto riot drew attention to deplorable conditions and therefore initiated changes, then wasn't such an outbreak justified? What about the war—what *about* the ideal of peace? When did loyalty turn into fanaticism?

"The ends do not justify the means," Seth told us many times. "In fact in those terms, the ends *are* the means." No violence was ever justified, Seth said—not ever. "There is never any justification for violence . . . never any justification for threats. The means create the end. And if the means are violent, the ends are violent." Yet, what do you do if somebody shoots first? . . .

During those years, while Ned and I were married, he struggled for months with the lengthy, complicated procedures required for the CO (Conscientious Objector) draft status—to no avail. Ned appealed his personal objections to military service before the district draft board in Buffalo. No dice: no CO. Now he would have to wait for the inevitable change in his college-student deferment. In the meantime, his moods leaped from deep despair to precarious exuberance as he dabbled intermittently with painting and tried to concentrate on his job in a local tree nursery.

The first class in December, 1970, fell on a cold, howling winter's night. Jane's living room was toasty warm, though, the radiators banged happily away in the big old-fashioned rooms, especially in the gargantuan tile bathroom. Class had standard jokes about that bathroom—the huge oval sink on its pedestal, the shower stall with its nine needle-nozzles; the toilet that would keep gurgling after a couple of flushes and often required the plumbing expertise of a class member to halt . . . but nothing seemed to reach Ned, not even this homey comraderie. He sat on the floor, in a corner, smoking cigarettes, wrapped in a cocoon of misery and anger.

In class for the first time that night were Joel and Alison Hess. At the time, Joel was involved in anti-war organizations at Cornell and was also preaching in a small rural church near his home. He seemed to be a very serious man, and during break he volunteered some very serious statements about good and evil—particularly evil, and how its characteristics ruled the world.

"The only hope we have is for good people to discipline their innate tendency to do bad things," Joel stated in summary.

"Oh—bullshit," I answered, cautiously. Immediately, Joel and I got into a furious argument, interrupted (much to the relief of the rest of the class) after several heated exchanges by Seth's booming voice.

"Now, the spontaneous self, the inner self left alone, is a good thing," Seth began, staring pointedly at Joel, "and we will not go into a definition of the word *good!* Left alone, the inner self keeps your body functioning and your eyesight keen; it keeps your balance perfect; it keeps you alive. It gives you a sense of joy and vitality and it fills you with a joy of All-That-Is, which, as most of you know, is my term for the word God!"

Boy! I thought, that guy's really getting it—and the first time he's in class, too! Hah! Much to my secret disappointment, however, I noticed that Joel wasn't too perturbed about it. I glanced at Ned. He seemed lost in another world.

"Left alone, then," Seth was saying, "you are a perfect creature—and you feel a oneness with nature. And when you walk down the street, you feel a unity between your fingertips and the leaftops and between your feet and the pavement beneath it. It is only when you meddle with the spontaneous self that difficulties arise—and these difficulties you may, if you prefer, call evil."

Joel nodded, thoughtfully.

"Evil arises, and we will not go into a definition of the word *evil,* when—and precisely when—you do not realize that the inner self is the source of joy, vitality, and creativity!" Seth went on. "At that point, indeed, when doubts enter in, then you mistrust yourself and the inner self that forms your physical image. Then when you do not accept the spontaneous self, you decide you will accept certain feelings and deny others. And those that you deny, that you do not regard as acceptable, these grow up within you until they achieve a strong charge; *and those repressed charges, individually and en masse, cause violence!*

"And if you want to equate the word *violence* with *evil,* then that is the origin of it; and it is mistrust of the spontaneous self—the inner self—that is within you all.

"Now, you see, we have visitors, and I am sounding severe," Seth said with humor, still staring at Joel. "I must therefore tell you that, since I am far older than any of you and far deader than most, you realize and sense the vitality that flows through this image [*Jane's*]; and sensing it, realize that this same energy is available to each of you! It is your heritage—the heritage of joy and spontaneity and creativity—therefore, use it! Recognize it in yourself and do not mistrust it."

"Well," Joel said as Seth withdrew, "I guess I agree that repressing your feelings leads to an explosive anger, but it seems to me that, recognizing this, the individual should strive to look for the goodness in himself and cultivate it a little bit—given the world situation and all . . . "

Abruptly, Seth was back, his own expansive expressions and gestures moving Jane's body in humorous incongruity to her ankle-length dress and dangling earrings. "We will see more of you!" Seth pronounced to Joel in a low, Peter Lorre-voice.

Joel raised his eyebrows, surprised.

"Now—listen to me," Seth continued in that grave, powerful tone. "You need not try so hard. If you trust the inner self, then you grow as a flower grows. The flower grows correctly, and it does not strive to grow, and it does not say to itself, 'I must grow two inches, so help me, by tomorrow night at twilight!' A flower *is*, and it allows itself to grow, and it is sure of its Is-ness and of the spirit of All-That-Is within it.

"Now, goodness is as natural as a flower that grows. If a flower stopped when the sun was shining down upon it, however, and if it began to consider and said—'Wait! Should I grow to the left, or should I grow to the right? Is it good that the sun shines down on me, or is it too easy for me to grow in the light of the sun, and therefore should I attempt to grow instead in the darkness? Should I grow two inches to the right, or two inches to the left? I must strive to grow! I must develop an ego and an intellect, and I must try to reach that sun that is God and I must work hard because if I do not strive, I shall not achieve—and I must achieve!'

"But, beside our intellectual, conscientious flower is an idiot of a flower! And the idiot of a flower stands and feels the sun upon its face and opens up its leaves and says, 'This is the sun, and it is good within me; it is the spirit of growth, and I'll follow it and give it freedom; and I care not whether I grow to the right or to the left, for in perfect trust with the spirit within me, I know I shall grow correctly.'

"And so it grows, our idiot flower, and it grows from within. And it is perfect and it is strong, but beside it is our intellectual and spiritual flower. And *this* flower says, 'Again! Three o'clock in the afternoon, the shadows are coming and the shadows are evil, and this sun is fading, and the night is coming, and the night is evil; and I must consider how best I can confound these adversaries . . . and it is easy to fail and not use my abilities and not to grow!'

"And lo and behold, in the morning the sun rises, and what do we find? Our idiot flower in full bloom in the morning sun and our other flower with one leaf like this [*Seth drooped his hand over the chair arm*] and one leaf like this [*his other arm stuck up in the air*] and head down, still considering the nature of good and evil and not trusting the spirit of vitality which is within it; and therefore, not listening to the inner voice . . . but questioning at every point and at every hour: 'In which way shall I go? Shall I accept the sunlight or the rain? Or are these evil forces?' And telling itself over and over again that to grow is difficult and to die is easy. Telling itself over and over and over—in metaphysical terms, now—that to be good is difficult and to be evil is easy.

"And that is a deception!"

"The idiot flower," Joel asked skeptically, "that just

stands there naturally and accepts its due—does it have a responsibility to try to enlighten his brother flower which seems to be caught in confusion?"

"It does indeed," Seth replied, "and it does by its example, for the other flower should look and say, 'How is it that my brother flower grows so beautifully in the sunlight?'

"Now, understand that I am speaking simply for an analogy," Seth said, "and I am not telling any of you that the intellect is wrong, or that you should not use it. Like any teacher, I am simply choosing an example. But the existence of our idiot flower is, in itself, an example, for I will tell you—in the simplest terms that I can tell you—that you can trust the inner spontaneous self. It is, in your terms, a spirit of All-That-Is. It knows how to grow. It grew you from a fetus to an adult, and it did so without your striving, and without your stopping it at every moment to say, 'Are you growing right? Is my left toe growing correctly or is it growing in the wrong direction?' If you would have had your say, the body never would have been formed correctly: you would have taken that much time to make up your minds . . . "

"Even though we feel the sense of spontaneity," Joel pursued, "do we have the option to react in view of it?"

"You go along with it!" Seth answered. "Unless you are a child, you will not enter the Kingdom of Heaven! Unless you are joyful, unless you live in trust of spirit, you are not whole. A little child shall lead them because the spontaneity of spirit knows All-That-Is . . . All-That-Is is not dignified! All-That-Is is not 'adult'! All-That-Is is not pompous; All-That-Is *is*, and in Is-ness comes . . . creativity. You can allow your intellect full freedom when it follows the spontaneity of your being.

"You follow the spontaneous self as long as you are conscious, in whatever life, or whatever existence. *But to evolve spiritually, you must consciously join with it, joyously and with abandon.*

"Now, my friend," Seth grinned at Joel, "Ruburt is not given to quoting from the Christian Bible or, indeed, of using Christian examples, but I will say this to you: there is a quote having to do with the lilies of the field.* Now when you do not trust in the spontaneous self you are like lilies in the field—our flower again—who suddenly begin to worry that they will *not* be fed, nor clothed, nor sup-

---

*From Matthew 6:28,29: "Consider the lilies of the field, how they grow: they toil not, neither do they spin: And yet I say unto you, That even Solomon in all his glory was not arrayed like one of these." (King James version)

324 / The War of the Idiot Flowers

ported, nor sheltered; and that the nutriments from which they take their existence might be taken away from them. You are supposed to believe that you are supported and sustained . . . by God, in your terms; by a spirit of vitality, or All-That-Is. To the extent that you do not believe this, you cut yourself off.

"Now, that is my immediate answer to you this evening, my young man, but you can find your own answers . . . in your own spontaneous self and [in] listening to the voice of All-That-Is within you!"

Class had heard Seth's "idiot flower" analogy before, but this night seemed to fill it with new meaning, perhaps because of Joel's forceful input on good versus evil. Discussions continued until past midnight: analogies about the flowers were all very nice, but what about riots and wars? . . . Class joked and exchanged thoughts about the practical applications involved in being "idiot" flowers: did this mean to just go out and do any old damn thing you please and to hell with the consequences? Did "any old thing you please" automatically connote evil? Were "consequences" automatically bad ones?

The following week brought up another facet of the "consequences" of spontaneity. Joel reported to class that during his workday, he'd found an associate asleep at his desk in the middle of an important project. Joel confessed that he'd felt like kicking the sleeping man's butt, even though, rationally, he knew *that* wasn't the solution. How, Joel wondered, could you go about changing spontaneous feelings like that into "nonviolent" ones?

Seth came through with an opening succession of jokes and terrible puns, finally telling Joel not to deny the part of himself "that wanted to wring the other man's neck.

"You were so frightened of the thought that you immediately inhibited it!" Seth went on, humorously. "Now, let us consider that thought and *why* you were so terrified of it. You were terrified of it because you are terrified of the idea that evil is more powerful than good and that one stray violent thought of yours was more important and more powerful than the vitality of good . . . . Your muscles tensed, your adrenaline production increased, [and] you wanted to wring his neck and you stood there and said, 'God bless you, my fine young fellow, may you live a long and happy life.'

"Now, telepathically, our fine young fellow knows exactly what you are feeling at the time!" Seth roared. "*You* are the one who is out of contact with your feelings and emotions at that point, however; for at this point of your 'spiritual progression,' you only imagine that you wish him good will. . . . Originally, you were mad enough to kick him.

"You have some idea in your head that good is gentle and bad is violent and that no violence can be good, and this is because, in your mind, violence and destruction are the same thing. Now by this analogy, you see, the soft voice is the holy voice and the loud voice is the wicked voice and . . . a strong desire is the bad desire and a weak [desire] the good one, so that you become afraid of projecting ideas outward, or desires outward; for in the back of your mind you think that what is powerful is evil and what is weak is good and must be protected and coddled and prayed for and begged for.

"Instead, what I am telling you is that the universe is a good universe . . . your own nature is a good nature and you can trust it . . . Be aware of your own feelings [*to Joel, in reference to the sleeping worker*] . . . then, as far as is possible, communicate those feelings verbally in whatever way you choose. Use anger as a means of communication; often it will lead you to results that you do not think of and, in your terms, beneficial results."

During that week—and stemming, I believe, from Seth's words on spontaneity and the expression of anger—Ned had a vivid dream in which he found himself filled with an overpowering, directionless rage; as though he were literally exploding with hostility. In the dream, he was standing by a creek. Bending over, he saw a beautiful multicolored fish appear in the rippling waters. In a flash, Ned leaped into the creek and kicked the fish over and over and over until suddenly he was drained of all anger and hate. His dream self then wept with relief, and he woke up feeling refreshed and at ease with himself for the first time in weeks.

In class the next Tuesday, Ned described this fish dream with relish. "And I kicked the shit out of it!" he said, with vehemence. "Then, everything just—released, let go. It felt great! It was like—wow, like I realized that I could get rid of all the hassles inside . . . by just *doing* it . . . "

Joel had been listening to Ned's dream with a grave, disapproving look on his face. "One thing makes me uncomfortable about that," he said, interrupting Ned's dissertation, "if it's true that our thoughts form realities and our dreams go on without us, or if this was some helpless probable fish in a probable reality, then I just don't see how you could have kicked that poor fish. I mean, I don't think I would have wanted to kill the thing, because I would think you'd be responsible for life in all of its forms, wouldn't you? And here, you let loose on the fish and you kicked it and killed it, in violence."

You couldn't help but remember Joel's sleeping worker and his near-miss with Joel's boot. But Ned—a tenderhearted person, particularly when it comes to animals—stared at Joel as if it were himself, and not his dream fish, being kicked. You could see Ned's good cheer deflate like a child's broken balloon.

"But I—" Ned stammered. I thought he was going to cry.

"Now!" Seth's voice cut in. "I come to the defense of Ned and the poor fish and of Ned, the poor fish!"

Ned smiled at Seth, obviously relieved.

"Our Ned chose a fish, subconsciously, for many reasons," Seth began. "First of all, the fish was a part of himself that he materialized within the dream state. It represented, to him, something quite different than the Christian fish [necklace] you [Joel] wear about your neck. The dream served several purposes. It allowed him to release aggression in a much *less* violent manner than he would have in the past. It also, however, allowed him to see the picture of his own aggression as it existed on a subconscious level of his mind. The aggression that he feared was not so great and big and powerful and black and hairy and threatening as he thought! Instead, it was a part of himself and very small—fish-size, you see, and easy to squash and kick!

"In this case, the fish was not a probable fish in another reality; it was a portion . . . of his own energy. Now, it would have been far more beneficial had he [Ned] been able to use that energy, keep it as part of himself, and transform it into a more constructive nature. However, the dream taught him that the violence within himself was not big and threatening and did not need to be feared. He could use it as a symbol to see how small it was in comparison to the whole inner self and how easy, therefore, to rid himself of it . . .

"Each individual life, all life, has its own built-in mechanisms against danger . . . You can become so afraid of violence that you overemphasize its effect; and, if you will excuse me, in doing so you are taking on the guise of the devil. It is the same thing, you see, as projecting upon a hypothetical devil all kinds of powers of destruction. You can do the same thing without realizing it by projecting into the idea of violence all powers, and then it seems to you that life has no ability to protect itself and that any stray thought of violence or disaster will immediately zoom home.

"Your poor little innocent flower: when it rains and thunders and storms come, does our little flower look up and say,

'Here comes that devil lightning and thunder'? It does not think that the thunder and the lightning and the wind and the rain are out to get it!

"It realizes that the strength and vitality of life is as much in lightning and thunder and the storm as in the sunshine, and it has the sense to realize that it *needs* the rain, even though the rain that comes down may rip off a couple of its leaves. You have much more protection than you realize!"

"Well," Joel said, "we appear quite vulnerable, though. I was thinking of the fish again. When you say the idiot flower may lose a leaf or two, but still have a great deal of protection, I was wondering—well, Ned's fish was only an image, but suppose I had a probable fish in some probable reality? What kind of protection would that fish have had against my violent acts?"

Seth regarded Joel for a long moment, and his voice turned somber. "Now, in the first place," he said, "there are several things you must understand. Some of these things you can misinterpret, and so I go lightly in class with them . . . but basically, you do violence to no one. Basically, you cannot hurt anything, but as long as you think that you can, then you must dwell within that reality.

"No one could hurt your friend's fish, even if it were a live one, in your terms. In your frame of reference, no thing, in your terms, is hurt without giving acceptance to the hurt; without attracting it, and without bringing it to itself; for within your frame of reference, you form your own reality. Not only human beings form their reality, but all consciousness forms its reality.

"This does not mean I am saying, kill, kill, kill," Seth admonished. "You do not understand the holy and sacred nature of life or energy and that you cannot misuse it. You may think you misuse it, but you are not allowed to misuse it. You are not allowed to destroy. While you live with these things, you must deal with them and bear their consequences. If you kill and believe that you kill, you will bear those consequences at this level of your development, but to think that you can destroy a consciousness would make the gods laugh. *You cannot destroy one flower seed, much less a man!*"

Joel didn't seem too convinced; class—and Seth—would bring up this issue of violence, aggression, and their consequences many times in the ensuing years. In 1973, for instance, Seth responded vigorously to a remark by Lauren DelMarie that "thoughts can kick people."

"And they [*people*] would kick them merrily back if you kicked them more often, [and] you would not need bombs—any of you!

"If you spontaneously let out your hostility when you felt it, you would not have this super charge that you felt you must throw out or be damned! It would not be so heavy on your head—or any of your heads! The problem is not what you think of as your negative thoughts, but your fear of them.

"Once you begin suppressing, you suppress all emotions to some degree, and set up barriers because you are afraid of the reality of yourself. *If you cannot express anger, you cannot express love*—not only that, you get the two confused!

"*The only revolution is a revolution of thought. The only changes made in your history, and in your nation, will be made through the change of your thoughts, and not through violent action . . . You cannot change your world from without, for you form it from within.*"

But the class session on Ned's fish dream affected him dramatically; afterwards, he said, he felt more "at home" with himself and could see his pent-up hostilities against "the Establishment" for what they were; as though the nameless "Them" existed out there in the same way that his fish had: in the dream-creeks of his own fears.

Two months after his fish dream, Ned was called up for his Army induction physical—and flunked it flat. In that respect, at least, his terrors and conflicts were over—and it seems no coincidence that the battleground he created for himself with the draft authorities dissolved soon after his dream confrontation with fishy aggression. Of course, this wasn't the last time—by any means—that class drew its own battle lines on the issues of violence, peace, loyalty, and aggression.

In 1974, Jane assigned each of us to write an essay depicting how our beliefs affected other people and their reactions to us as individuals. A few short papers (dealing mostly with sexual attachments) were read and discussed, but it seemed like the same old hash. Was beauty a set of personal beliefs, or a set of cultural standards? Did the opposite sex really care if you were fat, if your beliefs were right? Or was that a cop-out? The whole debate was getting pretty boring.

Then Jed Martz stood up and brought the house down.

"I saw little justification for the U.S. involvement in Southeast Asia on any grounds—ethical, economic, practical, theoretical, or otherwise," Jed read from his belief paper.* "I rejected

---

*Which I've quoted here in edited form.

President Eisenhower's Domino Theory (an ill-defined term). Due to these reasons I was not interested in doing my duty and serving my country in the Armed Forces. I also was not morally outraged enough to split to Canada or go to jail in protest . . .

"In my last term at college, I was called for a pre-induction physical. This was it—the big moment I'd dreaded for so long. I had to determine a plan of action. I thought of opting for a medical deferment since I'd had a double hernia and a pinched nerve in my back, but I knew I was in good health and that method wouldn't work. Then I decided I would have to play freaked out. I had never acted before and I knew I would have to be convincing. It was my strong belief that I was going to get out of the draft without having to leave the country or go to jail.

"I was called down at the same time as a friend of mine, Willie the Fireman. I stayed up all night and at five in the morning I dressed. I was unshaven. I put on sunglasses and a pink shirt and my flamingo-pink overalls. I wore no shoes or socks and a torn coat. I applied to my clothing and my person generous helpings of the following: scotch, mud, ketchup, vinegar, rubbing alcohol, urine and various other unusual cosmetics. I took the train, and the other passengers took one look or sniff in my direction and departed for the other end of the car. The one item that had the most distinct odor was a skin-disease cream called Leucoderm. I wanted to buy out the company and patent the product as a guaranteed draft repellent . . . I got some weird stares from Willie's parents [when I got to his house]. 'Your friend's here, and he's wearing his pajamas and doesn't have any shoes,' they said.

"When we got to the draft-board waiting room, Willie said pay no attention when your name is called, but go up to the desk for our papers after everybody else. We got to a room full of desks, and I sat at three different ones . . . I took the pencils from all of the desks around so the others had no pencils, whereas I had nine of them . . . I filled out the medical history form with checks and crosses in all the negative and all the affirmative columns. I also scribbled on the page and wrote lefty so I couldn't see how they could make any sense out of it. I checked off such items as homosexual tendencies, bedwetting, recurrent hallucinations, drug abuse, etc. Then we were to take the forms to a room where we were to strip down to our underpants (which I conveniently hadn't worn) and we were given a little cellophane bag to carry our valuables in.

"I walked into the room, and as everyone else hung up their clothes and got in line, I stood there staring at the ceiling.

330 / The War of the Idiot Flowers

After a while, someone came over and asked me what I was doing and I handed him the papers with the cellophane bag on top and stared at him. He told me to take my clothes off and I just stared at him in a petrified way and shook my head, no. They took me to a medical doctor who tried to persuade me to see the psychiatrist; I protested that I was deathly afraid of them. Finally I relented . . . The psychiatrist had long hair and a bushy mustache so I thought that he might be hip to me, but I stared at the floor and didn't look at him once and spoke in an almost inaudible voice. He looked at what I'd checked off: homosexual tendencies. 'Have you ever had sex with a male at any time?' he asked. I said, 'No, I want to, but I'm afraid.' He asked, 'Have you ever had hallucinations?' I said 'I've seen frogs—and colors.' 'Do you take drugs?' 'Sometimes.' 'Are you on drugs now?' 'No.' He was taken aback by that. He had difficulty believing that this was my normal behavior! Had I ever seen a psychiatrist? 'No, I'm afraid they want to hurt me.' Finally he gave me my papers after filling out a report; I read this while walking through the halls: 'withdrawn, incoherent, wearing dark glasses, describes vivid hallucinations.'

"I received a 4-F: not qualified for any military duty, period. I related these incidents to illustrate in a personal way how one can have beliefs that prove themselves successful in practical physical terms.

"Incidentally, I feel patriotic about this because I felt any military career would turn out (for me) along these lines for real."

Most class members, of course, had punctuated Jed's unperturbed reading with screaming whoops of laughter. Jed finished his essay and looked around the room quietly, not a hint of expression on his round, innocently bespeckled face.

"Oh, Jed," Florence MacIntyre said finally, her face contorted with disapproval. "How could you have degraded yourself so? *How could you have acted like that?*"

"Oh, come on!" someone shot back, but Jed just shrugged his shoulders, unoffended. "I didn't feel degraded," he said. "I felt that the draft and the war and all of that was more of a degradation, and I wasn't willing to do *that*."

"I just don't see how any intelligent person like yourself could *lower* himself to something like that," Florence stated. "How—I mean—don't you have any feelings of dignity? Or any feelings of loyalty to your country at *all*?"

"Yes, I think I do," Jed said. "That's why I did it." Others in the room were leaping to Jed's defense; few remarks were made (aloud) in agreement with Florence. Up boiled a heated argument. Voices rose to fever pitch. Faces on all sides turned red with anger. Everybody was shouting at once. Jane, for the most part, listened in silence.

"I thought Jed's attitude was pretty stinking," Harold Wiles remembers (although he didn't say much at the time). "I think he expended a lot more effort staying out of the service than he would if he'd gone in! All I remember was an underlying feeling of disgust for his methods and attitude and what he went through."

Predictably, as voices in the room got louder and louder, Seth whipped off Jane's glasses and shut off the whole brouhaha with his commanding "*Now!*"

With great precision, he placed Jane's new granny-glasses on the coffee table. "This has been your night. And it is still your night," he began. "But when all the young men refuse to kill for the sake of peace, and when all the women forbid their men to kill for the sake of peace, and when you realize that no peace will come through killing, and that the end does not justify the means, and when you grow full and light with thoughts of peace, *then* there will be an end to war! But as long as any men go to war for the sake of peace, there will be war. And as long as any woman teaches her sons how to go to war because of love of peace, there will be war.

"You make your world. When you populate your world with ideas of peace, then peace will grow. When you think thoughts of aggression, you attract aggression and you draw it out from others in daily contact, and on the part of nations.

"When you do not understand yourselves, you project what you do not understand upon others—upon your friends and associates—and then you become afraid of what you do not understand, not understanding that it is your own fear. And you do the same thing as a nation with other nations. There is no way to ensure peace but for every man, *every man*, to lay down his arms."

"But his behavior was just crazy!" Florence interjected angrily.

"To do what he did does indeed appear crazy. Idiot behavior in the world that you know!" Seth replied. "But it is very sane behavior. Our friend here [*Jed*] was not able to leap the barrier. He could not make a creative achievement out of going to war. And

I will tell you—" Seth turned directly to Harold, who until then had said nothing—"were you his age, and in the same war, you would have done in your own way, the same thing! You would have turned it into a creative endeavor indeed, and you would have helped lead that generation!"

"I never did quite get what Seth meant by that remark," Harold said, seven years later.

"Well, if Jed were my son, I'd be completely ashamed of him," Florence said, adamantly. "I've brought my son up to understand what loyalty and dignity are, and to do his duty when necessary! To feel a sense of responsibility! I would never want him to act insane!"

Florence MacIntyre

"If sanity is to lead your sons to death, then I would rather be insane any day," Seth told her. "And this is not to pick out our Lady of Florence, either. For in your own ways, and in different circumstances, your reasoning is often the same [*as Florence's*]. And many of you still think that peace must be quiet and dignified, and excitement is to be found only where there is not peace . . . so think of the ways in which our Lady of Florence's thinking applies to your own, in other areas of your activity and thoughts.

"A point I want to make: it takes aggressive energy to send forth thoughts and feelings of peace. So your idea of aggression is completely wrong. Aggression is action, and the thoughts of peace radiated outward takes aggression and joy and vitality . . . the thrust for peace is as natural as the thrust of a flower to grow up from the ground. Now, continue."

Jane came out of trance, and we started to repeat Seth's words to her—as best we could. "He said Jed was right when he acted crazy like that," one girl explained. "I guess he was telling us to be nonviolent."

Immediately, Seth reappeared. "Your very breath, in those terms, does a violence upon the air. A joyful violence!" Seth exchanged a round of smiles with Florence, who was quietly sipping wine, her face red and tense.

"You do not understand our Lady of Florence's position," Seth said, "and you use the same thinking yourselves in other areas, and it is this: supposing our fine American boys decide not to fight. But supposing our fine Russian or Chinese boys do not come to the same decision. So you are leaving yourselves open—so you must meet any threat, or be weak! So"—Seth gestured at Florence again—"I understand your position."

"You read my mind, Seth," Florence said. "I was just thinking, I hope Seth tells the enemy to put down their arms too."

"Now—" Seth answered quietly, gravely, "the 'enemy' does not need a Seth any more than you do to tell them to lay down their arms. They need their own inner selves. *And if one side lays down its arms, the other side will realize there is no need for arms.*

"You cannot understand this now, and yet I tell you that your preoccupation with arms, as a country, is received by others, and your own thoughts are materialized and you create wars in your minds that then must be fought with your flesh and your blood. And no drop of blood flows . . . that does not first flow in your mind, and in all of your minds!

"And there is no other way to have peace but to believe in peace. As I speak here, others also speak in other countries, as they have in other times. And you have not listened! And in not listening, you continue to create the reality that you have. And, in creating that reality in the world that you know, and in time as you understand it, you return again and again—sons who have been slain on the battleground are born as women, who then bring up their fine sons to repeat once again the old history.

"So it shall be done to you as you do. And, as you think, so is your world. The reality that you have is a replica of your thoughts. If you do not like the world, you must change your thoughts, and no exterior manipulation will change the face of your experience one iota if you do not change your dreams and your thoughts!

"You create the mountains. You create your bodies. You create the seasons and the continents and the rivers. You create—" Seth glanced down at Renée Levine and Stewie Gould—"Renée's smile, and the hand upon which Stewie's head rests. And the war and the pests, *all of the pests,* that seem to haunt mankind—war, and poverty—you create those.

"It is your world. Then change it—now!"

While class was trying to fill Jane in on Seth's comments, the main doorway downstairs banged open and we could hear footsteps coming up from the hall. To our surprise, Dan MacIntyre, Florence's son, walked in the door and sat down next to his mother. Dan hadn't been to class in a long time, and it was getting close to 11 o'clock besides. As Dan listened to explanations of what had been said, he started to fidget nervously. Finally, he and his mother regarded one another, rather shyly.

"What's going on—what did you tell them?" Dan asked good-naturedly.

"Well, Florence—tell him," Jane said.

Florence cleared her throat. "I was just telling them how I've taught you to have a sense of responsibility and loyalty to your country, that's all," she said.

"*What!?* Dan burst out, aghast. "You mean, about this crazy war?? *Are you serious?* Forget it! I'd *never* go—no way!!"

"*Dan-iel!*" Florence shouted in dismay, but instantly, Jane's glasses were waving in the air from a Sethian hand. "Let that be a lesson to you, in line with what I said earlier!" he said to her.

"I would still want him to have his dignity," Florence replied, her voice shaking.

"Of what kind?" Seth asked.

Florence looked down at her hands and didn't answer.

"A flower has dignity!" Seth continued, gently. "*You* have dignity! He [*Daniel*] has dignity! He has dignity no matter what he does, and he [*Jed*] had dignity when he pretended he was an idiot!"

Seth sat back in the chair and rocked back and forth, eyes closed, for several minutes before continuing. "As long as you believe in aggression and in force, in this country, you elect persons who believe in aggression and in force and who react to it, and so do the people in all the other nations," he said. "Unfortunately, you equate aggression with strength, so you are afraid to elect a peaceful man. And all the other countries feel the same, so they are afraid to put into power, by whatever means, peaceful men. So your world situation is the result of your individual beliefs, en masse.

"Now, when individually you believe in peace, and when you no longer believe that good is weak and evil is powerful, then on countrywide bases, you will put people into power who believe in the active nature of peace. And, again, there is no other answer.

"I am, basically, as you are, independent of flesh. But in your terms, and in your terms alone, you have issue—physical issue, that must deal with the time and the place that you have created. And as long as you believe that you must fight for peace, you will lose your issue.

"In greater terms, you know quite well that you cannot annihilate a consciousness. And all of those who die in war know well that they will die in war ahead of time. But still, in physical terms, all of that must be worked out, for the very point of physical existence is that you realize that your thoughts become matter while you are here, and matter can be vulnerable. And so through direct experience you learn what happens when you let thoughts and feelings of aggression have full play. I have said this in my book [*The Nature of Personal Reality*].

"An artist may create a warscape, and you can look at it, and it may be a masterpiece. But you are multidimensional creators! And when you create a warscape, then brushstrokes suffer, for *you are* the brushstrokes. And the guns are real, and the wounds are real. But it is an excellent representation—an excellent multidimensional creative endeavor!

"If you do not like the landscape, then you change the brushstrokes. You wipe out the oil. You make a new painting.

"And now, I bid you a fond good night—blessings and all!"

As class was leaving Jane's living room, Florence walked over to Jed and told him, "It's not that I don't like you, because I do like you. It's just that I don't understand how you could have done all that."

"It's okay," Jed said; his expression hadn't changed from its mild complaisance throughout the evening. "I don't mind. But I don't really understand your objections either, I guess."

I'm not sure that Florence, Jed, Harold, Daniel, or any of us really understood the full implications of Seth's remarks that night, but the point of it was drilled into us again in one of Jane's final classes—an "un-class," really, held on a Saturday night in July of 1975. It was then that Seth suggested that we start telling ourselves that we lived in a "safe universe."

A safe universe? In this age of the Bomb, was there really, in practical terms, any such thing?

"Now—each of you, to some degree or another here, believe that the universe is not safe, and therefore you must set up your defenses against it," Seth said that summer evening. "Now, the one-line, official consciousness with which you are familiar, says: 'The world is not safe. I cannot trust it. Nor can I trust the conditions of experience, or the conditions of my own existence; nor can I trust myself. I can look at a squirrel and rejoice, but I cannot look at myself and rejoice, for lo, I am filled with iniquity, and I am, to some extent, evil, and I must hide myself. I am not only evil, as myself, but I come from a tainted and flawed race, and my father and my mother are tainted before me, and I send these tragic flaws before me into the future; and therefore I must need protect myself, and I must set up my defense in whatever way I can, to protect myself in a universe that I cannot trust, and to protect myself from a self that is evil and flawed.'

"You have an entire civilization and world set up about those beliefs I have just given you: that the universe is not safe; that you must defend yourselves from enemies that come from without, and worst of all, from enemies that are within. And so indeed do you feel uneasy, and set up your barriers, and run as fast as you can, in whatever way given you, from those enemies *that are the result of a one-line official kind of consciousness.*

"*As long as you believe that you dwell in a universe that is a threat, you must defend yourself against it. As long as you believe that the self is flawed, and that your race is damned and evil, you must also defend yourself against yourself, and how can you then trust the voice of the psyche?*

"And, when I say to you, 'Be spontaneous,' how dare you take that step, when to be spontaneous would obviously give rise to all the lust, and all the passion, and all the murder, and all the hatred, to you quite obviously inherent in the human heart? And so you say, 'I will try to be spontaneous, but how can I? I believe that *I* am good, but how can I be good when I come from a race that is evil?'

"You try to say, 'The universe is safe,' and then you watch the news on television, or you read your newspaper, and you say, 'What lie is this? How can the universe be safe when I read about wholesale murder, and war, and trickery, and greed? How can I be myself, for if I am myself, will I not unleash unto the world only more of the horror that I see about me; for surely human nature cannot change, and human nature is evil. Look what evil it has already worked upon the planet in which I have my existence; then tell me, Seth, be spontaneous. What do you ask of me, and how can I therefore in this context stand upon the authority of my own psyche and say, "I insist that i am good"?'

"The official line of consciousness forms a world about it, and you perceive and experience that world, and it will always show you the results of the beliefs that are inherent in the official line of consciousness. While you devote yourself to that official line of consciousness, the world will always appear the same: evil, disastrous, bound only for damnation—whether through nuclear destruction, or the greater judgment of a fundamental god.

"The one-line stage of consciousness was necessary for reasons that Ruburt has given [in *Psychic Politics* and *Adventures in Consciousness*]. But that stage contained within it its own impetus. It set up challenges that could not be solved at that stage of consciousness, and that would automatically lead you into other strands of awareness. Only then can those contradictions make sense. Only then can you say, individually—and listen, now—'*I live in a safe universe.*'

"You need not say, 'The universe is safe,' for at your present level that will only enrage you! You say, instead, 'I live in a safe universe,' and so you shall. And those defenses that you set up against threats will crumble, for they will not be needed. But you *are* safe, and you are innocent, and you can become aware of that innocence.

"When you . . . leave the official one-line kind of consciousness as your criteria for reality, you will take it with you as one picture, or as one view; perhaps as a landscape that you have seen somewhere—a beautiful one that you love! But it will not be the entire picture. You must step out of that picture, while loving it and holding it tenderly in your hands."

CHAPTER THIRTEEN

Love Thine Ego As Thy Self—
Drugs, Religion, and Other Wages of Sin

BUDDHA SLUMPED

Buddha slumped,
Like an oak tree that is lightning struck,
his straight back
crumbled and snapped.
Buddha's face on my balloon
burst in just an afternoon.
Fruited Buddha
dropped one by one from off the bunch
and rolled beneath the couch to
lie with the dust.
My Buddha used to drive a truck.
He used to sell vacuum cleaners.
My Buddha loved children and dogs
but cats would just confuse him.
In sacred books
and photographs,
he wouldn't recognize himself.
Buddha slumped and
cracked the imitation bronzes.
I would die of laughter when
my roly-poly Buddha slumped.

—Dan Stimmerman, 1969

"I have said to you before, using—if you will forgive
me—your terms, that you are the black sheep of the
universe, because you no longer blame gods nor devils
nor circumstances for those effects in your life that you
do not like; nor bow down to gods, devils, or
circumstances in praise for those good conditions that
you have yourselves created. That therefore, you will
become conscious co-creators with an All-That-Is that
has little to do with the puny concepts in which God
has been entrapped for centuries, as far as your
religion and myths are concerned. For those myths
have also entrapped you who believed in them."

*—Seth in class,
March 26, 1974*

The war between the ego and the intuitions often cast its refugees onto the shores of Jane's class. Particularly during belief assignment readings, people would confess to agonies of guilt in one context or the other. Many were afraid to even experience emotion, let alone express it; on the other hand, some (especially those studying Eastern religions) struggled to suppress the ego so that "pure" emotion could "just flow." In one of his first classes, for instance, Ira Willis described his journey to India—where he'd joined a religious sect that required a severe initiation whipping by the guru leader. Ira had submitted. Later, he'd returned from India and tried Rolfian therapy—in which his body was punched, pounded, and squeezed to "get out the bad vibrations," in Ira's words.

By the early 70's, the drug scene was touching everyone's life in some fashion, and was a frequent topic of class debate. Were you wrecking your body, or were you delving into the rings of magic? Were drugs a filthy evil, or were they no different from the wine we sipped on Tuesday nights? Did they allow you new freedoms from the confines of the ego, or did they turn you into an antisocial nitwit? And although neither Jane nor Rob use marijuana or other drugs nor permitted their use in class, it was the format of this ongoing debate that provided us all with our first real insight into the rise of the drug culture: through the LSD trip of Lauren DelMarie.

It was a cold Tuesday in January of 1973. Class had been discussing violence and aggression, fear and anger, guilt and retribution. "Violence begets violence. Peace begets peace," Seth had admonished earlier. Several hypothetical situations were spun around the notion that beliefs form reality, and that violence was never justified. "Yeah, but what would you do if a rapist came into your house and grabbed your wife?" Warren Atkinson demanded. "Offer him a cup of coffee!" someone giggled. "No, really—what would you do? Let him go ahead and rape your wife rather than commit violence?" Warren pursued, a little heatedly. "I mean, how can you not justify self-defense?" Warren's wife, Camille, grinned at us. "Oh, brother," she sighed.

Seth then entered the conversation with words we'd heard before. "Do not get so piqued!" he told Warren. "A gentle reminder: You form your own reality. If a rapist comes to your door, then your own fears and anger and aggression have brought him there. You have broadcast your feelings, and he has picked them up. Your wife wants to be raped, or you want her to be raped. There is a reason—there are no accidents."

Seth withdrew, and class started discussing accidents,

anger, and all the little violences committed daily against the self. It was then that Lauren launched into the description that he was to allude to many times in the following months: a year before, Lauren had bought a tab of LSD from a New York City street dealer—and in a half-hour, his universe had gone insane.

"I laid down on my bed, and let me tell you, the walls were holes in space," Lauren said. "I looked at the dresser, and it was alive. I knew it was going to come across the room and get me—and then it *was* coming across the room, with the drawers opening and shutting, opening and shutting, to chew me up . . ."

Lauren said the trip lasted for hours, or days, or weeks: he couldn't tell. Time bent awry, and space warped before his eyes. "I screamed and screamed—I couldn't stop," Lauren said. "I didn't even know I couldn't stop until a long, long time afterwards, when I could feel how raw my throat was . . . I knew I was dead, worse than dead. I looked in the mirror and saw the flesh melt off my face. I saw the bones show through and my skull laugh at me. I saw my skin hanging rotten. I tore off my clothes and threw myself against the walls. Then I saw it—the ceiling fan. It was going around and around and around up there over my head. I couldn't take my eyes off it—*I knew what it was going to do!!* It was going to come down and cut me to ribbons. *And it did!* It came right down and it started slicing right through me, hack! hack! hack!—and I was being sliced like a roll of bologna, in pieces, and I could *feel* it, *I could feel those blades slicing through my skin and muscle and my bones and my guts!* I could see my blood and guts flying all over the room and splashing on the floor and the bed and the walls, and I screamed like a maniac—and I started smashing the mirrors with a hammer because that was the only way to save myself . . ."

When Lauren started smashing the mirrors, his mother called the police; by the time they arrived, Lauren was standing (in one piece) in a sea of broken glass, wearing nothing but a motorcycle helmet and cowboy boots, yelling, "Fuck you and the atom bomb too! Fuck you and the atom bomb too!" and swinging the hammer in all directions.

"The police didn't dare go in and get me," Lauren told a hushed class. "Finally my mother went into the room and punched me in the stomach and got the hammer away from me and they dragged me out—but all the time, I knew that I was in slices; I was screaming in agony and they tried to grab me, but when they touched me, it was like they put their hands on all this raw and bloody flesh—*and I couldn't stand it! I couldn't stand it!*"

The police took Lauren naked and screaming to the hospital, where he was confined for two weeks. "I didn't come down and I didn't come down," Lauren said. "I couldn't get out of the trip, and even after it finally wore off, I'd turn my eyes just right or think about what I'd seen and there it would be again, all that pain and torture and fear . . .

"I wanted to kill myself," Lauren admitted, "and the only thing—the only thing, *the only thing!!*—that kept me from jumping through a window or tearing my own throat out was the thought that I'd kill myself, and be dead, *and still be tripping*—I couldn't stand that thought; that there was no escape; no escape anyplace . . ."

Lauren DelMarie

Lauren stopped, swallowing back tears, his fingers digging into his knees. Nobody said a word. Finally, Richie spoke up in a church whisper. "Some of us understand what it took for Lauren to talk about that . . ." he started, reverently.

"Oh—*bullshit!!*" Florence MacIntyre's voice banged down like a gavel. "I'm sorry, Lauren," she said. "I just can't work up any sympathy for you at all. You knew what you were doing when you took that drug! You didn't have to take it. You knew what could happen! I don't understand why you expect us to feel sorry for you. You risked destroying yourself when you knew better, and that's why LSD is illegal. If you wanted to expand your consciousness or whatever, there are certainly other ways to do it."

Hmmm, I thought, wasn't that just like Florence, irritatingly pragmatic? . . . yet, I had to agree with her: why take the stuff and then whine about being victimized by it? Not like an earache, surely, where the pain was innocently encountered in the soul's marketplace . . .

"*Now!*" Seth's powerful voice boomed out, and we all jumped. Lauren turned pale; his throat muscles convulsed and his eyes seemed to bulge right out of his head. Jesus, I thought—he's terrified! What could Seth possibly say about any of this that could scare Lauren in anticipation?

"I have a few words to say to our Lady of Florence, and for some others here who may not understand," Seth began. "First of all, he [*Lauren*] is embarked upon the same search that you are embarked upon, only his methods were different," Seth told Florence. "You must try, gently, to understand this."

Florence wrinkled her nose. "Well—" she said, without enthusiasm, "I suppose I could *try.*"

"Now, you can take on penance and retribution, if you want to," Seth continued. "You can believe that you are sinful and evil and that in order to be good you must cleanse yourself; and you can then accept a method that will cleanse you. You [*Florence*] chose a hard road on your own of guilt and retribution; of torture quite as severe as his. You chose your own framework. You [*to Lauren*] chose *your* own! Neither would be necessary, if you understood the basic beauty of yourselves—the basic integrity and joy of your being.

"But when you do not understand that, then you will look for it through whatever doors are available and open. You will search for it as a dried animal searches for water in a desert."

Seth made an elaborate sweeping gesture to the rest of the class. "And now, I will let you continue. You are all on a trip! You have been on a trip since your birth, in your terms!"

Seth withdrew, and Lauren gave Jane a frantic explanation of his words. "I still don't understand—I mean, it just blows my *mind*—why I did it," Lauren wailed.

"That's what I mean!" Florence said. "I don't understand why you did it either."

"Yeah, but—" Lauren shook his head. "I mean, if I create my own reality, and there's some big Super-Lauren out there who knows what's going on, then why in *hell* would that whole self, or entity, or whatever, want me to go through all of that? I mean, what did I get out of it? Terror and agony—I mean, I flashed back into that trip for months after . . . "

Lauren looked up at Jane and stopped, giggling nervously. For several minutes, Seth had been sitting there quietly, just listening.

"I think that Lauren solved all of his problems in a very short time," someone remarked.

"He has not solved his problems in *that* quick a time," Seth answered. "He has learned what they are—but, continue!"

Conversation went on for five or ten minutes—with Jane in trance, Seth listening quietly. Finally, he turned to Florence.

"He looked to his drugs as you [*Florence*] look to your religion," Seth said. "When you turned to religion in the beginning, it was something you trusted; and yet, it seemed to open knowledge of other realities. It intrigued you. Today, let an old man like me tell you—the ideas grow a different way, but the reasons are the old _ones."

Seth looked down at Lauren, sitting on the floor, tears filling his eyes. "He went where his friends went, as you went where *your* friends went," Seth said to Florence. "But, you are looking for the same thing. And you are accepting the same burden in order to do so. You [*Florence*] faced ideas of guilt in your own way, and he in another. You thought you were doing what you should do, and, in his own way, so did he.

"This has nothing to do, however, with the fact that there are dangers in both endeavors, or that with the use of drugs, you automatically change the physical being of which you are a part. *And you are lucky*, for you [*Lauren*] are making your knowledge a part of you. But there is a dilemma with the use of such drugs, for part of the being knows what other portions do not know.

"But when you believe that you must test yourself, and when you believe that there must be demons, and good and evil, and contests, then you form them in your reality. But you [*Florence*] made a contest as he [*Lauren*] did—and many of you in your own ways have done the same.

"Now, because Lauren looks so long-faced, give us a moment," Seth said, his jovial nature returning. "There will be, then, a Song of No Contests." Jane slipped into a gentle Sumari song to

Lauren and Florence; the sounds were soothing and loving toward both. As the song ended, Jane wavered for a moment, half-in and half-out of trance, and then Seth's facial expressions were there once more.

"What do you mean by your use of your word 'lucky' when you spoke to Lauren?" Florence immediately demanded.

"I was saying that usually, in your physical life, you have a balance of knowledge," Seth said to her. "You operate with a group of beliefs. These beliefs seem to be consistent, so you operate—in your own mind at least—with some consistency.

"Now," Seth roared to us all, "I am not telling everyone to go out and get grass [*marijuana*], but grass is a natural ingredient, and acid [*LSD*] is not, in your terms. There are those who go on fasts and will not touch liquor or cigarettes and will not look an egg in the face, and who will take acid without a qualm! [*But*] it has various effects—few that you understand—and it brings to the forefront knowledge of the self with which you are not, at this point, equipped to deal. The resultant lack of balance can be disastrous.

"You were lucky," Seth repeated to Lauren. "I use the term 'lucky' in that you were graced to assimilate that knowledge in a way that you could at least bear, if not understand. But when you have mental experiences of the same kind of nature that are *not* brought about [by LSD], then *you* draw out from the cells that knowledge, and you are prepared to face it. And, drawing out from your cells that knowledge, you bring about, on your own account, certain changes in those cells that are otherwise brought about without preparation. Only those changes occur, then, that are natural to your stage of development."

Florence never did approve of Lauren's methods ("I still think you should have been smarter than that," she repeated later)—and Lauren himself would wonder aloud again and again why he'd done it. "How bad can your beliefs get, putting yourself through something like that?" he'd ask. It was a good question, and one that underlined our reactions to most bad experiences.

Actually, this wasn't the first time we'd heard Seth remark on LSD's effects. About a month before, Ronald Runyon, an author of occult books, visited class from the West Coast, and told us that he'd been offered a guided LSD experience by the administrator of the only hospital in the country where LSD could be legally given at that time, under controlled circumstances. "He thought it would be an extremely valuable spiritual experience for me," Ron says. "At the time, all my acquaintances in the Human Potential Movement were extolling LSD as a panacea."

Ron, a former member of the British Society of Psychical Research, had up to then refused to take the drug, although he said that he was tempted to try the "controlled" trip. Ron was describing the lectures he'd given on the unconscious, psychic, and drug-related phenomena, when Seth came through with several minutes of "telling analysis of my conversation," as Ron remembers it. Among other things, Seth cautioned Ron to stop using terms to hide from his own subjective experience, noting that, "the terms you dislike—the terms that anyone dislikes—you automatically dispense with, and you say, 'they are terms.'

"The terms that appeal to you, however, are the trickiest, for you very seldom examine them, and they become invisible beliefs, and you use them as lenses through which you then perceive and color your experience . . . and this applies to all of you and your beliefs." Seth concluded his advice by saying that Ron didn't need to take the LSD trip. "You do not need to find the answers from acid or from me—even when I am being acidy!" Seth finished, punfully.

Ronald Runyon

"Subsequently, and consequently, I did not visit [the hospital] for the LSD, nor have I had a single drug to this very day, which now seems wise in view of what Seth says in *Personal Reality* on how LSD alters the cellular structure of the brain,"[1] Ron says, adding that he went on to experience vivid dreams and other revelationary material on his own.

Later, however, in March of 1973, a class visitor described his work with a psychiatrist who administered LSD to patients suffering from certain psychological disorders. (Interestingly, Lauren didn't come to class that week.)

Matthew, the doctor's assistant at this particular institute, described the LSD treatments to us as a method of "purging nightmares," and that each patient was briefed beforehand on what he might encounter on his guided trip. At this point, Seth was in the conversation, pointing at Matthew with Jane's glasses.

"Now, I have a remark here to add in line with beliefs," Seth began. "The trip will get rougher and rougher, particularly when you believe that it will. And if you tell a patient that he can expect to face the deep problems and nightmares of his being, so will he meet them in exaggerated forms; not only using LSD of course, but in many therapeutic situations."

"Well, Seth," Matthew said, "if you don't warn the people about the possible difficulties in advance, when they do occur—as I think they would anyway to some extent—it might be even more difficult to re-establish contact with them. That's why we say, 'If something bad happens, remember that I'm here with you.' "

"Make sure, however," Seth replied, "that you reinforce the idea of a friendly helper there, not the idea that you are going to expect to have such material automatically arise to be dealt with. You are taking for granted that there is only one way to get out of a bad place. It is also important that you realize the nature of the ego."

Here, Seth leaned back in the chair and started rocking, one foot on the blue rug and one foot on the top rung. "While you think that the ego is a stepchild of the self; while you think of it as an outsider who must be swept aside so that this great energy and knowledge can flow through you, then you set up a situation of opposites that need not apply, for the ego can learn far more than you give it credit for and it can assimilate that kind of experience when the individual realizes that it is able to. There is no need for what you *think* of as the ego to be swept aside and annihilated, even in a symbolic death.

"Now, there are two schools. One says that the intellect . . . must dissect and rip apart and that . . . the intellect is all and everything, and that all can be understood using the mind alone. You think of this school as the American school, as the Western school; and it is the school that most of you, to one degree or another, try so desperately to escape.

"On the other hand, there is a school that says the intellect and the ego are nothing; [that] we would be better off without them; [that] the truth is not known to the ego or to the intellect or to the mind; [that] it is all feeling—*and both schools are equally wrong!* And as long as you have systems dealing with one or the other, the poor physical person is caught in between. Either his mind is tended to, *or* his feelings."

Seth leaned forward and beamed gleefully at Matthew. "The latest—if you will excuse me—*caper,* is the Eastern one," Seth said loudly, with a sly emphasis. "And while it seems to you that I should go along with this because you think I am not physical and therefore must be so spiritual, the fact remains [that] it is just as distorted as what you all think of as the Western idea of the dominating intellect. Each of you knows that you are creatures of mind, consciousness, feeling!

"I have said often to many of you: if a man tells you that you are guilty, he is a false prophet; if he tells you to look to him and not to yourself, he is a false prophet; if he tells you to ignore your mind, turn aside from it and trust only your feelings, he is leading you astray. If he tells you to ignore one portion of your being for another, regardless of the portion, he is cutting you up into pieces and you are letting him do it and smiling and saying, 'Allah!' the whole time—or whatever the word might be.

"You are entire beings blessed with consciousness and feelings, with intellect, with thought—and meant to use them both and all, joyfully!"

The conversation between class and Seth continued for nearly half an hour, with Seth at one point returning to Matthew's therapy technique. "Now, for the record, and simply in my opinion, I would not recommend high doses of acid to anyone, regardless of the therapy involved," Seth told Matthew. "Small doses with supervision and a good guide, yes. But I also think that your good doctor will come to these conclusions on his own, and I think that what he is doing is teaching him many things, and others involved with the group; and because he believes in the framework in which he is operating, he has done some good. But he has done some good in *spite* of the method and because of the goodness and strength of his own personality, which could be just as effective without these methods."

Grabbing the chair and placing Jane's feet firmly on the rug, Seth pulled the rocker around to face Matthew squarely. "Now, people oftentimes live through personal disasters—natural disasters—in which they are pitted against nature as they know it—hurricanes, floods, earthquakes," Seth said to him. "There are no accidents, so on other levels they chose those circumstances, whether they realize it or not, with their conscious beliefs.

"Those who encounter the mental or psychic equivalent of a natural disaster, then, also know what they are doing and have their reasons. And so your patients accept acid for their own reasons, which may not be the reasons they tell you, or the reasons you think they have accepted! And so there is a give-and-take between the beliefs of the therapist who gives the acid and the beliefs of the patient who accepts it; and so there is a common meeting ground that you think you are aware of but have not as yet even encountered. I say, 'you,' meaning everyone involved.

"In a bad trip, you have—using, now, an analogy—a forced psychological disaster in which two agents are necessary in terms of the therapy in which you operate. One of course is the therapist, and the other is the patient. Now, no matter how nicely you speak to the patient and say, 'My dear friend, this is all for your own good—*take this medicine, it is hell and you will die!*'—he knows what you are offering him and he takes it from you—" Seth made an encompassing gesture to the rest of us—"as Ira took the beating from his guru, because he believes in guilt and he believes that this magic will remove it."

Before closing his evening's remarks, Seth then looked around at the Boys from New York. "Where is my friend the Pied Piper [*Lauren*] this evening?" Seth said. "Tell him that I asked."

"Yeah, he shouldda heard this!" one of the Boys replied. And so any other group might have considered it coincidence that a year later, when class was reading aloud from portions of Seth's *Personal Reality* manuscript, Lauren innocently volunteered for Chapter Ten—which turned out to deal with the effects of massive doses of LSD on the psyche. As he read, Lauren started to garble words, cough, and otherwise react so strongly to Seth's pointed dissertation that he finally had to pass the material to Will Petrosky—who read but a few sentences before Seth interrupted the narrative and turned his dark, intense eyes to Lauren:

"Now, instead of the next massive dose [of LSD], there are many people who think that the next occult school will do it; or the next religion; or the next political party; or the next new medicine; or the next wonder drug; or the next new improved god will all do it," Seth boomed. "Excedrin will do it if you believe in it! Acid will do it if you believe in it, but *you* will do it if you believe it!

"And each person . . . will for himself see what he has put up before himself instead of himself—what beliefs, what god, what product, what medicine man, what father, what mother—"

"What diet!" interjected Jean Strand.

"—what diet," Seth continued smoothly, "what vitamin; and each [of you] will follow [your] own journey . . . yet, the magic is you. And if you allow others to believe that magic is, instead, an idea or a pill or medal or a god, then you will spend your life searching for it. And if you find a medal, and you say, 'This is my magic, and it will protect me,' you are safe until you lose the medal or until you question it. And then you think, 'There is no magic, and it has fled from the world, and where is my protection?'

"Now, I want to make a note . . . what I said applies to massive doses of acid. The same chemical disorientation, however, can also occur with quite accepted medical drugs, where the messages are literally scrambled on a biological basis. The self tries to solve a particular problem. In so doing, it may end up with a physical difficulty. The physical difficulty is meant to remind the personality of the inner problem behind it. The difficulty will be cleared up when the inner problem is.

"If, instead, a drug is used to camouflage the ailment—or in your terms, to heal it, to cure it, to get rid of it—the inner self is in a quandary, for it knows the problem has not been solved though the symptoms have disappeared," Seth continued. "The drug used to cure the body *may*, in many instances, obscure the problem, and confuse the body and the mind. Therefore, another ailment must be taken on that will symbolically, and quite practically, materialize the problem in your reality. So the patient will get another ailment.

"If this ailment is also obscured or cured through the drug, whatever it may be, then the inner self is in a further quandary, and it will continue to try to materialize the problem so that it can be solved. The communication between the mental, psychic, and physical portions of the being can, in such instances, be obscured.

"Now, that does not always apply: for someone with a severe difficulty, believing in the effectiveness of your doctors, may be given a wonder drug and believe in it so [fully] that when the symptoms are completely annihilated, he . . . feels secure enough to solve the inner problem. In such a case, however, he has effectively *used* the drug to heal his mind and his body. The drug has not done it.

"This does not mean that you cannot take advantage of such drugs. It does mean that when you do, you are operating within a framework of reality that still, to some extent, divides you from the reality of your own being.

"Peyote, used naturally by [certain native groups], had an entirely different idea behind it than most of you have about [that] drug," Seth added. "It was not expected to annihilate an ego. It was used within a social framework in which it was perfectly natural. There was no paranoia connected with it.

"So the reason [why] you use a drug is highly important. When you use peyote, you expect it to give you, again, a new occult, forbidden knowledge. When the natives used it, they expected it to give them the wisdom of the leaves and the flowers; to activate within themselves the nature that they *know* they possess; and it was as natural as when you eat bacon and eggs. Therein lies the difference in your beliefs.

"And—you are safe," Seth said, turning again to Lauren. "Relax, all of you. You do yourselves no good by rehashing the past in a negative manner. It would do each of you good, in fact, as you go to sleep at night, to say to yourself, 'I am couched safely in the pool of my being; therefore, I am secure and I can move with the greatest ease and freedom in all the dimensions of my reality. The past has no power over me, for I will live secure in the power of the present and in the knowledge of my own power and reality.'

"We have spoken of massive doses of acid. There are some of you who have taken massive doses of religion. The results are the same. You have taken massive doses of guilt in whatever framework. There are people in this room who have had experiences quite as frightening as any of [*the New York Boys*]. They did not take a pill. There were no physical injections involved. Yet there was an assault upon the foundations of consciousness."

And during a class soon thereafter, following a discussion on beliefs about the body, Seth added: "You plunged into your creaturehood at your birth. It [*your creaturehood*] keeps your eyes open and your lips smiling as you look at me. It is the essence of your being. It keeps you alive. If you cannot trust that which keeps you alive, then what can you trust? It keeps your fingers wiggling. It is the unknowing knowing that rushes within you at every moment, and you can trust it above all things. It does not come from others. You will not find it in books, or concepts, or precepts! It comes from the intimate experience of your own being. When you are alone, *feel* it. Go along with it joyfully, and say, 'I give myself up to my life!' And with that attitude, all other things that you need to know will come to you."

Seth then sat back in the chair and closed Jane's eyes. "Another small point—to some of you," he said dryly. "This is not to Florence. This is not to Arnold. This is not to Harold. This is not to Helene—because they know better! But it is to some of you—and I will close my saintly eyes so that I give no naughty, great, ponderous, dangerous secrets away; far be it from me! But for some, it is always fun to have a crutch about.

"Now, the crutch may be grass, or it may be acid. But it says: 'I will only experience my creaturehood fully when I use this . . . and, the way I use this, I can turn on, and I can feel the reality that surrounds me—and that is my being! But . . . I cannot do this by myself. It is not a part of my being. I need this, or this, or this. Only then will the magic work.'

"A squirrel is filled with the reality and present joy of his being, and none of you today has seen a squirrel with a hypodermic needle up in a tree! He does not need it, either. He does not need peyote. He does not need acid. He does not need grass—because he is that which he is, and he is full of the joy of his being, and not afraid of it. And as he scampers through the branches, he is not afraid of falling down, either, because he trusts his own being. And he knows, without your fine intellect, that he has a place in this universe—that a place was made for him, and that his being is sacred and joyful and alive.

"Now, if religion separates you from the joy of your being, then it is detrimental. If you think you need a particular religion in order to justify your physical being, then it is detrimental. If you think you need grass to do the same, then that is detrimental. If you think you need to justify your existence through whatever means, for whatever reason, then you do not understand the joyful, playful, spirituality of yourself or of your being!"

In spite of the emphasis of the New York Boys' questions on drug use, however, none of them ever came to class in a "stoned" condition, and despite their nonconforming protests, almost all of their group held regular 9-to-5 jobs. But because of their experiences, class dealt with subjects that had been relatively untouched before their arrival. Oddly enough, the New York bunch also precipitated some of Seth's most intriguing comments on religion, religious hierarchies, and the divisions between intellect, intuitions, and emotion created within such systems.

Before they'd started attending Jane's class, most of the New York Boys had belonged to a Manhattan Gnostic study group run by a charismatic man named Arturo. Before students could enter his class, Arturo, like Ira's guru, demanded certain "initiation" rites: according to Rudy, Richie, Lauren, and the others, people had to be "ready"—but since Arturo's class goings-on were kept secret, exactly what one was supposed to get "ready" for was largely a mystery. After Arturo thought enough progress had been achieved, he directed his students to read specified books at specified stages, and warned participants not to share their gleaned knowledge with anyone. In Arturo's universe, a person was filled with evil, as were dreaming, revelation, and even thought itself—all part of a cosmic set-up fraught with danger, demons, and potential annihilation.

The New York Boys were strongly affected by Arturo ("he scared us shitless," as Richie put it)—and during their first classes in Elmira, they talked about him at length. The contrasts between Arturo and Jane especially fascinated them, as though such contrasts were an astounding thing to find. And while some members of more conventional religions might have wondered (and did, aloud, in class) how anyone could go along with Arturo's brand of nonsense, it was the New York group's preoccupation with him that, like the "druggie" stories, brought our ideas out of the hushed whisper of theory and into the realms of immediate daily experience. Despite all of Arturo's dramatic impact, his intent was not that much different from the Sunday-morning Jehovah who habitually rained hellfire, floods, and infanticide upon dissenters.

"Listen to your own being," Seth told Richie one night in 1972. "He who lords it over others makes himself into a false god. And he who drinks with gluttony the tribute of others needs it worse than drugs. And he who confuses you, confuses himself. And he who speaks in ambiguous terms [as Arturo did to his students] does so because he does not see clearly!

"The man who says—or the spirit who says—'I alone have the truth, and these are the maps, and this is the only way,' or implies it through his teaching or his actions, does not have the way. The man or the spirit who sets himself up above you, is not above you. There is no above or below, in those terms . . . Any man who tells you, 'The knowledge is secret, and I will not tell it to the violets, or the roses, or the clouds, or the sea gulls,' does not have the knowledge. It is as free as the air that flows . . . through your cosmic cheeks. It belongs to you. He who sets up closets of secrecy has nothing worth hiding.

"The joy of vitality should not be hidden, nor the ways to use it. The wind speaks the secrets constantly. Who is there, therefore, that would enclose them in a cult or a book? The secrets are all about you. Who is there, therefore, who would dare say, 'They are for a few—or would teach you that? The secrets sing through your blood. They are your heritage! Let no man call himself priest, or semi-god or demi-god. You are the gods! Do yourself just honor.

"In one of the Sumari songs, it is written: 'The gods do not come kneeling; therefore, do not kneel.'[2] The gods sing within your own being. My voice is no more than the truth that the leaves sing; or the sound that the flowers make as they grow—but you do not listen to the leaves—you do not listen to the flowers! So I speak in their behalf, and not my own. And in your behalf, for yourselves. So do not enclose yourselves in closets of personalities or beliefs, but open up the doors of your being. There [are] . . . no lords of the universe . . . *you* are the lords of the universe. Stride out bravely through your own mind and claim your kingdom."

Richie had been listening to all of this with studied intensity. "Does that mean that whatever knowledge I gain, I can impart to whatever friends I feel I should impart it to?" he asked.

"You can indeed!" Seth answered. "I have never put boundaries of secrecy about what *I* say! It is published!"

Yet the hold of Arturo's personality was strong on those who had known him—and seemed to call to his former students even more after he dropped dead on a Manhattan sidewalk not long after his former group had started commuting to Jane's class. The manner of Arturo's death frightened them more than ever (but again, the strange deaths of men claiming to be gods have affected a lot of people throughout history).

"There is no difference what guilt you are told [to believe in]," Seth told Lauren one night when discussion had turned again to Arturo and his teaching methods. "As long as *you* believe in guilt, then you are trapped by it. And whenever you meet anyone, king or pauper, who says that you are evil, then run fast! They may say you are evil because of Original Sin. They may say you are evil because you are possessed of a demon. They may say that you are evil because your stars are not right, or because you are human and filled with flesh!

"Whenever anyone tries to make you feel less than you are; when they make you believe in your deficiencies and enforce them, rather than encourage your strengths and your abilities; then run as fast as you can. When they encourage your dependence upon a group instead of your dependence upon the glory that is yourself, then run as fast as you can!"

In another class conversation, Joy Mankowitz, who had also studied gnosticism, remarked that Arturo believed in "a rigid structure of reality." To this, Seth bounded into the discussion: "It is *easy* to give you a rigid structure," he said to her. "Then someone says to you that reality is such-and-such a way, and all you have to do is follow the proper path!

New York "Boy"
Joy Mankowitz

"But I am far more insidious than your Arturo. For I make you find your own reality and your own way, and I take away all the comfortable and the uncomfortable rules and laws, and I return you to the authority of yourself. And how you all try to avoid that authority! And how you say, 'I hear nothing,' and 'I see nothing,' when that authority speaks!

"It is easier to listen to others who say you must crook your nose, and wiggle your thighs, or you must say, 'Allah!'; or you must wiggle your ear; [or] speak to the gods in the silence; you must breathe properly; you must eat in the way I tell you; you must sleep in the way I tell you; you must visit with the people [whom] I tell you you must visit with—*because you are all evil! And you are evil because you are alive!*

"Now, how can you beat that?

"If someone tells you that you are evil because you are alive, and you believe it, then you are indeed in a quandary. Now, I tell you [that] you are blessed because you are alive. And I am blessed because *I* am alive! And my vitality is your vitality, and it speaks through your gut as it speaks through your mind and your being, for it is your own. I merely let you taste the vitality of your own being so that you can draw sustenance and knowledge from yourselves. And that is your own joy, and your own right to be, and your own vitality, that is as secret as a trumpet—that is as dignified as a squirrel: It is the magic of your own being—the knowing that you know—the *is-ness* of yourselves!"

Seth withdrew. "What was this?" Jane asked, lighting a cigarette. Listening to the explanation, Jane pursed her lips a little in exasperation. She was only too aware of how people tended to set up new gods: new drugs, new religions—new spirits.

"Well," Richie was saying of Arturo, "I suppose that if you believed yourself to be evil as long as you're alive, then there's only one way out of that, which is to die—and Arturo did exactly that, didn't he? But in the meantime, he filled us with all of these unanswerable questions about the—"

Seth re-appeared so suddenly that his first few words disappeared in the frantic tape-recorder scramble. ". . . whenever you sacrifice yourselves, or make yourselves unhappy, miserable, ill, and filled with questions that you cannot answer, [it is] because you do not *want* answers, to put yourselves in . . . positions that are impossible," he told Richie and the others. "All of this because you have been taught that you are guilty because you are alive!

"Whether you get this idea from religion or science, the results are the same. And so my message is, simply, *you are blessed because you are*. You can be joyful because you *are*. You have a *reason* here because you *are* here.

"Whenever anyone tells you that authority resides outside of yourself, do not believe him. When anyone tells you, though the world tells you, that your joy resides outside of you, do not believe them or the world. Your salvation does not depend upon another. You have never lost your soul. You *are* your souls. You are your souls in flesh.

"Your bodies are your souls in flesh. Do them honor. Whoever tells you that the body is soiled, do not listen to him. You can trust your bodies as you can trust your soul. In your reality, the body is the garment that the soul wears.

"Now," Seth said, loudly, a wry grin on Jane's face, "I will have to tell you some jokes or return the class to Ruburt to get some decent laughs and giggles out of you!" The New York group, most of them sitting glumly on the floor, didn't—for once—react. "You look as if you have been in a church!" Seth concluded humorously.

More than a year later, Seth added to this body of material on gods, the ego, and physical reality as he commented on a class discussion on man-animal relationships and ancient Greek myths. "The source of your reality, as you understand it, lies within your psyche," Seth began. "Gods—as you understand them, in your terms, at your present state of development, and using your terms—represent the level of your consciousness. Your psyche is a mirror of the gods.

"Until you understand to some extent the miracle of your own existence, then you will manufacture gods who are beneath your own greater capabilities. While you think in terms of one self, then you will create the idea of a one-line [*or linear*] god, confined by your ideas of personhood.

"While you think you are being plunged into a life of sin and denial and of lower vibrations, then you will be forced to think in terms of being saved from that life. Then you will need to manufacture a god who must be killed for your sins, because you believe in the necessity of sacrifice. Symbolically, that is important—that in Western civilization as you understand it, you would find it necessary to create a god who must then be physically betrayed and crucified. You would not do that to your [own] children!"

"Why *would* we do such a thing as that, as crucify a Christ?" asked a student.

"The framework of your beliefs and your consciousness brought you to that impasse," Seth answered. "When your consciousness seemed to be stuck inside your head, then you must think in terms of one personhood, and you must project outward a god who was greater than you only in degree. If you could be cruel, that god with his greater power could be far more cruel. He could annihilate thousands and cause floods. He could send all of you to an eternal hell. If you could be kind to those that you love, then this god could also be kind and bless you—as long as you followed his rules, as you blessed your children as long as they followed your rules.

"As you begin—and you are [beginning]—to catch a glimpse of your own greater reality, however, so will you be able to glimpse an even greater reality in which your existence plays its part, and perhaps begin to conceive why godhead is multi-personal: a multi-personhood large enough to contain not only your species, but others.

"Your religions are based on the idea that you are basically bad. You are afraid of your feelings because you think that your being is evil, and yet most of you, with some exceptions!—" Here, Seth turned a mock-severe glare on Pam, who earlier had been confessing that she hated insects, hard as she tried not to "—[most] will look at the animals and grant them the greatest of moral superiority and say, 'That is good, and that is natural,' and deny to yourselves the same goodness and the same rightness and the same nature.

"Therefore, again, after this jolly chat, do I return you to your own beings—but realize that the free vitality that leaps in this room is your hope. The free vitality and the unstructured nature of these classes has a reason. Spontaneity does indeed know its own order. When you grow from a fetus to a grown adult, you grow spontaneously and truly. You are not part frog, with a dog's leg and an ear of corn! Spontaneity knows its own order, and when I say 'unstructured,' I really mean that the spontaneity of yourselves will then flow into its own natural structure—one that is not put upon you from without, but the creativity of your own changing forms."

In a following class, the subject of prejudice among the races of humankind came up. One member spoke of his childhood Hebrew schooling. "Something that always made me wonder if God was playing with a full deck was this business of referring to the Jews as His Chosen People," Gary said. "I mean, how 'chosen' can you be if God lets you be wiped out continuously over the centuries, right?"

"Yeah, Gary," Jane started, "but what about—oops, just a minute," she said, "somebody's got something to say on that." Off came her glasses.

"Now!" Seth roared at his loudest, "when the god said to me, 'You are my chosen child, and therefore, you must suffer,' that is when I would look around for another god, and say, 'I thank you kindly—but take your gift someplace else! There must be someone else you like better than me! Indeed, I am unworthy of such great benefits!' And I would run and hide, if I had to run through the centuries!"

Shrieks of laughter nearly drowned out Seth's last words. Seth waited patiently until the laughter and banter died down. "Now, I have been quiet [tonight]," he continued at last, referring to the late hour, "because it is good for you to listen to yourselves, and encounter your own beliefs, and see your feelings and your ideas in motion. The ideas of the gods change, as consciousness changes, and, for all of my jokes, you cannot, indeed, blame the gods—as you think of them—overmuch, for you projected them out there, and then responded; and they always were exactly what you wanted them to be at any given time.

"This has nothing to do with All-That-Is, or All-That-You-Are; but the gods as you have understood them through the centuries represent comfort blankets with shapes and forms and designs that came alive and danced through the framework of the universe for you, given vitality by your own beliefs.

"That is all right! It is great, creative play in its way! And, looking outward at those gods, you could see your own psyche projected. That has nothing to do with the energy within you that enabled you to create those gods, or the greater All-That-Is, from which you came.

"So, do not blame the gods overmuch, for the same great God of which we spoke earlier [*of the 'Chosen People'*] might indeed look down and shake His head and say, 'What kind of people have thus created me, that they want Me to whip them and take all of their sheep, and cause floods and tribulation? When will they learn, that I might grow?'

"But always there was, and is, the energy of your own be-ing—if you want to think of it that way; the great source psyche from which your own psyche springs; the great exuberant energy by which your gods were created as you work out the nature of your own being and creativity.

"And so at least, then, theoretically, there are gods still yearning to be born; [who] say, 'I await my people who will expect me to have the honesty and fairness that I would expect in a decent parent; the honesty and the decency I would expect if a flower could speak; a people who will not tell me to slay their enemies; a people who will not tell me to destroy; but who will instead say, 'Bless [thy] people and bless the Earth, and all the creatures upon it.'

"I would, then, if I were speaking for those unborn gods, request with their voice, a people who would not say, 'Set me then in domination above all the creatures of the Earth,' but instead say, 'Let me understand all the creatures of the Earth and see their own sacred individuality and meaning.'

"*And those gods are still unborn and awaiting your desire.*"

NOTES FOR CHAPTER THIRTEEN

1. These effects are discussed in Chapter 10 of *The Nature of Personal Reality*.

2. Because I wanted to include this poem here, Jane searched through her poetry books for it, but never found these lines anywhere. "It's the damndest thing, because these lines sound so familiar," she said. "The only thing I can think of is that Seth was referring to a Sumari poem that I haven't written yet—but is *there*, somewhere, in my psyche, 'waiting' for me to get to it. . . ."

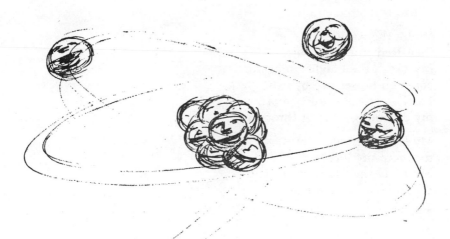

CHAPTER FOURTEEN

Togetherness in Space: Class Dreams
and Co-Creations

A TUDOR SONG

The morning rose in mist,
the sleepers rising from their beds—
went out with still their dreaming
going on inside their heads.

It is not strange,
the light remains
in darkness as in day;
and weaves a spell
in dreams that tell
of lost forgotten strains.

White the royal color once,
then Red, the royal hue,
My Lord, the knights in armor
come on horses two by two.
I woke—it was a misty morn—
my dreaming was not through!

My Lord was once my enemy,
to whom my love is due.
My Lady was my serving maid—
I'll serve her as I'm true.

The Circle's swung,
my life is done—
I bid you all adieu.

                    —Dan Stimmerman, 1973

"I am in class and I ask Jane a question I had wanted
to ask Seth: 'Having two conflicting sets of beliefs,
how does one go about getting a decision?' Jane
answers as Seth. 'You can't put an egg in soup
overnight,' he says."

—*Class dream of Darren Stephens,*
October 5, 1973

"In Elmira, Jane has a new apartment. We look at this
thing that looks like a washing machine but is a fish
tank. I say, 'But there are no fish!' Then there are
loads of fish, seals, crocodiles, all around . . . . Seth
materializes, 'Now!' he says to me, 'You are doing very
well. But I have one piece of advice: You should not
put detergent in a fish tank!'"

—*Class dream of Will Petrosky*
April 24, 1974

"When I speak of dreaming, I am not speaking of something that is less real or vital
than the reality that you know. So when I
say to you, 'You are dreaming when you
think you are awake,' I am not inferring
that one is a more valid reality than the
other. I am saying that when you are
constantly concentrating in the manner that
you understand, that you are also doing
dream work—that you are involved on
other levels of consciousness beside the one
that you know."

—*Seth in Class,*
August 7, 1973

Science assures us that everyone dreams, whether or not we remember doing so; and that a person who is kept from dreaming will rapidly become psychotic. (You have to wonder just how psychotic scientists let their subjects *get* before this heady conclusion was reached, but never mind.) More passionately, humankind has variously regarded dreams with awe and fear; as literal portents of the future; as nonsensical fantasies; or (as in Freud's smooth updating of ancient anxieties) as doorways to the dungeons of the unconscious, filled with unholy ghosts of repressed desires.

In the self-awareness surge of the sixties, bookstores began to blossom with dream-interpretation books, dream analysts appeared on television talk shows, and dream-therapy seminars sprang up everywhere. Unofficially, at least, it seemed that subjective experience was gaining some sort of conscious recognition. Then, in May of 1979, a Cincinnati car rental manager made the most famous dream "hit" of modern times. For ten nights in a row, David Booth's dreams were filled in detail with the gruesome crash of an American Airlines DC-10. In his dreams, Booth saw the jetliner take off, but sensed that it was in trouble "because its engines did not sound right." Then, in his dream, Booth looked across an open field, saw the plane bank to the right, turn over, and crash to the ground in a ball of orange-red flame and gray smoke.

"There was never any doubt to me that something was going to happen," Booth told reporters later. So sure was he of impending disaster that he called Federal Aviation officials with his dream story three days before the actual crash, on May 25, of an American Airlines DC-10 at Chicago's O'Hare International Airport. Nobody treated Booth with disdain—but nobody ran out to check DC-10 engines, either.[1] On the day of the crash—when the jet lost a wing engine on take-off, banked sharply to the *left,* turned over and exploded upside down in a field—Booth's disaster dreams quit.

Precognition, especially the foreknowledge of disasters, has always been the main fascination of dreams; and even though none of the dreams recorded by class members over the years achieved the notoriety of David Booth's,[2] we all had our share of precognition. Humorously enough, a flurry of these occurred just before I sent out the questionnaire forms for this book in January and February of 1979: Several former class members dreamed of the project before they were consciously aware of it.

"You might be interested to know that I had a dream in which I foresaw my participation in your writing project," reported Geoffery Beam, whose dream experience during class years was practically nil. "In the dream, I was assisting Jane with some work she was doing, and was also doing typing for another writer—a woman [*Geoffery's questionnaire response was typewritten*]. I could not identify the woman, but knew she was working on material connected with Jane's work. I also saw the opportunity to give vent to some of my rather pawky humor. This was fully three days before the arrival of your letter in the mail." And the night before she received my questionnaire, Betty DiAngelo dreamed "of class members singing to me . . . . in very loud dramatic voices. The song was 'Blue Moon.' I still don't believe it—I don't even know the words to this song or particularly like it—it's not quite from my time era. The song was a spoof-type thing; I was being indulged, as I . . . [had been] feeling sorry for myself. I was duly chagrined, while they were having a great time over the whole thing. Well, the next day Tim and I were driving down a back road in Vestal. I saw a bar that had a huge sign in blue cursive writing: 'the Blue Moon Lounge!' I had never seen this place before—not since it's been the Blue Moon; it used to be O'Hara's. And that day, your letter came in the mail, asking me to remember things from the past, and changes I had made, involving class.

Still, class members did record some clear-cut precognition over the years.[3] "I look outside—I discover that while I had slept, it had rained so that all the land was flooded," Bernice Zale wrote in her dream notebook on June 19, 1972—four days before "the flood that couldn't happen" inundated New York's Southern Tier. "The school was floating like the ark on the flood waters . . . New York State expected to go under the sea . . . ." Interestingly, the Chemung River reached its flood stage during the *night* of June 23—while people slept. (At 5 A.M. police and firemen woke up riverside neighborhoods, delivering evacuation orders through bullhorns.)

Similarly, Joel Hess reported that "In April or May of 1972, I had a vivid dream in which there was a very bad flood. A river or a stream that ran between steep banks overflowed when it rained several days [*as it did that June: Hurricane Agnes "stuck" over the northeast and sent down more than eleven inches of rain in less than four days*]. Water ran through streets, cars and trucks were washed away, all commerce stopped, utilities were shut down, people became refugees like we are always seeing where there is an earthquake or volcano . . . .

"Families were walking alongside washed-out roads, carrying household furnishings, packs of clothing," Joel's dream continued. "Then there was martial law and soldiers armed with guns patrolling. I also saw people trying to leave the community by water, in boats, and pulling up to . . . a school or other public building in boats, as if it were a dock or wharf, and getting out. The water was brown, chocolate-colored . . .

"This was a vivid dream of the type that, once you start to write it down, more and more cascades out of your memory so that you write and write and become imprisoned by the task of writing . . . You begin to wish you hadn't had the goddamn dream in the first place," Joel says. "Well, this one was clearly loaded with symbolism: fear of the awesome power of nature over an insecure, uncertain, paranoid me . . . surely the dream had been all symbolism! Little did I realize that a month or so later, all those things would happen, literally, in Elmira. . . .

"P.S. Did you know that Marsha [*Joel's present wife*] had a flood dream about a week before the second flood [*a less drastic hurricane-induced flood that washed through parts of Elmira and Corning, New York, in September of 1975*]? We are standing on top of the big hill behind our house on the [Chemung] river and saw the entire valley flooded, animals and vehicles floating by. It was a clear, sunny day with lots of fluffy white clouds in the sky. Well, when [this flood occurred], the sun was out and there were clouds; the rain had long since stopped. But the trailer part of a tractor-trailer truck floated past our house, a rabbit [*which Joel rescued*] was trapped in the rising waters of our cellar, we rowed *over* our [flooded] car in our rowboat, and we had some [dead] cows wash up into the yard. Another 'symbolic' dream turns real. Both accounts are written down.

"We are not into 'tragedy' dreams or impressions as some people are and do not normally pick up on negative stuff," Joel concludes. "These were blockbusters, though!"

It would be interesting to find out how many people in the New York–Pennsylvania area dreamed of floods in the weeks and months before the physical fact; or if anyone acted on the advice of such dreams. Holly Palmer, who with her husband Don attended class three times, reports a precognitive dream of Don's 1977 death that had very definite messages of action in it: "In the dream, my husband and I were attending a party at what seemed like a country club," Holly writes. "Many standing around, talking, eating, etc. Don was not feeling well and was lying out on a library table, and I was frantically trying to get help—looking for a telephone to call a doctor—but was frustrated, moving from room to room without finding a phone. Woke up.

"Discussed this dream the next day with Dr. Ann Faraday [*an author of dream and other 'psychic' books*]. We came to the conclusion that it may or may not be precognitive, but that I was asking myself to write down some phone numbers. . . . Well, I didn't do it, and when Don had his very quick attack, I was lost on who to call—we had been in the community only a year, knew very few people, and had no doctor. Don, having always been a practicing Christian Scientist, had told me several times not to call a doctor if he decided to leave. So finally I called a neighbor. My neighbors got there in ten minutes and *they* didn't know who to call. Call to the only Doc in town was answered by a machine. Finally called the sheriff. It was an hour and ten minutes before the authorities got there and pronounced him dead."

Matt Adams notes that he *expects* dreams to "alert me to major developments—to prepare me as it were—and so I was, when my mother died [*in 1977*] . . .

"My mother had been suffering from emphysema for some time and was generally weak and lethargic, but hardly on death's doorstep. In the dream, I woke to the sound of the telephone ringing," Matt reports. "The bedside table was not to the right of the bed, as it is in the 'real' world, but on the left . . . On it was the telephone (which in real life is in the kitchen) and a clock, whose dial read 5 A.M.

"It was my father calling, to say that my mother had died. In the dream, I hung up and began to cry, when I heard my mother's voice. I then realized that if I put myself into a light trance, I'd be able to hear her better. She walked in, wearing a dressing gown, and sat on the side of the bed. We talked for a few minutes. She explained to me not to worry; that she did intuitively understand the survival of bodily death (something she did not ever discuss in life; didn't believe in it) and was well on her way to a new incarnation. In fact, she began growing a dark bluish-black beard! When I expressed surprise, she said it was one of her past aspects bleeding through her present image. When she departed, I woke up, *bang*, and was quite amazed to see that the bedside clock in the real world read exactly 5 A.M.!

"The dream was so vivid and precise that I called my father later in the day, just to make sure things were okay. He explained that my mother was going into the hospital later that week for some tests to see what could be done for her edema. . . .

"It was all her choice, of course. On her way out the door to the hospital, she remarked to my father that she might not come back, and once in her private room—with oxygen at hand, with all her needs taken care of—she literally relaxed to death and was gone in ten days' time. When my father telephoned to tell me she had died during the night, he did wake me up—but at 7 A.M., not 5:00. Yet from what the doctors said, I later estimated that the time of death was between 4:30 and 5:30 A.M. . . . ."[4]

Other kinds of precognitives, involving symbolism or odd exchanges between waking and sleeping selves, also abound in dream journals. "The reason I came to ESP class was because I had read Jane's books, *Seth Speaks* and *The Seth Material*," says Derek Bartholomew. "I called her from a phone booth along a busy highway. . . . As I was talking to her, I realized that by coming to one of her classes, I was fulfilling a dream episode in which I attended a class of hers. I was already keeping a dream notebook, and in one of my dreams, I was in a class situation. I was nearly overwhelmed when I first met her in class and she so closely resembled the teachers of my dreams! Just in repeating that event, I still get a sense of energy in it that is continuing.

"When I was about nine or ten," Derek adds, "I recall looking out a window in our house that faces the east. The sun was still low on the horizon, and above it were some clouds. Somehow in front of, and in a way superimposed over, the clouds above the sun was a great shining, golden castle. It had high domes and towers rising into the air, with flags waving in the breeze above them. After watching the scene for a minute, I called excitedly to my parents and brothers. When they came to the window, all they saw was a sun with a few clouds in the bright blue sky. When I tried to describe what I had seen, my mother made some comment about clouds ˌooking like animals or other shapes, but they couldn't see what I was seeing. To me it was as real as the sun shining or some tree or rock or a house, but they were blind to it." In October of 1974, when Seth first challenged us to start forming our own "inner"—but "*not* imaginary"—city, Derek's first thought was of his childhood city-sighting. Was there an element of precognition in his experience?

"I've had so many extraordinary dreams . . . since classes have ended," Betty DiAngelo says. "But on September 22, 1976, I had a precognitive dream that I'd completely forgotten until doing this [book] questionnaire. In the dream, Tim and I were at an amusement park where there were crowds of people and many children. There was one child—an infant really—on a roller coaster. The child was crying and was animal-like in some way, as if it were a combination monkey/child, or some other small animal. It had lots of dark hair.

Betty DiAngelo

"I became upset over the child's crying and stopped in front of the roller coaster. Finally I said to a group of people standing there, 'Whose child is that?' They looked at me disgustedly, and one of them said, 'Why, don't you know? It is yours!' At which point I picked up the child, and Tim and I walked off.

"I had this dream a year to the day before my daughter's birth. At the time of the dream, I had no interest—or thought I didn't—in having another child. In fact, the idea was not intellectually appealing. . . . A few months previous, I had been having weird physical ailments. My doctor had suggested a mammogram, and I stopped going to him, hoping to figure out my health problems by myself. What I uncovered was that part of me wanted to have another child and another part didn't [*and note the roller-coaster imagery*]. I was completely ignoring my feelings on the subject. This dream perhaps helped me to make up my mind—though at the time I didn't see any connection and had even forgotten it. And now I see many coincidences . . . my daughter did have lots of dark hair when she was born, even on her arms and shoulders; it eventually went away. She is also very tiny and quite affectionate.

Tim and I used to laugh, especially during her crawling stage, when she seemed more like a little puppy than a child. . . . "

"I started having clairvoyant dreams and psychic experiences frequently after beginning the Seth/Jane classes," says Charlene Pine. "They must have gone on for years before, but class drew my attention to them, and also helped me change some limiting beliefs about my abilities.

"Since that time, and in the present, I have class dreams involving Jane, Seth, Rob, and others. I get a lot of helpful information; and especially at stressful times, Jane or Seth delivers a 'heavy.' I realize, of course, the nature of my inner self working, but very often these dreams are right before (the very *night* before) a letter arrives from Jane. I do feel that the classes, or call it the relationship, continues. . . . Sometimes myself, Kurt, Richie, Rudy, and others still have class dreams in the same week or night. . . ."

My own dream notebooks include numerous "little" examples of precognition that evoke the class "predictions" experiment more than portents or warnings, but specific examples of precognitive material do appear. In 1972, I was working in an Elmira print shop, setting up forms for the local hospital's operating room supply requisitions. One night, I dreamed that a man my parents had known for many years died during an operation. In my dream, the man expired while lying in a pool of his own blood. The next day, my mother called to tell me that this man had indeed died during an operation the day before—*and* that he'd hemorrhaged to death; doctors had been unable to stop the bleeding. Had my hospital-form typesetting job helped fine-tune my inner senses to the man's predicament?

Also in 1972, I had a dream in which Jane and I 'saw' a new kind of power plant; an apparatus that would float in the ocean and somehow use the flow of ocean water to provide energy. I told Jane that this might be done through the separation of water from the salts and minerals. Upon awakening, I drew a picture of this set-up (see Figure 11). Five months later, an article appeared in the "Technology" section of the April 1973 *Saturday Review/ Sciences* magazine on the proposed FLOPP ("Floating Power Platform"). This device, being developed at the Scripps Institution of Oceanography, was supposed to generate nuclear power in offshore clusters of "floating pop bottle" vertical holding tanks. This supposedly earthquake-proof mechanism would use cool sea water, the article explained, for necessary circulation within the plant. The diagram accompanying the article (see Figure 12) has a startling likeness to my dream-drawing, even to the hoses, or cables, between the tanks and shoreline.

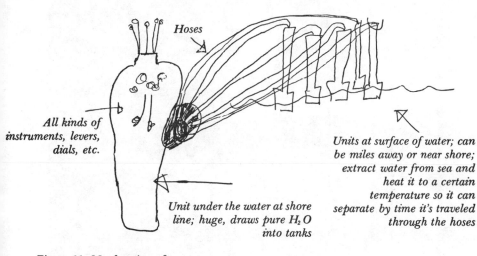

Hoses

All kinds of instruments, levers, dials, etc.

Unit under the water at shore line; huge, draws pure H_2O into tanks

Units at surface of water; can be miles away or near shore; extract water from sea and heat it to a certain temperature so it can separate by time it's traveled through the hoses

Figure 11. My drawing of a power plant as glimpsed in the dream state

Another "little" precognitive dream appears in my note-book for Monday, August 8, 1974: "Jane and Rob tell me they're having trouble with the roof of their apartment. Their landlord has offered to put in a drop-ceiling because water is leaking through." The next night, I noted, "It was raining as I drove to class. As soon as I arrived, I used the bathroom. I then wandered into Rob's studio [*which was off the bathroom*] to look at some paintings. Water was leaking through the studio ceiling and onto some photographs. Jane and Rob hadn't known that the roof had developed a leak."

The actual phenomenon of "class dreams"—sets of re-markable coincidences in which we dreamed about one another in class settings, usually with Jane or Jane-as-Seth at its head—started to occur almost as soon as class began (as any group will tend to dream of itself). By fall of 1971, however, there was a steady acceler-ation of these dreams that sprang from more than Tuesday-night togetherness. Sometimes one or two class members would simply dream about each other, or one person would dream of another in a situation that turned out to have actually happened in the physical

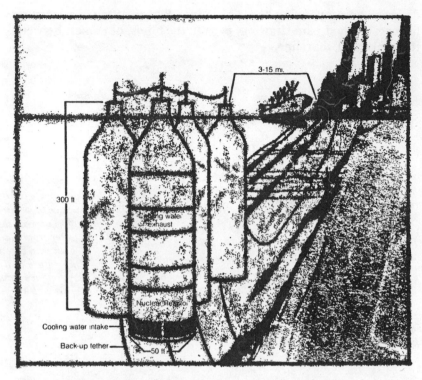

Figure 12. Corresponding drawing of a proposed nuclear plant

world—a bit of clairvoyance. As time went on, though, we'd discover that during the week, anywhere from three to four members to nearly everyone in the class had recorded dreams that correlated—right down to settings, dialogues, issues discussed, activities, symbolism, and events.

From the earliest days of class, dreams and dream interpretation occupied much of our discussion. Personal dream analysis was offered by class members, Jane, or Seth; but more than avenues of self-help, dreams were treated as an area of consciousness that held the most fundamental clues, questions, and answers to the nature of identity. Who is the dreaming self? Do dreams go on without the dreamer? How 'real' is a dream? How universal are dream events? And always, Seth coaxed, teased, and admonished us to remember our dreams and write them down; and in particular, to suggest that we might meet in the dream state and be wide-awake and aware enough there to experiment with our consciousness—with our *dream* consciousness.

"Our regular students have been experiencing an extra bonus," Seth explained early in 1971. "You are beginning your own dream classes, as you know. Some of you already know the evenings in which you will work and the area in which you will be involved. As you learn to live spontaneously on a physical level, so automatically you will be able to build up [dream classes] . . . You are all multidimensional realities. *You are learning to use your consciousness to become conscious co-creators of your own reality.* And some of you . . . after [physical] class will be involved in some adventures that I hope you will remember!"

One week in the fall of 1971, not long after the appearance of Sumari, Janice Simmonds reported "a significant-feeling dream of an apple tree being pruned." That was all there was to it, she said—just an apple tree being pruned. "Doesn't sound like anything, does it?" she smiled shyly. But then Rob, who had started to come to a few classes now and then, said that *he'd* had a dream on the same night as Janice's in which he'd seen huge *peeled* apples growing on a tree. "I was also told that *kito* is the Sumari word meaning *apple*, or one phase of an apple's appearance," Rob said. "In this case, I guess it means apple-ready-for-eating." Rob had hardly finished speaking when Pete Sawyer, an artist, burst into a description of the painting he'd been working on all week—a still life of an enormous blue apple! None of the three had communicated with one another at all during the week—in the usual terms.

"Around this time," says Nadine Renard, "I participated in a 'class' dream. In that week's class, out of twenty-six to twenty-eight people there, thirteen people including myself had [recorded dreams] that included three or more points in common, [including]: (1) an Oriental person in a prominent position; (2) having to go into a basement or downstairs; (3) orange or yellow flowers someplace [in the dream setting]." During that fall, Bernice Zale and I recorded many similar dreams involving the two of us; an Oriental teacher appeared in many of her dreams; and both of us had numerous dream settings down in basements or fallout shelters. She had not been to class in several months. And even though Ned and I were separated by this time, we still recorded similar dreams: in his dream notebook (which he loaned to me for this book), Ned notes a dream for March 5, 1971, in which the two of us were being held captive in a garage by threatening men. In his dream, Ned managed to keep the threats at bay by forming a circle of class members. I looked the dates up in my dream books for that time: on March 7, 1971, I had a dream in which Ned, class member Alison Hess, and I were defending ourselves—from inside a garage—against "Mafiatypes"; in my dream,we managed to escape— to Jane's class— by car. Both Ned and I had noted that we'd realized during the dream that it *was* a dream.[5]

In the same time period, I had a class dream in which Seth discussed the "creative inner meanings"of destruction, decay, and aging. In my dream, I sat next to Joel Hess and muttered asides to him as a movie of an H-bomb explosion was shown as a demonstration. A few days later, my notes state, Joel described a class dream to me that he'd had on the same night as mine— *and in which Seth had lectured on the meaning of destruction.* Joel specifically remembered talking to me in the dream about the Bomb. On the night of August 8, 1971, I found myself with Jane and another class member, sitting in a field. Unexpressed fury that I'd felt on the Tuesday before for this person rose up inside me until I felt choked. "Go ahead, Sue," Jane said— and I really started to let the person have it; in fact, I woke *up* with a loud yell. Later that day, Jane called to tell me that she'd remembered a class dream in which we were all sitting outdoors and that we'd dealt with "the nature of emotion." But by then, it wasn't unusual for Jane and me to find ourselves dreaming about each other. Many times, we would also discover that I'd record a Seth-session dream containing specific information to me, or to someone else, on the same night that Jane remembered dreaming about *having* a Seth session. Sometimes, she would recall bits of the Sethian conversation— which would correspond with *my* notes. "Sometimes I wake up and feel as though Seth has been carrying on all night long," Jane says— while adding that she's only dreamed once of Seth from an exterior-observer point of view (and even then, he was in disguise). And this Seth-session dreaming also happened with other class members— again, with specific information recalled on both sides.

"I don't recall any class dreams," Matt Adams reports, "although I do remember a most unusual one that involved a cocktail party on the roof of a fairly tall building in, I assume, New York. I spoke briefly with Seth, who was dressed in a three-piece suit, very elegant and prosperous and quite out of keeping with Rob's more informal portrait! This was not a class, exactly, but a reception for people interested in Seth and Jane's work.

"Once, Jane and I dreamed of the same city— a dusty, dry place where large signs with gold letters on a black surface were hung out like battle flags over the street. But we concluded that each of us had been in a slightly different part of town! The streets were long and straight, and few if any buildings were over two stories tall. It was not earlier than the nineteenth century, or it could have been just 'now-time'—I really don't recall much except those black-ground signs, each with only a few letters upon them."

Class dreams were a fascinating part of our "ESP" experience, but we never fully investigated their implications—if that were indeed possible in a lifetime. And time *was* the crux: there simply wasn't enough of it. You could literally spend the entire Tuesday night analyzing one tiny dream detail that we'd had in common. Where class dreaming would have led to over a period of, say, twenty or thirty years—had class lasted that long—is anyone's guess; my speculation is that Seth's challenge for us to "dream an Inner City" (see Chapter 10 of Volume 1) was meant *in part* to propel us into something long-term and heretofore unheard of, whether class continued or not. Certainly, Seth made constant references to "the Experiment" and its relationship to our dreams.

For instance, one August night in 1971, Seth punctuated a lengthy discussion of dreams with some surprising remarks about their directions. "We mentioned some time ago an experiment," he began, interrupting some salacious speculations on the "meaning" of sex dreams. "Now, the visitors that have been here until this evening had a part to play in that experiment. Other portions of the experiment, however, are concerned with your dream states and those individuals that you are meeting [in dreams]. Besides the associates and friends that you know in your daily waking life, you also have quite a legitimate relationship with people that you do *not* know as you go about your daily concerns. And you perform work of which you are unaware as you go about your daily way.

"Now, some of you are ready to meet these other associates. They are people living on the face of the earth at this time; people that you have never met physically and probably will never meet in those terms, but you are involved often as apprentices in joint endeavors, and it is time that you become aware to some extent of your relationship.[b] Therefore, I want you to take particular notice of people in your dreams who are strangers to you. You may encounter them in class dreams. You may also encounter them, however, in dreams that seem to have no great meaning. These people cooperate with you as you cooperate with them. You are involved [in] many activities: helping people who have died, in your terms; speaking to others who are quite alive, in the dream state; learning to understand and manipulate subjective realities."

Seth rocked back in Jane's chair, crossing Jane's legs with delicate grace, as if he were naturally familiar with the mechanics of a mini-skirt. "Now, there are two main possibilities that can emerge here," he continued, "and these people can become quite real to you. You have begun to become aware of some of your own reincarnational existences [in dreams]. Because of this, you have been able to relate to yourself and to others in a more effective manner and understand others from a different point of view. Now, however, you should also become aware of other personalities who work with you when your normally conscious ego is quieted. Some of you already have clues.

Seth

"This requires some study and means that you will have to remember your dreams much more effectively than some of you are doing!" Seth scowled his familiar mock-stern scowl, pursing Jane's lips and scrunching her eyebrows together in an expression that Jane herself never used. "And I am giving you the impetus!" he roared. "When possible, think of these persons . . . so that in your daily waking life you can receive some more intuitional information as to the kind of work and endeavors in which you are all involved."

Seth paused, closing his eyes. For a moment, Jane's body sat motionless, hinting of the Seth II personality. Besides, that mysterious "Experiment" had been mentioned again—a favorite word of this other personality.[7] Was this going to slide into a Seth II speech?

"We want you to become aware of all your activities, not simply your conscious ones," Seth said finally, opening Jane's eyes and staring out in his usual animated manner. "You are using abilities in that work that you are not using—as yet—in your conscious lives, and I want you to become aware of what these abilities are. They can also help you deal more effectively with physical reality, and help you understand it far better. You may find, several of you, yourselves involved in the same work in the dream state. And so, also, keep track of whatever class members may appear within these dreams. Then, when you are doing well in class, you will be able to relate not only to some reincarnational selves [*which we had been experimenting with at this time*], but to the inner self and to its activities; and use these activities to enrich your normal daily encounters and to increase the nature and extent of your perceptions."

Joel Hess cleared his throat. "You said, '*We* want you to be aware,' et cetera," he repeated. "Would you explain the 'we' a little bit?"

Seth shook Jane's head, grinning at Joel. "Not at this time," he replied. "I will, however, later."

"After we think about it a while?" Joel offered humorously.

"Indeed," Seth said dryly. "I notice it did not miss your attention, however."

Gert Barber spoke up. "In the dream state, these, ah, *strangers* or associates—would we put on them a face that we would be able to relate to, say a member of our family?" she asked.

Seth stared at her with a small, tender smile, holding the room in silence. It almost seemed as though Gert's question had reminded him of something else; some memory welling up in his Sethian mind that momentarily distracted him. "They will appear to you as strangers, and not as people that you know," he said after a moment. In closing, he advised us also to watch out in our waking life for "strangers who approach you without effort, concerning mutual friends—and for clues, awake and asleep, on the nature of 'the Experiment.'" Was this tricky, evocative dream challenge reflecting Seth's knowledge of, or "memory" of, the impending Sumari development that Jane would deliver that November?

Whatever it comprised, Seth's "experiment" hint worked its usual understated charms: class dreams seemed to explode upon us. Suddenly our dream records were filled with correlations; strangers virtually overpopulated our dream landscapes; odd waking encounters leaped into our awareness—were we actually meeting more "strangers" than usual, or were we just more conscious of them now?

For example, on August 9, I had a class dream with many strangers in it. Each one of us, familiar members and otherwise, were supposed to list all unknown people who'd appeared in our dreams lately. In my dream, Joel Hess *described* a dream with strangers and their concern about a winter coat. I described—in my dream—a similar dream involving a coat that Seth took off and handed to Joel. To my dream self, it seemed that we were actually describing as-yet undiscovered layers of perception, and that the "strangers" in our midst were dream-selves from other probability systems.

The next day, a typewriter salesman came to my house to discuss the machine that I was going to rent for an in-home typing business that I had for a while. During the conversation, the salesman stood up and removed his topcoat with a humorous flourish, saying that the cool breeze that morning had fooled him into wearing it. Later on, he mentioned a minister who'd been preaching in a small church near his home. The minister turned out to be Joel Hess. And I also discovered in the course of our conversation that the company secretary who had been taking my calls about this machine was a friend from my high school class—the salesman, of course, "a stranger who approached with effort," for an encounter that included mention of two "mutual friends."

That Tuesday, Joel remembered only that he'd had a class dream the night of August 9. But at Jane's that night for the first time was a woman who had graduated with me from high school. Upon checking my records—we usually brought our dream notebooks with us to class—I discovered that I'd had a class dream on August 10 in which several members of my high school class appeared. I hadn't seen any of them since 1963.

Several weeks later, I had a dream in which I found myself stopping at a gas station on my way to Jane and Rob's. Instead of paying the attendant—a man whom my dream self observed as "a stranger"—I handed him a book with the name of a family friend written on the first page. I hadn't seen this person in more than ten years. The station attendant immediately pointed to the name and said, "He's dead."

"My gosh, is that telepathy or clairvoyance?" my dream self said. I told the attendant to call Jane Roberts about coming to ESP class and then drove there myself, where conversation centered around the "sound" of molecules. A wind was blowing hard against the old house. We then discussed the death of my friend and how he would adjust to his new state.

On the afternoon of the day I recorded this dream, my mother called to tell me that, unknown to me, this friend *had* died the day before. All Jane remembered was a dream in which she could hear Seth giving information to someone she didn't know on how to manipulate one's consciousness.

Just after the appearance of Sumari that November, I wrote down a dream in which Jill Ryan, a woman who'd been to class once and disliked it intensely, was attending a Seth session. In physical life Jill was a stage director, costume designer, and choreographer for a theater troupe; in my dream, Seth seemed to be telling her why she disliked ESP class and its apparent lack of structure. Seth then gave me information on Sumari and the accomplishments of this "family." On the same night, Bernice Zale had a dream involving a group of people dancing in a strange place. In the dream, I told her that she "has often been connected in some way to dancing." Bernice then walked to her town's elementary school, where a professor—i.e., a male teacher figure—gave her some information about the Sumari family and another family of consciousness, described in Bernice's notes as "Beverly, or something close to it." Besides the immediate correlations between the dreams, it's interesting to note that one of the families of consciousness Seth listed four years later in *The "Unknown" Reality* is the "Borledim"—which he says provides the parent, or earth stock, for the race.

It was typical of these class dreams, as they began to snowball, that we often recalled them in vast, involved detail, dialogue included, sometimes for dozens of notebook pages. (It was during this time, for instance, that I had the "Counterpart Library Dream," as I later called it, as related in Appendix 9.) Class members who sent me their dream records—Betty DiAngelo in particular, who hand-copied a thick sheaf of dreams for me—said that they'd chosen *representative* dreams out of their records; it was all they had time to do. "Sue, how can I?" Camille Atkinson responded to my request for class dream material. "There were hundreds. A life-time of dreams. Where would I start? I had had dreams of class in and out of all my life—of course I didn't know it, but I knew it once I got to class!" And then there were members who didn't remember class dreams—or many dreams at all. Yet the dreams that I did collect, particularly from 1973 and 1974, intertwine in detail after detail.

Some of these occurred on the same night; many others during the same Tuesday-to-Tuesday *week*—which we saw as correlating "hits."

For example, in the class of August 14, 1973, we compared notes and discovered that more than half of those present—at least a dozen people—had been dreaming during the week about policemen. Several of us had dreams in which we were in jail cells; others remembered spy-story scenarios of trying to steal secret government documents; still others found themselves being searched by the police for unnamed crimes. Specifically, on the night of August 14, George Rhoads and I compared these remarkably similar dream situations: In mine, George and I flew to Hawaii, where a man met us in the airport and demanded to know George's name. I immediately told George not to divulge his name to "just any old person on the street"—that it would be dangerous to do so. But then I discovered that the threatening man had gone to Syracuse University when I did, and that he was doing an Urban Renewal study in Hawaii. As he told me this, the airport turned into the Newhouse Journalism School complex at S.U. George and I then walked away and found some friends living at the bottom of a snowy, slushy crater, where a wild moose was running around and around the edge.

George's dream that night began with his arriving, by plane, in Argentina, "with a friend to visit her parents. Part of this was a trip around the world that I was making alone. I went down a long hill in the country, and as I went it turned into a city. I saw some policemen holding some ragged-looking men—making an arrest. Then the road went through a zoo, and I drove on what appeared to be cobblestones. It was dried shit, though, and creatures were burrowing beneath it in the liquid part. They popped up, but the surface hardened again." And according to my notes, two other class members' police dreams that week included notes on slogging through layers of slushy manure.

"Now *you* choose the theme for your dreams—I do not!" Seth burst in as we were discussing these dreams that Tuesday. "And, for a while, class will provide the theme for your class dreams—that is, *you* will provide the theme, as you have done. Each of you, in your own way, will interpret the theme and develop it and learn your own lessons from it. And you did very well. Most of the correlations are obvious. Let me make, however, a few remarks.

"Creativity is permissive, it is free, and it is playful. And, out of the playfulness and its permissiveness, it finds its own joyful structure, and that structure is spontaneous. But—it *is* a structure. Now, a dance forms a structure. Creativity does not find a *rigid* structure.

"Authority and the police, and the police state, represented many things to each of you individually; and yet, if you police your ideas and your beliefs, you put yourself in prison. And if you are afraid to listen to the beliefs of others to which you do not agree, you make your own bars. And, if you cannot react playfully to those who hold other beliefs than [yours], then you have a lot to learn about being Sumari!

"The dream state is a free, creative state. Yet, even in it, you can experience rigid barriers and beliefs; but facing those, and realizing what they are, you can also realize the power of your own creativity. See how well you took one theme and elaborated upon it in your dreams, for your own purposes, and then for class purposes! For what you learned, you communicated to others, and many of you who do not remember class dreams—had some!

"The rigid, authoritative image—you can project it outward, or you can see it as a tendency within yourself. If you are able to treat it playfully when you meet it on the outside, you will be able to treat it playfully when you meet it on the inside! And you will not feel the need to pin [anyone] to the wall!

"Now, the Sumari are creative. They are creative, inventative [*sic*], joyful, and they are sometimes impatient. As I did say, they do not stay around to mow the grass. But mowing the grass in certain levels of reality is quite important. And to stand around and laugh at those who mow the grass, and tend to what *you* have begun—to laugh at the caretakers—is never anything to be proud of.

"As last week you chose the theme for your dream, so you shall this [forthcoming] week. And I will not tell you what the theme is, for it will be your own. But there will indeed be—*with* your enthusiastic cooperation!—a time when you will transcend yourselves, and your abilities in your 'now,' and clearly have a dream experience in which the events and the circumstances and the environment all agree. *You do not seem to understand completely that your dreams are real*, and have their validity. Or even . . . that your intent—your intent—itself has a reality that builds up in energy at other levels of existence, and works for you.

"Now, not only are your dreams individual, and indi-vidual-ly important; as far as class is concerned, there is a mass ge-stalt in which your individual dreams have an even greater meaning, and in which each of you are doing your part in erecting realities that you do not as yet understand.

"Now . . . I return you to this dreaming class, and I hope that your other selves wake up and remember what *they* dreamed of, and the dream class that *they* attended; and when they are asked what dreams they had, and on what night, in your terms, they remember *this* class!"

Continuing in its ongoing fashion that following week, class dream recall once again had dozens of points in common—but this time, not so much between people, places, or things, but with symbolism and ideas: a kind of mirror-image correspondence. My records note that several of us reported dreams dealing with the rela-tionship between the physical body's cells and the cellular structure of the dream-image body, while five others had widely varying dream encounters concerning the nature of self-discipline and how much of that elusive quality one must have in order to do anything at all—"In order not to become a bum," one student finished his dream description, a worried frown wrinkling his brow. In each remembered dream, there seemed to be a reference to a foreign country.

By then, of course, we were expecting some kind of col-lective dream analysis from Seth.

"Good evening!" he began, removing Jane's much-handled glasses. "The first lesson that you have taught yourselves in the dream state has to do with the continuity of your own *experience* in the dream state—the simple fact that so many of you had experi-ences using the same symbols and the same ideas; that you agreed upon so many objective issues appearing within your dreams. You did not agree upon the same room, or the same people, but the simi-larities were obvious to each of you. You can see for yourselves how, in the dream state, you were working with issues that concern you. You can see also a great correlation and give-and-take as you created your own images, allowed others to borrow them, borrowed some for yourselves. And out of the whole cloth, each of you made original dreams that were, on the other hand, like no other; and yet, the same issues were often found—and as you spoke, they became obvious.

"Now, there are certain things that you must agree upon in physical reality: the tables, the chairs, yourselves as you look. There are many things upon which you agree, and when you speak, you agree upon what is said—generally. What I want you to understand is that in the dream state also there are agreements. There are things upon which you agree. There is order in what may seem to be chaos. And, [*to Camille, who hadn't remembered any dreams that week*] there is memory in what at times may seem to be amnesia! I want you to see the similarity, the give-and-take, and the communication—the order—that has appeared in your dreams. Then I want you to see if you can decide what the individual issues—such as the foreign nationalities—mean.

"You have witnessed a very simple demonstration that *you* have given *yourselves* about the nature of the dream state, and your own continuing work and play and validity within it—the continuity that exists between the waking and the dream state as you think of it. You are not momentarily insane—not when you are asleep! Some of you [*to Rudy*] may be insane when you are awake and walk through glass . . . but you cannot say that you are insane when you are asleep, or that there is no order!

"Now, our regular students recognize my humor," Seth continued, "so they know when I am joking and when I am not; so I am not saying that you are 'insane' when you are awake! I want you to recognize the continuity of your consciousness as it passes through these thresholds of activity, however.

"Now, oftentimes, dreaming, you are not aware of your waking self; but waking, you are not often aware of your dreaming self! Try now, for example, without any [dream] record, to remember your dream activities—but when you are dreaming, try to remember your waking activities! And yet, there is great continuity, in your terms, for of course both exist at once.

"I have something to say to each of you, and all of you. In many areas of your lives, you go to learn discipline. You are taught by another and by a teacher and by a great authority. You are taught to become disciplined. In this class, there are other issues involved, and now I will tell you the terrible truth!

"For I am an un-teacher. And an un-teacher un-ravels you, or lets you unravel yourselves, back to the truths of your being. An un-teacher helps you un-learn your 'discipline.' An un-teacher, hopefully—and it is a difficult task that I embark upon, playfully—an un-teacher, hopefully, lets you lead yourselves toward the freedom of your being. So, when you are used to discipline, you may, for a while, feel un-done, or without a foundation. And then, when you let your disciplines go, you feel the great foundation of your own being, and its greater freedom.

"There is a purpose to this class, as all of you know, and for all of my talk, you see, you still have not un-learned enough. For when I tell you that you create your own reality, none of you are really sufficiently secure in that belief to take advantage of it as yet; to grasp this great creative freedom of yourselves, and use it to make the life that you presently [live] be the most creative and joyful for yourself and others. And so you give yourselves and others excuses, and you are in this position because of that, or you are in this position because of that person, or because of your background.

"Now, this applies to everyone here, Ruburt included—to each of you. When you thoroughly recognize the majestic freedom of your own being, and your own creative power, then you recognize yourselves as creators, creating your daily life and joyfully helping create the mass experience of the world as you know it. And then, you are ready to say 'I act out of the full joyful knowledge of my creativity.' Then you do not blame events or others or circumstances. Then you are able to thank yourselves for the joys of your being, and the glory of your days. You are able to say to the smallest cell within the ear, 'I give you greeting. I am thankful for our joint creativity; for our eternal knowledge which is ever new.' . . .

"And your dreams will help you point the way to your own freedom—and they *are* pointing the way to your own freedom.

"Again, from my reality to yours: if there is one gift that I would give you, it is the reflection of yourselves as I see you, returned to you so that you could sense, as I do, the miraculous joy and freedom, and trust it. If you make mistakes, they are your own mistakes, and you can learn from them. If you make decisions, they are your own decisions; you can make new ones. If you are afraid of making decisions, you cannot learn from them.

"Your dreams for this week will clarify the issues involved in your past week's dreams. So—bring all of your records. You are piling up dream goodies for yourself. You are your own teachers; these are your dreams, not mine. Mine are like winds that blow about the universe, and that are seen in different shapes and forms, according to your perspective, and upon which hilltop you happen to stand.

"I give you, each of you, my deepest regards; and through my knowledge of your integrity, reassure you of that integrity, when you doubt it—for there is no need to doubt it. In the dream state, you will be reassured, and by yourselves; the selves you *think*, again, you have forgotten; the selves you hope you are, but the selves you are afraid you will never be. Those selves *are*, and they will speak to you and reassure you in the dream state, as they speak now when you are awake—but you do not listen.

"And your dreams also, in their way, nourish worlds. There is no waste. Your dreams and your thoughts have reality."

During *that* next week as we discovered the following Tuesday, (August 28), our dreams seemed to be filled with debates and lectures delivered by class members. On August 25, for example, I dreamed of Jed Martz giving a speech on how dumb basketball was compared to the academic "rightness" of classroom learning; Rudy Storch kept interrupting with a sermonette on *The Bhagavadgita*. My dream-self finally told Jed that there was no real difference between a mental activity and a physical one; but *I* was interrupted by Bernice Zale, who wanted to tell me the story of a new bathroom innovation—in which the toilet seat was changed weekly by a traveling toilet-seat changer. That next Tuesday, several of us related dreams involving the relationship between mental and physical activities; and all of them seemed to include one class member or other lecturing the rest of us on the fine points of some hilariously silly topic. "It's getting to be like the *Oversoul 7* dream tribunal,[8] you know it?" Phil Levine remarked during the discussion.

"Good evening! Seth interjected at this point. "And before class is finished, you will discover what good teachers you all are, and how wily you carry out your own themes in the dream state, and how they correlate. You see, finally, that your inner self is a friend. You will also discover that *you* are the self. Each of you, in your way, will come to your own realization . . . and when your own inspiration and experiences come to you, then they teach you in a way that I cannot teach you. For it is your own experience. It is your self meeting your self.

"You [*Phil*] used the word 'dream tribunal.' And some time, you will each realize the true, deep, dark secret, and hidden aspects that lurk within *Oversoul Seven* and how it so insidiously works upon your psyche, and leads you to dream tribunals. What do you think you are heading for with your dreams in this class? And that is the only clue I will give you.

"And . . . if you think you have trouble explaining this class to your friends, you should imagine the difficulty I have with *my* colleagues!

"Some of my colleagues are also very serious and given to hard work; and they all have their own ideas of teaching, and of training, and they all think they have the way that works best. I think I have a way, and so I do not bother them. They think they have the right way. So my way always changes. *That* way, sometimes it must be the right way! I speak humorously in terms I think you can relate to about my colleagues, for of course they do not exist in that way at all. But, it is a good way to get an idea across. I do not exist in that way either!

"Now, you come here, and you listen to me speak," Seth continued. "You hear a voice. Certainly you all agree that you hear a voice. And your instruments [*tape recorders*] pick up a voice. Yet, if you try to find me—*this* loudspeaker—you cannot find me. You cannot find me in your reality in the same way that you *think* you can find each other. In rational, intellectual terms alone, and using the terms the way [they are] usually used, you are learning a lot from someone who has no reality, and that is a good trick on your part!

"Finding yourselves is something else, and yet akin to what I am speaking of. For, you see, your physical images are reflected in a looking glass. And yet you know what you are looking at is not the self you know, but only a part of the self that you know. For where in your body are you—in your nose, or your toe—in all of it? If you cut off an arm, what happens to the part of you that was in the arm? Where did it go? If you are in the cells and atoms and molecules that compose you today, what happens when those atoms and molecules change completely, and your physical organs are composed of entirely new atoms and molecules? Where has your self gone then?

"You perceive omens. What are you but omens of yourself? Creations felt from the inside? But to try to look at yourselves from the outside, [you] therefore never recognize who you are. You are apports. You come from other dimensions of reality into this one. Then why does it bother you so if you imagine a bird coming from another reality into this one?[9] Where do the new flowers come from each spring?

"It is a fairytale to tell yourselves that they come from the seeds that were put here last year, which came from the seeds that were put there last year, that came from the seeds . . . et cetera.

For you are left with the old question of where the first seed came from, or the first apple. What is to prevent—what *is* to prevent—a mysterious bird from entering into your reality and forming a new species? Only your beliefs that that isn't possible. Yet again, if it is impossible, then where did the first bird come from, or the first seed, or the first before the first?"

Kurt Johns

     Seth turned to Kurt Johns, whom he'd affectionately called "the Indian" ever since Kurt had reported dreams and other intuitive glimpses of an Indian-self he thought he might have been. "Where is your Indian?" Seth asked, smiling at Kurt. "He has his own joyful reality, and his own being. And as I have told you often, your own thoughts materialize in other systems than your own. You seed other realities of which you are not aware. You form aspects of yourself, and so are you also aspects—while being your own individual selves.

     "When you open the doors to your perception, you see *this* reality more clearly. You also begin to glimpse varieties of possibilities inherent within this system, not usually perceived. You see the form that your thoughts take. You project them outward as omens, and then follow them. They are joyful and friendly. Inner symbolism becomes real, and varied, and alive. Living signs that you then follow, but that form their own reality.

     "Now—I return you to your own Indians!"

CLASS DREAMS AND NOTES:
A SAMPLE OF CORRELATIONS

For the week (Tuesday to Tuesday) of December 8–15, 1970:
December 9, Ned Watkins: "With a group of people, plus Seth. People are ancient cave-dwellers. Place was cave-like, no windows or wood. Seth explained meanings, and later I re-explained everything to someone."

December 9, SMW: "With group of people at a cafe; Jane there. Huge map of the world on the floor. Seth comes through and explains where there is evidence of ancient civilizations — he says some is buried in caves in Spain. We stand on the land area on the map. Seth explains this location in detail. Later, we disperse and re-explain it all to others."

For the week of March 31–April 7, 1970:
April 3, Ned Watkins: "Sue and I are swimming naked near a McDonald's. Another girl is there. I tell her to write to me — she's an old girlfriend. I talk to her for a while. A giant had told me that he would help me go out-of-body."

April 3, SMW: "Ned and I are swimming naked by Pudgies' Pizza place. Another girl is there. She is wearing glasses. Ned seems interested in her. We try to go out-of-body."

For the week of November 20–27, 1973:
November 20, Darren Stephens: "I have a room in a very big house that turns out to be Jane's. We are tending to a small white unicorn and her baby, who lives with me. Sue W. comes to visit. Before I can tell her about them, the unicorns get out. A large gray cat and her kitten threatens them."

November 20, SMW: "We have a tame lion in my parents' large house. Class is there. The lion does something he shouldn't."

For the week of February 5–12, 1974:
February 8, SMW: "A dream in which I was put into suspended animation by a group of oddly dressed twenty-first century people for a voyage into space. One of these people was dressed like a cowboy . . . Later, we were all on a yacht and a Greek gangster character threw us into the water. We didn't drown, however, but managed to get to

shore after many trials. At the end, my grandmother Mullin [dead for two years by then] appeared and I couldn't figure out how she got there—was she dead or not? Had she died, or was she about to?"

February 8, Priscilla Lantini: "I had a dream that my husband and I were shot and killed by gangsters. We were both dead on the spot, but I couldn't die. I got right back up again, although I knew I was dead."

Priscilla also notes that "Eddie Feinstein, one of the Boys from New York, had a similar dream [during that week] in which he was in a war and killed and could not die. He told of this at class that week and [said] he thought he heard Seth say in the dream, 'The Mona Lisa is very, very heavy.' Seth came through and told Artie that that was *his* interpretation of what he thought Seth might say . . . "

[" . . . And so, you should, by rights, tell *me* what it means!" Seth told Eddie that night. "But, for now, I will give you a clue: 'Sweetness and light come hard.' It is my interpretation of your interpretation!

["But," Seth went on, "it is easy for others to talk and tell you it is easy to be spontaneous, and easy to get out of your body. Therefore, the responsibility, it seems to you, is stronger. If there were trials put in front of you; if I said it is difficult to get out of your body; if I gave you trials and said you must do thus-and-so, and *then* get out of your body, you would feel safe because, after all, it would not happen right away! You may not pass the trial! But when I say it is easy to do so, and tell you that you have the ability, then you face, in yourself, you *own* obstructions and your own fears—and they are heavy!"]

"Then," Priscilla continues, "Eddie asked Seth about a dream he'd had during that week in which he'd been participating in a war." [However, Eddie said, the weapons used in this war seemed to be shooting a liquid rather than conventional bullets. "I was shot," Eddie said, "and lay down to die—but I couldn't! The result was sort of like not being able to get out-of-body . . . " Eddie stopped and laughed, light dawning on his face.

["Do you need me?" Seth roared.

["I didn't see the connection before," Eddie said. "Of course!"]

For the week of February 19–26, 1974:
February 20, Betty DiAngelo: "While going to sleep, I picked up that a class is going on. I see Richie Kendall very clearly. We are

speaking in Sumari, and there is a greeting that sounds like 'Shamah.'"

February 20, SMW: "A strange class dream at a party. Carl Jones is running around kissing the girls. A new *Oversoul Seven* has come out. Sumari says this, meant for Jane: 'S' ventala mendala vert*u*.'"

For the week of March 12–19, 1974:
March 12, Betty DiAngelo: "Class in a large dim hall that was separated, with large double doors. In the other half was a large group of people also having a Seth session — a different 'family of consciousness.' Theirs had religious overtones. I sneak into their meeting and hear them ridiculing us . . . "
     [*Note: Betty did not attend the March 12 class, which featured a Sumari "initiation" song to newcomers.*]

March 13, George Rhoads: "Has to do with a class. A race; people on an elevated conveyor, or little swings, standing up. Some parts are dangerous and speedy . . . We end up in a kind of dark, dim supermarket. Large. An exhibition hall. Paintings by friends. I stop at one. An empty skin, white with big nose and bald head — a fool. Maybe that was the title. An airplane model hangs nearby."

March 19, Betty DiAngelo: I am having a discussion, argument really, with a new girl in class over organic versus inorganic food [*an issue that was of prime consideration to George at the time*]. The dream seemed filled with strange happenings . . . Mary Strand, Tim, and I leave together . . . remember crossing some water that was near a roller coaster. Also cutting through a car dealer's lot with models on display."

For the week of April 16–23, 1974:
April 20, SMW: "A strange sort of dream correlation. I recorded for last night's dreams, 'mystical, deep; something about June and Joyce [girlfriends from sophomore year at Syracuse], and the Engadine Valley in Switzerland.[10] Strong feeling of communication with past, present, and future. Convoluted physical event.'
     "The next day, I received a letter, dated April 20, from my college roommate, Ellen R. The two of us went on a trip to Europe after our sophomore year at Syracuse. We worked for two months in the laundry room of a Swiss resort hotel, located in a mountain pass in the western part of the Engadine. We'd reminded one another many times of that trip, of course, but had never

spoken about the strange kinds of *inner* journeys that European junket had awakened in us—I remember, for example, a vivid sense of absolute familiarity as we stood in the Innsbruck train station, our first stop after leaving Switzerland.

"Ellen records few dreams and has never been to Jane's class or read her books [*in 1974*]. Here, I'll quote from her letter:

> 'Dear Sue: The oddest thing just happened, and I know of no one else to tell it to but you, because you are the only one who will believe me—at least I think you'll believe me. I swear that it is true.
>
> 'The day that we [*Ellen and her husband, Max*] moved into this apartment, on July 14, 1971, two things were stolen from us during our move. At least we assumed they were stolen because we packed them on the moving truck at 87th Street, but they never arrived here. One was a green carpet sweeper my brother had given us a few weeks before, and the other was my 320 Polaroid camera, my wedding gift from [*Max and friends*].
>
> 'Well, the losses were sad, but not the end of the world. I use my regular vacuum cleaner to do the floors, and we bought me a Square-Shooter Polaroid camera to replace the other.
>
> 'Today [*April 20th*] I was hanging up clothes in my closet, and my 320 Polaroid was there, hanging on a clothing rack right next to the door!
>
> 'Sure, you're thinking, Ellen is a slob, and she probably hung it there when she moved in and didn't notice it until today. BUT THAT IS NOT WHAT HAP-PENED!! I always use that clothing hook and I have cleaned my closet lots of times, and even Max has cleaned my closet, and when we first moved in we searched the entire apartment, including my closet, for the missing articles.
>
> 'So, now I have two Polaroid cameras and I don't believe my eyes. The only believable explanation for me is that some other-worldly being borrowed the camera for a while, and now returned it! Can *you* think of another explanation? I really am *not* putting you on—this really did just happen to me! And I am reeling from disbelief!
>
> L, Ellen'

"To compound this odd bit of telepathy, or whatevever it was—had I picked up on Ellen's camera hijinks in my dream?— when I called Jane to tell her about this experience, she told me that during her nap that afternoon, she'd had a brief dream of me in Europe, a context in which Jane never associates me at all. Jane and I agreed, though, that if there were truly no other explanation for the camera's sudden re-appearance—if it didn't turn out that someone had found it and put it on the closet hook without comment, for instance [*and no other such explanation ever did arise*]—then it seemed like a kind of portent, or symbolic event, of new directions, or probabilities for Ellen and Max; 'the intertwining of past, present, and future,' Jane said. [*And indeed, they did take new directions together; in 1978 they moved to another city, where today they each have new careers; the series of events that led them there started about the time of this incident*]. And for whatever reason, it seemed that Jane and I had tuned in on this inner and outer 'turn' in Ellen's life.

"By the way, this explanation [*much of it deleted here*], sounded 'right' to Ellen at the time, even though I hadn't discussed such things as probabilities and simultaneous time with her before . . . ''

For the week of June 11–18, 1974:
June 12, Betty DiAngelo: "Class very crowded and in a different place than Jane's apartment. Tim and I were told we had missed G. [a local poli-sci professor who specializes in the Mid-East]."

June 13, Derek Batholomew: "Diane Best and I were with Ira Willis and the rest of the class at an ocean beach. After we had walked along the sand for a while, Diane and I went off with some of the others to watch a movie. I don't recall what it was about, but there were a lot of people in the auditorium."

June 13, SMW: "Long, long dream in which I have a small-animal veterinarian clinic. Strange stainless steel surgery objects appear. Many people come to the house. A horse walks in to see me, on his own. Several members of class come in from a camping trip. George Rhoads and I dance to a waltz in the kitchen while a meal is being prepared."

June 16, SMW: "A long dream about Diane Best and Ira Willis. Ira sits down in my strawberry patch and talks about the school for 'famous' people he's teaching in. Diane appears, larger than life, over his right shoulder, her hair covered by a tight cloth scarf, carrying a tray of biscuits. The three of us, along with [class member] Deeana Bowman, take a journey in two small red children's wagons. Much talk about Diane and power (particularly physical power) and her interpretations of Sumari. We discuss the Mid-East and the tense situation there."

June 18, Derek Bartholomew: "Class dream, but only unusual detail I recalled was that Willy, Jane's cat, was allowed to attend too."

June 18, George Rhoads: "I notice [William] Styron [*author of* The Confessions of Nat Turner *and* Sophie's Choice, *and a friend of George's*] in class. He is there with two similar friends. A houseful of people. A meal prepared by some women. Big white biscuits and butter—a different kind of meal, but I eat it. Large biceps on Geoffery B.—that Seth gave [him]. I sit around with special new things I got from dream—stainless steel barbed wire? Un-material flowers . . ."

For the week of September 17–24, 1974:
September 20, Betty DiAngelo: "In class we are discussing animals in connection with humans. A couple from San Francisco relates an encounter in which a large snake crawled through their bedroom window and their goat promptly did it in and made a messy job of it. I then related that Tim and I had a similar happening, but it was our cat that killed the snake."

September 24, SMW: "A mother poodle is being persecuted by everyone. She comes in my bedroom window. I try to save her, and end up only saving her two pups. But they look so much like her that I have to get them away fast so no one will shoot them. I go into a needlepoint store and see a huge book on medieval needlepoint patterns. I see tapestries with unicorns, goats, mermaids on them. Then I come to an elevator to another universe. Class members Phil Levine and Pete Sawyer [*who moved to Elmira in the early 70's from his hometown, San Francisco*] are running it. It's crowded. I think of the messy end scene of the Jack the Ripper movie I once saw, in which J. the R. gets squashed under an elevator and blood runs out from underneath it."

        [*Note: Tim and Betty were not in class at this time—they were taking a cross-country vacation.*]

For the week of September 24–October 1, 1974:
September 26, Derek Bartholomew: "The class was moved into a

large building where we were to be shown a movie of diabolical understanding (I'm still not sure what I meant by that). The movie was made in 1916 and was in black and white. We couldn't understand the language of the movie, so a large man brought out a scroll and began to read from it. Soon this became incomprehensible because of the man's accent. . . . We left shortly after the movie was over."

September 26, SMW: "In a large house with ornate, overcrowded antiques, polished floors, bright blue wallpaper with goldweave designs, scrollwork on doorways. A party going on for many people, including class members. Then I find myself, George Rhoads, and another girl bailing out of a World War I airplane. We land near a theater and go in. A large audience is watching an X-rated movie made in WW I era. This seems to culminate in everyone's feeling sexy except me, and I feel that I must not have understood what was going on."

For the week of December 16–23, 1974:
December 16, SMW: "My mother and I are in Peru when a volcano erupts [*I have a cousin, a Catholic priest, who lives in Peru*]. I see this clearly. Lava flows; ash fills the air. We find a little fancy car. The ash touches our car and it's magic; we escape to the Old City section of Luxembourg, where we see hanging gardens, vines growing on the old houses, etc."

December 16, Betty DiAngelo: "Seth is telling us that the atmosphere is very heavy with unhealthy contaminants, particularly dangerous for small children. The class is outdoors—the atmosphere here is one of arbors, passageways, and gardens."

December 23, Will Petrosky: "Class. A giant party. Some magic dust is sprinkled. A giant Kali [*a Hindu god*] appears and does a dance."

For the week of March 4–11, 1975:
March 4, George Rhoads: "Excavation of a cellar to reveal ancient bas-reliefs, sculptures, and texts. The group meeting there made other writings as well. I meet there with a group, my father included, to see some objects brought to us for our inspection—long pieces of steel rod with mirrors at either end and in the middle. I guessed rightly that these were truck mirrors, double periscopes, allowing the driver to see behind him from high or low . . ."

March 5, Derek Bartholomew: "I was driving along the road with some class members, stopping to visit various museums to look at the artists' works."

March 5, George Rhoads: "A group of several people go to a field where there is a sort of tacky Stonehenge made of plywood and cardboard. People are hang-gliding in the distance. We want to take some of the plywood and make hang-gliders. Then in a big room — apartment? — somebody helps us make hang-gliders out of a 2 × 4 fastened together at one end with a bolt."

March 5, SMW: "Two airplanes zoom in circles over the house. Oddly shaped, like hang-gliders, they are from another time and space, I think. One rams the other and threatens to crash into the house. I run down the driveway. I see that the house and property are really carefully maintained museums; illusions preserved in the middle of a giant and filthy city. It occurs to me that this is a pretty tacky way to preserve history — to make a 'Looking-Glass Zoo' out of us."

For the week of December 31–January 7, 1975:

On January 3, a relative of mine was rushed to the hospital for emergency surgery, suffering a perforated bowel and peritonitis. My relative recovered; on Sunday, January 5, I recorded the following dream:

"I am part of a research team teaching animals how to read. A shot of a substance called KGB gives their brain cells the ability to do this. Mice and then possums write letters. I say something to someone about consciousness having freedom to take great leaps. All this seems connected with [my relative's] symptoms and reasons for the emergency situation."

Unknown to me, George Rhoads recorded this dream on Sunday, Jan. 5: "I put a hole in a fence to let animals run through and away from a car fire on the other side of the fence. The fire was then put out with sound."

As I was driving back home to Dundee that Sunday afternoon, I saw a fire truck pull up, sirens blaring, next to a car with a flaming motor. Later, in class, I thought how the two dreams and the incident with the truck could connect with my relative's operation — the hole in the fence (abdomen?) that is opened to let the animals (emotions?) out, away from the fire (infection?) which is then put out with sound (as George's car motor fire was — motor equaling the body; truck equaling technology?). In my dream, the animals' cells were given a shot by medical researchers to make them more intellectual — to bring their natural animal (emotional?) instincts and

the human quality of intellect (as my dream defined it) closer together. Was this the unofficial intent behind my relative's physical
troubles?

Seth did give some fascinating dream interpretations in
class—sometimes before the person had explained the dream to anyone, including Jane (an interesting example of trance telepathy). But more than interpretations, Seth—and the entire class
context—gave members invaluable help in learning *how* to dream;
in learning how to open up, and interpret for ourselves, that entire
sphere of consciousness. For some of us, this was no easy feat.

One June night in 1973, Seth came through with an eloquent soliloquy on the "reality" of dreaming. It was, as usual, pertinent and profound, but as he finished, Florence MacIntyre spoke
up: "If this is such an important part of our life, then why can't we
remember more of that part?" she asked. "I remember nothing of
it." Even recalling a tiny portion of a dream in the space of months
was an achievement for her, Florence sighed.

"Now, you asked the question in a general manner, but it
cannot be answered in that way," Seth said, smiling at her. "So, the
answer that we will give our Lady of Florence will be a personal one.
But each of you had better apply it to your own lives and beliefs."

Seth sat back in the chair, closed Jane's eyes, and cupped
her chin in hand. "You are still afraid of the inner self," he began.
"You still do not trust your dreams, and you are afraid of them. You
do not *want* to remember them. When you give yourself suggestions
that you will remember your dreams, many of you do not mean
it—" Seth opened his eyes and looked at Florence "—as *you* do not
mean it. You are afraid of what you might meet, and you are still
afraid of one particular dream, and you know the one to which I am
referring.

"You *can* change the ending of the dream by understanding the nature of reality—that *you* form it. While you are afraid of
dream reality, you are afraid of what you think of as 'real' reality.
The dream [*of Florence's*] beautifully poses your dilemma in physical life, but you are afraid of solving it or even facing it either in
physical reality or in dream reality.

"Now, this applies to many of you. You can give yourself
suggestions for centuries, and say, 'I will remember my dreams,'
while at the same time you think, 'Dreams are dangerous. They are

a part of me that I do not want to know.' And if that is what you really believe, you will not pay any heed to your [own] suggestions!

"You must believe in the power and energy and strength and glory of your being, and know that problems are challenges for you to solve. They are there to be solved! Then face them joyfully, and yourself, knowing that when you know your entire self, waking or sleeping, you will be pleased—as in the old legend, God was pleased when he created the world.

"It is only when you do not know yourself that you fear [that] you are evil, and [are] afraid to look within yourself. But when you open up those doors, you are amazed by the immensity and grace of your own being."

"What," asked a student, "is *beyond* our dimension of consciousness?"

The class burst into laughter. As if we didn't have enough troubles grasping *this* one! "The laugh," Seth answered loudly, "is the answer!

"Now, practically speaking, of course, there is a solution," Seth continued to Florence and the rest of us, "and it is this: *Stop cowering*!! Do not cower before your own belief that the inner self is frightening, or that you are a bad person, or that while you are good, there are bad things hidden down there. Tell yourself, and convince yourself, that since you are a part of All-That-Is, you are—in your own way, now—a unique expression of All-That-Is; and there is nothing in All-That-Is to be afraid of; and there is nothing in yourself to be afraid of. Tell yourself that often, and think and feel that, and it will get through to you. But the more you tell yourself that you are frightened of your dreams, while telling yourself that you want to remember them, you are in a quandary. And again, this applies to all of you."

Stewie Gould spoke up this time. "When I dream, and then wake up, I sort of take it all for granted. It's so obvious that I'll remember the dream that I don't even write it down—and I go back to sleep and then I wake up and realize that I *don't* remember it and should have written it down! How come that happens?"

"That applies to everyone," Seth answered. "The problem and the solution. The problem is simply that you fool yourself. You know very well, because it has happened many times, that if you do not write it down you will forget it—and only part of you wants to."

"I usually tell myself," Stewie said. "But then, I seem to make a judgment, like, if it's good, I'll write it down; if it's a bad dream, then I won't."

"*That* is your problem!" Seth stated. "You should not make the judgment! Simply write [the dreams] down!

"Now, Ruburt has said this often, and it applies again to all of you. The very habit [that is] set up as you write down your dreams and recall them, opens up channels between what you *think* of, now, as your conscious and unconscious selves. The training teaches you to switch from one level of reality to another, and to bring back your goodies in both hands. Whether or not the dream is important in your terms, you can use this training."

And in the course of this dream "training," it was perhaps inevitable that Seth appeared in our dreams with such punctual frequency, either as the cherubic gentleman depicted in Rob's painting (reproduced in *The Seth Material*), as Jane-in-trance, or in some dream-scape combination of the two. Seth was, of course, such an outstanding feature of class that it would have been unnatural if he and Jane had been missing from class dreams. Yet, did Seth, as an independent entity, actually walk into our dreams in the way that we walked into Jane's living room? The question is a tricky one, since it deals as well with the questions of how "real" were our *own* appearances in class dreams—and again, with the "reality" of mental events.

I think, of course, that we freely used Seth—as well as Jane and Rob—as easily recognizable, reassuring, and consistent dream-symbols: direction, self-knowledge, and personal power neatly wrapped up in familiar personae. And as he cautioned us so many times to do, this was one method of following the "Seth in ourselves." The difference, in my opinion, between these dream appearances and the kind of report that Jane so often gets—wherein Seth has spoken to, or through, someone else, or materialized at a seance in Chicago—has to do, in part, with the assumptions of the perceivers.

True, people anywhere can use Seth (or Jesus, or Mr. Spock, or most anyone) for a meeting with their own inner knowledge—and successfully, with good and valid insights. But the Seth-Jane-Rob phenomenon, as it develops and investigates the realms of consciousness, is only partly an experience in mediumship (as the term is usually defined). Group dreaming, the exploration of probabilities, the "building" of an "Inner City" (see Chapter 10) and other such exercises challenging the boundaries of physical reality were tried out in class for a reason: our experiences gave an immediate re-flection of how inner logic, turned outward into the daily world, can give us a real understanding of the underpinnings of existence, and some practical reassurance that the individual can indeed make a "difference" within his private moments.

"Now within yourselves, you each have your wise old man," Seth told us once of his image in our dreams. "You each have within yourself your eternal child. You each have within yourself windows that open into your own realities—even those realities that you cannot translate in your terms. I am a vehicle, as the wind is a vehicle. I am a window, as that window is. I am composed of what you are, and what I am.

"And it is true to say, as I have said, that the flowers speak with an eloquent voice, if only you would listen, and that the flowers are also what you are, if you knew it. Part of a rosebud a month ago may now be something else entirely. And the cells that now glow through your arm may have been the cheeks of a Chinaman, or a waving twig in the wind. You speak for the twig, as you go about your day. And I speak for you as I go about my quite different day.

"But each of you grows out in all directions. You . . . send out feelers, and communication and energy comes back to you as you send out communication and energy. And more comes to you through my voice than the words, as many of you know by now. The words make sense to you, and you listen to me. But within the words, where the mind finds no reason, there are also communications; and you accept those also and acquiesce to them, because they are a part of your own greater reality.

"And when I speak, I rouse the grand old wise man in each of you so that you will listen to him, for he speaks within your dreams in whatever guise you want. But do not forget there is [also] the wise old woman!

"Your dreams are the other side of your waking life, as your waking life is the other side of your dream life. Remember that whether you are awake or dreaming. If you remember that when you are dreaming, you will become awake and alive; and if you re-member that when you are awake, you will become dreaming and alive!

"You are now dreaming that you are awake. In your dreams I speak to you—in your dream of wakefulness. When you dream, you dream that you dream; and you dream that I speak to you in your dreams. You are awake, whether you believe you are

402 / Class Dreams and Co-Creations

awake or dreaming. You are creating realities, whether or not you
pretend that you are *dreaming* realities.

"The atoms and molecules within you dream that there
are people. How real their dream is to you! How deep a trance is
your life! How deep a trance, in your terms, is the life of a dream!

"How real is a dream? What makes you think that there is
any difference between what you think of as a dream, and what you
think of as reality? You assume that a dream is less real; yet through
what you think of as your dreaming life, you make your physical life.
You do the work in your dreams that allows you to survive in physical terms. You choose in a dream state the probable realities that
you will then make physical. You work harder in your dreams—but
playfully!

"I will not say more. I want you to feel what I have said.
Where would you be but for the atom's dream?

"If atoms dream their joint dreams of you, who do you
dream of, and what realities do you form? Now, the dream of the
atoms is a gestalt dream while still individual, and you dream individually; and yet you meet in dreams, and there are mass dreams. I
am asking you questions now, but unlike you, I do not demand instant answers!

"What I want you to tell me is this: How aware are your
atoms of your individual lives, and how aware are the products of
your dreaming lives of your realities . . . and you of them? Do stars
dream?

"That is your assignment. The entire group of questions.
Look for the answers through your intellect, your intuition; and address the questions to yourselves before you dream."

NOTES FOR CHAPTER FOURTEEN

1. Would it *ever* be "practical" to immediately ground all
DC-10 airplanes on the basis of one dreamer's phone call? Yet with different beliefs concerning the nature of the psyche, perhaps the *quality* of
David Booth's dreams—as well as his own feelings of certainty—would
have been recognized, and something more done. As it was, after the
Chicago crash an FAA investigation did reveal a structural weakness in the
wing engine design and DC-10s *were* grounded for general inspection after
this air disaster; perhaps Booth's dream contained the intensity of a larger
danger.

Another instance of "official" dream recognition occurred two months after the DC-10 crash: a Connecticut woman reported her vision of a Niagara Falls catastrophe. According to news accounts, she saw a dam of rocks above the falls collapse and an onrush of water drown a group of deaf children aboard the *Maid of the Mist* cruise boat. The Army Corps of Engineers made a check of the retaining wall in question, but found nothing wrong. Several hours later, however, a rusty seismic sensor gave a false warning of a rock fracture on Terrapin Point overlook. That area was closed until further investigation proved that it was a mechanism malfunction and not impending rock slippage.

But what *had* the woman picked up? Probabilities? A warning that the sensor should be fixed, as the DC-10 design needed fixing? A sense of doom pervading her life, combined with a need for drama and the kind of media exposure that David Booth had briefly attained? Yet again, in this incident, the vision was treated with some respect—in this last case, checked out.

2. In conjunction with the newspaper accounts of David Booth's experience, George Rhoads sent me the following note: "Reading about the dreams predicting the DC-10 crash of the 25th of May, I recalled a terrible nightmare I had on [May] 15th. I quote it as I wrote it:

"'The ruin of a large building. Very high ceilings, roofs full of holes, some huge. Vast scale. At first, all was well. Paul [*George's son*] took me to a room where there were things he'd had as a child—souvenirs, old things. He told me there were machines—huge boilers—at the upper part of the building. I went to see. Great rocking beams and engines hundreds of feet high, in ruins. Boilers extending into the distance, pipes. Then something fell from a high place—a piece of machinery—and when it fell, it made a shower of sparks and a terrible impact. Then other things fell, and people were being crushed. I ran downstairs. A man was waiting for me, to lead me out. Paul was still in the upper part. Dust and noise and crashing everywhere. I yelled for Paul, so he could find the way, but no answer. I went back, but could not get far because of the dust and noise. People dying. The man was with me, waiting. . . .

"I woke from this dream yelling and crying. The deaths—the terror—were quite vivid!'"

It's interesting speculation that George's dream might have been his own personal, internalized foreknowledge of a more public event. Speculation—but nothing specific. An added point to consider, however: One of the 275 people who died in the crash was author Judith Wax, who had published her first book, *Starting in the Middle*, just months before she died. The book deals fairly exclusively with beliefs that see senility, disease, and general decay as "rational" inevitabilities to be contended with by "middle age"—starting in one's early forties! Ms. Wax and George are of a contemporary age; George also counts several well-known writers among his many artist friends. Private fears and public ones, connected? Again, interesting speculation—"You create the reality you know, individually, and en masse"—but nothing more.

3. During class years, nearly everyone kept dream records, which we read from almost every week. With the exception of couples, or with those few members who came in social contact during the week, there was little dream comparison between Tuesdays, although if something really exciting happened, students would call up Jane with dream descriptions. But in general, the dreams we read aloud or recounted during class were new to other members.

In the time between the last regular classes and my questionnaire's request for dream records, however, many members lost their notebooks, or—ye gods and little fishes!!!—*threw them away*. Some didn't have the considerable time necessary to copy them for me; others didn't answer that part of the questionnaire or didn't remember their dreams in the first place—or (my aching brain!) didn't *date* their dreams when they occurred. Some, like Betty DiAngelo, Darren Stephens, Derek Bartholomew, George Rhoads and others, generously and laboriously copied the dreams I asked for; and of course I had all of my own dream notebooks, my correlation notes and those made by others; and remarks made by Harold Wiles on the class session copies. Therefore, these dream chapters' histories are made up of that combination of records. It does, of course, leave out many connecting dreams because of simple lack of space. Someday I'd like to see all of class members' dreams made available for study; it would be a fascinating—if unbelievably time-consuming—piece of research.

4. "Later," Matt notes, "Seth said that the dream had been valid—(no shit, Sherlock!)—and that the communication had come from a different layer of my mother's personality. . . . " In fact, Seth made several remarks about Matt's mother during a book dictation session not long after her death:

"In your terms . . . Matt's mother made her decision [*to die*] approximately three years [before the event]," Seth said. "A large portion of her intent and focus *began* to be directed elsewhere. In your probability, the official death has just occurred. Three years ago, however, that personality also took another turn, where another decision, to live, was made. In that probability, Matt's parents moved to Florida. A pivotal point came in the parents' relationship with each other. In your terms, the parents pulled from the past into the present certain elements that had a long time ago united them. That probability, however, is not what is considered the official one.

"Such things are almost impossible to explain. When consciousness splits off from itself, the 'original' is not less, but a new synthesis occurs. Such psychological births take place often even in one life, quite escaping your notice. The mother to whom Matt related in usual terms ended this particular Earth experience, and begins another experience with the memories up until the time of death.

"The other portion of that personality represents points of contact and relationship between the parents which regrouped, and *that* woman will live on into her eighties, dying with her memories of Florida. This of course presupposes Matt's probable father, who also made the Florida trip. Psychological dynamics govern such issues, and emotional forces as they group and regroup. Largely unconsciously, Matt's mother began three years ago in your reality to plan what in your terms will be her future life, and the energy not used here was utilized to form a large overall pattern into which the next-life experiences could flow. It was at that deep level that she contacted Matt in the dream state.

"The self is quite able to keep track of its own journeys into various realities and times, and feels no confusion. All mental or psychological actions occur from your standpoint with a rapidity and native balance that may appear awkward only when you try to define such activity. In those terms, each instant of life seeks completion and fulfillment, when obviously within your time context and limitations this is an impossibility. You only keep track of a small portion of the action, then.

"Probabilities merge and intersect at every point of your lifetime. You have, in one life period, literally thousands of alternate probable life paths *that you take,* as legitimately as you take the life path that you officially recognize."

5. Coming "awake" in dreams is an experience that you can train yourself to do—by suggesting, simply, that you will do so! Or tell yourself that when you dream of a certain person, place, or thing—say, any time you encounter something inharmonious (such as wallpaper on the walls that you painted over ten years ago)—that you'll become aware that you are dreaming. It's an indescribably profound experience; for one thing, it establishes a link of *knowing* between your dreaming and waking self and tends to give you a certain kind of "courage" in dream exploration (and, who knows?—maybe in the waking state too).

6. This seems to be another early allusion to the counterpart concept (see Chapter 18). It also reminds me of my childhood dream-discussion groups, which were almost completely comprised of strangers.

7. Again, see Chapter 10, Volume 1, of this book.

8. In Jane's novel, *The Education of Oversoul 7,* the Earthly personalities—or aspects—of the entity Oversoul Seven unite across time and space in dream "meetings," or tribunals.

9. According to Matt Adams, Seth was alluding to some strange experiences that Jane, Rob, and Matt had been discussing earlier that day, before class. "During a lunch hour not too long before," he writes, "I had been walking in a New Jersey park overlooking the Hudson River. With me was a friend named Frank, who was rather more skeptical

and orthodox than I was. It was a bright sunny day. We were gazing out through a gap in the trees at the river below when, all at once, a bird glided out of a tree less than 30 feet away, at just about eye level.

"It was a twice the size of a blue jay, with perhaps a two-foot wingspread. Its bill was quite thick, cantaloupe-orange, and blunt at the tip like a puffin's or flamingo's. It had a woodpecker-like crest on its head, and its feathers were vivid blue. But strangest of all were the widely separated *squarish* white spots, nearly an inch across, over its wings and back.

"In sight for perhaps two seconds, the bird swooped silently up into the foliage of another tree and was lost to sight. Frank and I looked at each other and almost in the same breath, asked, 'Did you see *that*?' All the way back to the office, we racked our brains, thinking of every species of bird that could possibly match what we'd seen and uncomfortably concluded that there simply wasn't any! Later, the writer Brad Steiger told me that perhaps I had seen 'the great speckled bird.'

"But while this sighting was still annoyingly fresh in my mind, I related it to Jane and Rob, who said that once a bird that neither of them could identify had gotten into Rob's painting studio. Jane cited the old Irish belief that a bird in a house presages a death in the family; though I don't recall whether their unknown bird foreflew the demise of either of their parents. In any case, the whole question of unlikely *oiseaux* was definitely in the air that Tuesday night."

10. The Engadine Valley in southwestern Switzerland includes such well-known resorts as St. Moritz and Davos. One of the peculiarities of

the region is its native language, Romansch, which has no clearly defined origins, unlike the German- and Latin-based languages that surround it. Some linguists believe that Romansch may be more related to Finnish than to the other Romance languages; but its existence in the Engadine still presents something of a mystery. This kind of linguistic oddity always fascinated me; and seemed to represent, long before I could put it into words, the convolutions of time and space that are hidden, generally, within the privacy of one's own psyche. Perhaps this is partly responsible for the connection that suggests itself between Jane's dream and mine, and Ellen's experience with the camera.

11. See *Psychic Politics*, Chapter 17, for Jane's record of another "probable class," or series of correlating dreams.

CHAPTER
FIFTEEN

Further Expeditions: Out-of-Bodies
and the Gates of Horn

REPETITION OF OUR CONSTANT CREATIONS

We are the changes of life
blinking in and out so quickly we don't notice
the repetition of constant creations
massaging us to sanity.

We are one big happy who-done-it wonder people
cruising thru our selves shaking hands.

Extended penis and intended vagina
puzzle-fit interlocking minds
weathered smooth from timeless tumblings.

The dream of what we are
we are.

— Barrie Gellis, 1972

"I am out-of-body over green countryside—fly over a
smoggy city. I try to get to Elmira . . . with Lauren.
Seth is three feet high and gives a rap on probable
realities. *Then* I meet a probable Jane—who lives with
her mother and daughter!"

— Will Petrosky's out-of-body,
November 21, 1974

"True Dreams from the Gates of—*wha-a-a-a-t?!*"

Once again, those old red flags were waving in my brain. Fire alarms, air-raid sirens, and Don't Walk signs were sounding off, too. Just the night before, I'd happened to see part of a television documentary on a Meher Baba clan—in which his disciples were dancing around a large photograph of Baba while throwing rose petals and rice (organic wild, most likely) at the picture's feet. I'd nearly screamed with embarrassed horror: is *that* what our ESP class looked like to other people? Were *we* just sitting worshipfully around Jane/Seth's feet, throwing symbolic rose petals in hopeful exchange for the Answers to Life? Were we just another squawk in the general roar that some had distainfully labeled "Me-ism?"

Actually, I'm sure that this kind of feeling—in less exaggerated form—crossed every class member's mind at one time or another; and basically, it demonstrated the sense of balance that we were learning to achieve. But this *thing*, this new dream suggestion that Seth had just made to us, had really set me off—even though I would soon discover that I related easily, as most class members did, to its dreaming impetus.

We had been discussing our beliefs about "true responsibility" and love on that May Tuesday in 1974, when Seth entered the conversation. "When you say 'I love you' because you think you have a *responsibility* to say, 'I love you,' when you do not feel the emotion behind those words," Seth reminded us forceably, *"then you are a liar,* and the other person knows it! You are not responding to that person, and it may be that alone—your private response—was what they wanted, and not your lies. . . . "

Ah, love! That great, eternal, perplexing, consuming, belief-ridden, self-rending subject! Lies and truths, loves and hates. "If there are no divisions to the self," someone had remarked earlier, "then why is it that you can love and hate a person at the same time?" An old question, endlessly drawn and quartered. "If there are no divisions to the self," someone else had retorted, "then why is it that you *never* feel just one simple thing about anything or anyone? You mean to say we're all doomed to feel twenty thousand ways about everything because that's the way the 'undivided' self *is?*"

Then, without preamble, Seth gave us the dream hint that had tripped my warning bells: "During the week, before you sleep, tell yourself—if you want to—that you will have a 'True Dream from the Gates of Horn,'" he said. "Now, that is an ancient suggestion, given by the Egyptians: The Gates of Horn. I do not

want to tell you what it means yet, simply to ask you to give yourselves the suggestion—those of you who want to!—for a True
Dream, that will help harmonize the portions of your being. That is
part of the suggestion! Ask for a True Dream that comes from the
Gates of Horn, [and] that will help harmonize the portions of your
being."

Seth closed Jane's eyes; Jane immediately opened them.
Someone filled her in on the "Gates of Horn," while I sat sullenly,
feeling lousy. Everyone else had taken to the idea at once. All *I* could
think of was the Baba group, dancing around that huge, ridiculous
photograph. I didn't respond this way very often to things that went
on in class, but when I did, it tended to be toward the extreme.
Right then, I wanted to quit class and go home. And yet . . . always, that annoying "And yet."

"Well, that sounds interesting," Jane said of the Gates of
Horn—lightly, without much enthusiasm. "I'm all for harmonizing
portions of my being, you know?" Then she looked at me and smiled,
instantly discerning the nature of my grumps, and shrugged. "Who
knows?" she offered me, laughing. "Sometimes I *depend* on you to
react like that," she added affectionately, then turned to answer
someone else's question.

After class, I drove home alone, trying to sort out my
doubts. What difference did a dream suggestion make, after all? If
you didn't really like the suggestion, then no matter *what* you told
yourself before falling asleep, you wouldn't use it. Your self protects
yourself very nicely that way—except, another part of me noted, in
the case of nightmares . . . well, even nightmares were edifying . . .
But what portions of my being would be involved? What was meant
by "harmony," anyway? What in hell bothered me so much? Faced
with the possibility that True Dreams from the Gates of Horn, or
wherever, could actually help harmonize the warring parts of my
being, was I balking, preferring the clashes of indecision to resolu-
tion? Was I simply getting too introverted lately, too analytical?

Odd, I mused, that the day before this class, I'd had an
irritatingly persistent buzzing sensation in my left ear. I'd gone to the
local hospital emergency room to see if an insect or something were
stuck in there . . . but there was nothing; the noise had finally just
stopped. This was the same ear that I'd had abscesses in twice before;
and—funny thing, really—who had shown up in tonight's class but
Juanita, who'd also had ear problems that Tuesday in 1971, when
Seth had given us both hints for the symptoms' causes—which, in my
case, had involved love and/or the warring portions of my self.
Hmmmm. And then—oh, but this was too much—I'd found out *that*

morning that the doctor who'd treated me that last time in 1971 had died of a lingering malignancy the Tuesday before. Like a waking correlation. Like a strange harmony of circumstances. Well . . .

As usual, I shouldn't have worried. "True Dreams from the Gates of Horn" became indeed some of the most ecstatic, joyous, and profound dreams that we recorded; used particularly in times of stress, and interpreted in light of our daily events, "TD/GH" dreams were labeled by all who experienced them as "different—*completely different*"—in their emotional intent and relationship to you, the waking/sleeping being.

"I realized," says Betty DiAngelo, "that my TD/GH dreams all deal with nature in some way; the two realities always kept merging and I would have a difficult time writing [the dreams] down because of this . . . I think the fascination I have for paintings by Rousseau . . . is because all those throbbing jungle scenes are TD/GH -type inspirations . . .

"On May 29th, 1974 [*the night following Seth's first mention of TD/GH*]," Betty says, "I had a dream of my sister; that *she* had a TD/GH, discovering her inner self, being close to nature and her roots as a human in physical reality. Impossible to describe, but the feeling was 'the source she springs from.' Then on June 19th: throughout this dream, I kept waking up . . . seems it was late at night and I kept awakening (also) within the dream, as motorcycles outside kept annoying me. At one point I went out on the porch, only it was a large patio, cluttered with chairs. My neighbors were there too—the noise was keeping them awake. I went back inside and went to bed, then awakened again, as I heard loud radio music from [my daughter's] room. I went to check . . . someone was staring in her window—a girl. I told Tim . . . and also thought, 'I must figure out why this is happening.' Then I woke up for real. It was 2 A.M. and it was pouring out; a beautiful summer rain. I shut the window because the [rain] noise was too loud, and fell back into the dream.

"I found myself outside. [There was] a large plastic dome on the lawn. A firefly was trapped inside. There was one on the outside too, fluttering as if to get at the other firefly. I watched, transfixed. Before [I could] free the trapped firefly, it got out on its own. The two fireflies then went off together a beautiful scene. Then it was raining, in the dream . . . [then] Tim and I were back in bed, watching people flash on our door . . . an Indian chief, very dignified—all historical people. All the time I was aware of the unceasing rain outside.

"Then I heard something in our kitchen, such as a cat

scratching on the window screen, but it was a strange girl . . . then the front door bell rang. Tim and I looked at each other: this was peculiar, all these visitors at 3 A.M., and we were somewhat alarmed. [But] there was a crowd outside . . . and the feeling was that I knew the purpose and message, but it was elusive. Half of the crowd were the neighborhood children; they all had glowing and shining faces and . . . they brought me gifts. The rain had stopped. There were puddles all over; the night was misty and magical — yet the rain stopping had something to do with a matter resolved, or completed. The mystery unraveled, the children went home. There was singing . . .

"Then I awoke from the dream and was lying in bed, mulling it over, when I heard my name spoken very loudly — and very slowly, like a record on the wrong speed. The voice was not human, but more like a computer would sound — very deep. Then I walked [for real] out on our porch. It was almost 5:00 A.M. The atmosphere was the same as in the dream. I looked up in the sky and saw two stars (in Gemini), and I knew they had some connection with the two fireflies in the dream . . .

"Also, later in September, I gave myself a TD/GH suggestion. [The dream began with] something about white slave trade . . . another girl and I escaped down a deserted road. We found refuge in the basement of a dilapidated old house where others were also hiding. There were several old people, two young girls, ages thirteen or fourteen, a toddler of three years, and a nurse. Tim came in to warn us 'the attack' would begin soon . . .

"I was dismayed to see that the basement wasn't entirely underground, but most of the foundation was exposed. The walls were whitewashed. Each person seemed to be very quiet and in his or her own shell. The teen-age girls were dancing a ballet quietly and then put on an old record. I said to myself, 'I know there must be some reason why I am here with this particular group of people whom I don't know, but what?' I was almost overcome with sadness upon looking at the beautiful three-year-old child, who had lots of dark curly hair. I picked her up and crouched with her behind a piano — as if that would afford us some protection. The bombs started up, and it was a constant, horrific noise like a huge machine gun. I knew, as did everyone else, that we were the target and had no chance of survival.

"I felt my consciousness being obliterated — and wondered if I were dead—I no longer felt the child next to me—I knew my body must be hurt, but I felt nothing. When I awoke from the dream I continued to hear the noise of the bombs and sense what I felt like—that the person who died sort of became alive, or awoke again, within me.

"The actual death was not as traumatic as I supposed death to be," Betty concludes.

On that Friday, May 31 (after grudgingly making the TD/GH suggestion), I recorded this set of dreams, many with strange feelings—many indescribable: "Class is in a strange cottage-like room. We are doing beliefs that somehow have to do with a large plastic turtle. Eddie Feinstein reads his beliefs from the turtle's shell and hands it to me.[1]

"I half-wake up, and feel something like a large animal running up the side of the bed, along the headboard, and down on the floor next to my feet and back again. I fall back into the dream, and walk through some woods into a huge underground area. I come to a desk, behind which sits a receptionist. 'Is this the True Dream of the Gates of Horn place?' I ask.

"'Yes, it is,' the receptionist says kindly.

"'Can you tell me if Jane Roberts has been here?' I ask.

"She looks through a register of names. 'Nope—no Jane Roberts,' she says.

"'Well, how about a Jane Butts?' I ask. The woman looks again. 'Oh, yes, she was here a little while ago with about twenty-two people,' the woman says. 'And what is your name?'

"I tell her, nervously. She turns some pages. 'Yes,' she says, 'you were here also.' She smiles rather mysteriously. I go down the hall and finally see class members walking along, and catch up with them. We all seem headed for this 'True Dream' event, up ahead in this tunnel. Before we get there, however, we come to a man sitting by a fingerprinting machine. He tries to get me to put my fingertips on a series of circles on some special paper for record-ing purposes, but I won't do it. 'I don't put up with this kind of junk awake, so why should I have to when I'm asleep?' I snarl. Sean catches up with us. He's still in his pajamas and won't get dressed.

"We end up sitting around in a garden. Jean Strand and I discuss leg-shaving. We go to class through a rabbit hole. I tell Jean that this is how *Alice in Wonderland* was written—from a dream through the Gates of Horn. Seth is giving a talk on 'masks'—meaning divisions in the self.

"To me, Seth says: 'You put your mask on and off like a moth before a flame.' To Tim DiAngelo, he says, 'You are only beginning to see that you wear one.' And to Florence MacIntyre: 'And you, who wear your mask proudly, as a mask of distinction.' The scene is repeated several times.

"Then this dream falls into another of 'deep inner rooms,' with the same people there. The house we're in resembles my grandmother's old house on Elmira's west side. My aunt takes me aside and shows me a room in this house that she says was mine years ago. For an instant, I don't recognize this room—I realize that it wasn't 'actually' in the house—and then I feel this room being created in my past—I *feel* it spilling out of this dream, my dream, and backwards into physical 'fact' where it becomes a familiar memory, and deeply comforting. My aunt hands me a white rag doll. I hold it and it 'becomes' familiar in the same way. I know that there is no way to describe this once I wake up, because the room and the doll will have become factual, logical circumstance for everyone in my family, too. The room will have been there always, and to say otherwise will seem crazy. But I *know* that both were—are—created NOW, in this TD/GH. Class members agree that this is the nature of reality, awake or asleep."

Priscilla Lantini

"Around the end of September 1974," recalls Priscilla Lantini, "I had a TD/GH that involved a city I was landscaping. It was beautiful, that week of class. I found that others had dreamed of a city they were creating.[2] We ended up [in the dream] calling it 'Sumari City,' but it was my house and I created it. To get in the front door, you had to slide down a tube or cone, maybe eight or nine feet high, ending in a large white door with a gold knocker. Also in this house was a sunporch with a babbling brook running underneath it. You could see looking through the windows where it went under and where it came out. The sunporch was full of mattresses and pillows, sheets and blankets. The room was full of the wonderful smells of the forest . . . "

From these beginnings, "True Dreams" came to be used by class members as the infallible call-for-help dreams; as a special "signal" to the inner self that direction, answers—harmony—was needed. TD/GH requests always seemed to result in vivid, direct information—"You don't ask unless you *really want to know!*" a student once remarked, a little incisively.[3]

An extension of these TD/GH dreams was another suggestion, or "present" given by Seth that December. "I have, in my way, a Christmas gift for you," he told us. "Now, when I give gifts, I ask something in return, so between now and the first of your new year— I am giving you leeway—each of you will have, if you want it, a gift: a particular dream that will stand out from all others; that will have meaning for you alone, and set you on your own path, and help you find your own tone. But you must be willing to accept it. I give it to you on behalf of yourself."

Class members who reported a "Christmas Dream" did indeed feel that it stood out from other dreams during those December weeks. Betty DiAngelo recalled a "mystical class dream" set outdoors on a friend's farm in Pennsylvania. "It's a self-sufficient farm— the symbolism was parallel and obvious," she says. "I carried the meaning of that dream in my head for months." "The Christmas dream—very real," Ralph Lorton notes. "Very clear; *more real* than life. I have not pursued the meaning enough. In [the dream], I was three to four thousand feet over a section of the Mediterranean Sea and hovered near Jordan–Israel. [I saw a map below, with three rivers flowing into the ocean]—the names of tribes of people who moved slowly inland and mixed with others: *Pinces* and *Cimre*. I never worked hard enough to follow up this meaning . . . "

"My Christmas Dream," says Rudy Storch, "was [about] a man of nobility . . . doing something magical. People were trying to ally themselves with planets. Me and someone else allied themselves with the moon and another planet. This man 'of good position' was manipulating (or setting up) marbles in a specific way on an object. The marbles (or stones) corresponded to the planets in some way. The man explained to me that since I was allied with the moon, and due to his manipulations, that I would be ABSOLUTE-LY SAFE from all harm forever.

"As he was explaining this, I felt incredibly safe and powerful, and began to *understand* with certainty that I was indeed safe.

"The setting altered somewhat, and we were now in England. The man was now reciting incantations. A throne appeared on a platform with a lance beside it. The man said to me, 'Well, I'm not sure, but I think if you step right over there, you will be the King of England.'

"The next thing I knew, I was riding on horseback with the lance. Everything was extremely detailed and vivid. I was feeling incredibly exhilarated and powerful. Up ahead, I saw a magical good knight about to pierce a magical barrier (like a force field). He pierced right through it with his lance. With a feeling of reckless confidence and power, I sped after him and pierced the barrier myself. The knight then proceeded to ride through a second barrier. I hesitated, and then attempted to follow him. I had a little trouble piercing this barrier, but succeeded. Up ahead was a brilliantly glowing area which I knew to be the 'Galileo Lion.' As I approached, I saw an exquisitely carved statue of a lion—large, textured, silvery, glowing, and awesome to behold. I knew that it was a magical lion and that if I said the word 'Gold,' I would animate the seemingly inanimate lion. I said 'Gold,' and the sculpture sprang to life. But it would not go beyond the boundary of a circle that surrounded it."

Rudy—who had done some physical "barrier-piercing" on a restaurant's plate-glass window nearly two years before (Chapter 6, Volume 1)—assessed this dream as one of "great personal import" for him. "Seth often urged us to feel the 'magic of our being,'" he says. "Indeed, Seth's concept that we create our own reality is as magical as you can get! Although this [Christmas] dream sounds like a cross between an Errol Flynn movie and *The Seven Voyages of Sinbad,* it helped to put me in touch with a feeling of my own magic power and the 'magic' of the universe. I also felt that the dream helped put me in touch with the unlimited energy available to each individual. In addition, it provided me with a valuable intuitive experience: a 'direct knowing' that I was *safe.*"

"'True Dreams from the Gates of Horn' come whenever I suggest to myself that I have them," says George Rhoads. "These always produce important revelations or experiences that reflect a shift in perspective, an expansion. Daily events take on a dream aspect, and I am able to interpret these events as I would those of a sleeping dream. I am more attuned to the weather, animals, other people, and my own body. All these speak through [an] inner voice.

"Several times in class I have entered a different area of consciousness in which my focus widened to include all sensations equally, my own thoughts becoming one small event among many at once. With this came an inner quiet, a calm and crystalline attention."

"Now, the suggestion that I gave you, was given, of course, for a reason," Seth told us of the Gates of Horn dreams. "Those dreams will involve you with beliefs *behind* your daily reality; and, in certain form, you will see *how* you form that reality, and your most intimate living relationships. There will be, therefore, a correlation between those dreams, your beliefs, and your daily experience.

"I want you to continue the suggestion as given, and then to interpret the dreams in the light of your beliefs and your daily private experience. Later there will be other suggestions, dealing with other levels of reality, as you will interpret them in the dream state.

"Each of you must do this work—this play!—for yourself. It will teach you invaluable information *if* you allow it to. We are beginning a new series of exercises that will involve the dream state and your waking reality. And those of you who are able to follow will later be able to make appointments and keep them in the dream state. But the work—or play—however you consider it, must be done. You must therefore become intimately acquainted with the particular dreams that come to you from what we refer to as the Gates of Horn. Both the Gates of Ivory and the Gates of Horn, historically, in your terms only, were used by the Egyptians. Their idea was that dreams from the Gates of Horn were 'true,' and dreams from the Gates of Ivory were 'not.' But we [in class] are dealing with different definitions!

"Now, listen. As you meet here in the waking state, so you do indeed meet, many of you, in the dream state, at other levels of actuality. You exchange ideas. You help each other. You have, in those terms, an interior family. Now, for those of you who do not like the idea of families, the analogy may not be a pleasant one!

"However, the fact remains that in the dream state, many of you meet each other. You have a common bond, for you understand that you create your own reality. [And] each time you remember to wake up and record a dream, you are doing something with your consciousness, and it is important. For you think enough of your interior life to consciously record it as a physical event in your time. And with your beliefs, that is important . . .

"Now it seems safer, in your terms, to become aware of dream experience than it does to become aware of waking experience. Yet, in any given five-minute period of your life, you perceive information that you do not accept—it is not official information. You are aware of realities, and instead of accepting them, you say, 'No—you do not fit in here.'

"So you do not have to dream in order to become aware of other realities. You must simply allow your consciousness some freedom. Then in the middle of your ordinary activities, you can become familiar with other kinds of reality that are, in other terms, quite familiar to you. You are simply in the habit of blocking these out, and they represent strong portions of your own reality and being.

"*You may find yourselves with a random thought that does not seem to fit in with what you are doing or thinking at the time, and so you dismiss it. It seems random because it does not appear to fit in with your organized picture of reality, but it is an important mosaic that you throw away.*

"So I also joyfully, and playfully, and creatively challenge you (even Jed over there!) to become more and more aware of your waking experience, and of those stray thoughts that come, like thieves in the night. They are not official. You do not accept them. The intellect says, 'Oh, no!'

"*Listen* to those thoughts. Open your mind a mite further—in your ordinary waking life, in the middle of your ordinary pursuits, and see what miracles are there; and I say *miracles*. Miracles, because they can help you transform your own understanding, and your own reality. And you have been blind to them because you fear you will lose your identity. Your identity, instead, you see, can grow and include such experiences.

"Now I told you that class was quickening, so the time is ripe for each of you. So . . . be gentle with your own experience. Do not be such a disciplinarian that when stray thoughts or intuitions come to you, you dismiss them. The fields of your own being are filled with flowers that you do not recognize. You do not stop to look at them or smell their odors. They are not official flowers or official thoughts. Sometimes you try to be too practical!

"There is no disagreement between your official reality and those unofficial realities that sometimes sneak through!"[4]

Another dream-related area where class members experimented with pre-sleep suggestion and inner "training" of a sort involved the phenomenon of consciousness projection, or out-of-body states. We assumed from the beginning that our consciousness, or self, was *expressed through* the physical body but not dependent upon it for existence, so this "training"—or experimenting—was not so much concerned with proving the so-called impossible as in maintaining a balanced, aware stance and seeing what was *possible:* what we could get; how far we could go.

Many class members reported that after falling asleep, they frequently found themselves in fully alert out-of-body states. Others struggled with "trying to get out" and got nowhere, or achieved a half-in, half-out dream-like stage with ghostly arms and legs sticking up above physical ones, strange crackling and snapping noises roaring in their ears. But when the out-of-body happened, it was unmistakable—it was a conscious, coherent perspective of objective and subjective attention.

"In college [while out-of-body] I climbed over my bunk bed and saw myself in the mirror," Nadine Renard recalls. "I was very frightened as I didn't know what I was doing—difficulty getting back in my body. This happened on about five occasions in the same room. [I also] had a boyfriend who had the ability to leave his body at will and describe what I was doing in Hornell [New York] when he was in Buffalo . . . he 'visited' me once at my sister's in Philadelphia and later described it . . .

"[During class], Jane wanted us all to meet OOB [out-of-body] at her apartment at 2 A.M.," Nadine recalls. "I arrived (airborne, I don't know how) at the door and entered [her] living room. No one there—room was straightened and clean. I waited a while for the others [and] . . . decided to go home. I entered my body easily with no fear, but mad because nobody else came! I was no longer afraid of OOBs, but had much more difficulty leaving body at will. Sometimes I couldn't and got a lot of 'static' in head. I entered easily on return, but I was usually disappointed because I couldn't find people!"

"I seemed to have had a few successes with conscious out-of-bodies," Betty DiAngelo says. "I didn't work with it a lot—was kind of uncomfortable with it, seeing my body lying there while I was out of it. But I'm aware of OOBs—a lot of OOBs—as they seem to occur quite frequently. I always experience the tremendous speed and [a] roaring sound—it's at that point that I usually become aware of them: when I'm journeying *back*.

"[For instance], on January 14, 1974, I fell asleep [in the afternoon] by mistake—I meant only to rest my eyes a few minutes. I realized [my daughter] Ivy was awake and playing in her bedroom. I tried desperately to wake up and couldn't, so I tried to go OOB and check on her. I did. Her bedroom in the OOB was an incredible mess, with piles of clothes and toys strewn all over. Ivy was on the floor playing, but she looked like a little old man and had a white beard! The shock made me wake up. I ran into the bedroom and she wasn't there—but happily playing on the living room floor and looking out the picture window . . .

"[In] our very first class in July of 1971, we did an exercise . . . Jane led us on a mental journey. I saw a beautiful, straight, tree-lined road that looked the way I imagine the lush English countryside does. On two other occasions when we did the same thing, I felt myself climbing a hill, crossing over a shallow stream to the other side, where there were many pine trees. It was very much like the property where we live now . . ."

On January 18, 1975, Rudy Storch decided to take a nap, with the suggestion that he'd go OOB and receive some reincarnational information. As often happens in the moments preceding a projection experience, Rudy fell into a dream scene. "Me, Richie, and a few friends were at an amusement park," he recalls. "A woman was running an attraction that went through time. . . . We rounded a corner where they had two signs, 'Jazz' and 'Classical.' I thought it was going to be the music we heard on our journey. I went rushing through the entrance (a portal) and found myself flying. I realized that I was OOB.

"I felt extremely clear, alert, and full of energy. I told Richie that I knew for sure that we were OOB because I did it all the time and it felt the same. . . . I saw . . . a big burly pirate . . . [who] looked at me and said that his name was Charles Ansen and that he took over the Panama Canal. (Later, I looked up Panama in an encyclopedia and there is a city called Ancen there.) [Then] I met an aristocrat (man) dressed in fancy clothes from the past, English or French. . . . I think he was afraid of me. . . . Then I was outdoors, in the woods. I met a big, friendly wilderness man. He knew that I was OOB. We embraced. I recognized him on some level, but when I woke up, did not know who it was."

For me, out-of-bodies usually start from a half-awake state, in which I can feel myself "sliding" out of my physical body. This is often accompanied by a loud buzzing noise that seems to come at me across the room, ending with a *snap!* behind my right ear and an immediate *whoosh!* as I'm propelled out. One of the most vivid—and poignant—OOBs I experienced was on August 30, 1974, just a few days before my son started kindergarten.

From my notes: "Terrific series of out-of-bodies. I go back and forth, out of body, in bed. At first, I raise my (non-physical) legs up out of the bed, and feel the two 'sets' of legs clearly and consciously, and the two 'sets' of movement within them. I pull myself away from the rest of my body and wander out into the yard, where a voice says, 'Class members are being called!'

"No moon, but a dark and velvety landscape. I think: What are the dreams of other consciousnesses? Of men on other planets? The blind? Animals? I fly through the night, see Seneca Lake below, and dive down into it. It is wet, but with a touch like warm oil, not wet in usual terms. Dark under the surface. I sense the presence of fish. Do they dream?

"Back in my body. I open my eyes, close them. I let that electric-charge feeling overtake me again and I sit up, OOB. Sean is sitting on the end of the bed, also OOB.

"'Sean,' I say, 'I am flying out the window now. Will you come?'

"'No, Mama,' he says, 'I want to stay with your body, here, while you go.'

"'It's safe,' I say, looking at it, but I don't coax him. I float out the door and over the hills again. Am aware of class members—Jean Strand, Gert Barber, Ira Willis.

"Then I'm aware of the weight of my sleeping cat, Tyrone, on my body's knees, even though I'm not *in* my body. I'm suddenly standing next to the bed again. Sean is still there, waiting. 'Let's go now,' I say. He gets up, and we fly out the window together. To my surprise, this time it's a sunny day out. I think, 'This must be symbolic for both of us.' I look at Sean as we fly over the hedge. He is fifteen or sixteen. He grins. I realize, in a rush of nostalgia, that my baby is grown. 'Don't worry about it, Mama,' Sean says. He pours water from a small glass into a large container, a symbolic gesture that I understand, having to do with the accumulation of years and its purposes.

"Still, I am wistful. 'So soon?' I say. I look down at the cornfield passing below us. 'Mama,' Sean says, 'that once never leaves you.' He goes in another direction. I see him drift over the lake, exploring on his own. I am glad, though sad also. But I feel more secure, knowing he has this kind of understanding.

"Just then I find myself in front of a wall of some sort. It's strange, out here in the fields: another symbolic object? I do what I've done before in front of walls while OOB: I 'line up my molecules'—consciously meshing the molecules of this body-self with the wall's—and go through it. It's very thick, but I feel myself pass through, or among, its atoms and molecules, and I come out in a stand of young trees. I feel ease and confidence. . . ."

"I am still trying for out-of-bodies," reports Priscilla Lantini, "but I can brag of one in my lifetime and that was one night at class when Jane said that anyone who wanted to follow her out [*during an expansion-of-consciousness exercise*] could go. I waited to see if I could. I knew something was happening when all of a sudden I could not hear the breathing of people around me. Then my body seemed to blow up like a giant balloon and first thing I knew I sailed up through this giant body and out through its head, which seemed to be like a cone.

"I was in the night sky, looking down through the tree branches to the street. A few minutes later, we all returned. I loved it and hated to see it end. When the class discussed it, I found out that some of the others went way up and picked stars. I thought that must be great, but I'm still tickled to death that I went as far as I did."

George Rhoads says his impressive out-of-body experiences have been in the dream state. "Awake, I did once leave a sickbed to fly in circles and loops around the room. This was amusing, but did not have the consciousness-expanding quality of certain dreams. In these, I enter worlds or atmospheres densely rich with association. These places evoke a lifetime of memories—maybe many lifetimes.

"One such place," George says, "is a campus: old ivied buildings, tall trees. Here I wander through familiar halls, each room, each door like an old friend. Memories seem to reside in the very wood and stone and soil of these places. Maybe they are windows to experiences that are outside of the full awareness of the focus of this lifetime.

"During class years, I developed abilities I now use routinely. I 'receive' beneficial material, mainly during my dream interpretation sessions. At first this material came in the mental voice of Seth, startling and amazing. Now it just comes to mind with an easy shift of consciousness. This was part of the training in out-of-bodies and TD/GH sessions . . . "

One cold March Tuesday in 1973, a visitor in class followed our reading of some "body belief" papers with some descriptions of his *out*-of-body experiences; in the process, he commented that he used the OOB state for problem-solving and for "leaving the burden of the body behind"to find "pure" information. You hardly needed a course in Sethian cues to know that these remarks were almost guaranteed to bring him forth; and when Seth finally did enter the conversation, it was a profound one, indeed.

"It is quite an esoteric idea to play around with the out-of-body state, and it is fun," Seth began. "*But* in order to find the reason for your own beliefs, you must look into the contents of your sardonic!—conscious mind. For the answers are known to you, and they are not buried in the deepest recesses of your being—only if you think they are! You know, consciously, much more that you let yourself know you know. The closets are in your *conscious mind,* and these closets are formed when you say, 'I know it, but I will pretend that I do not know it.'

"Now sometimes, in dreams, you will receive your answers; but not if the conscious mind is still allowed to hide its own contents," Seth continued. "*You* are the one who must open the door and accept the dream information; and you will not do so unless you are ready for the encounter with yourself. And the encounter with yourself is a bold and exciting one; and it does not look to others, but to the knowledge within yourself as a species. In those terms, you have a developed and self-conscious mind for a reason!

"Few people are aware of the abilities of that consciousness, and the ways in which it directs your unconscious knowledge. For it directs great power, but that power is released according to your beliefs about yourself, and the world that you know.

"I invite you to be truly self-conscious: *to accept your creaturehood.* For within that creaturehood lies all the secrets to your spirituality and the doors of your awareness. It is why you have a conscious mind, and bodies.

"You come here and you are going to understand and investigate the nature of reality. Now, you hope that this includes out-of-body encounters. You would be willing to deal with demons, even, who come out of the blue to greet you. Some of you have been willing to encounter cosmic monsters! But! *All* of you show some reluctance in encountering your own creaturehood—facing life and death, and birth, and the moments that *seem* to flow one before the other. If you have not the courage to encounter your own emotions and the reality of your own being *now,* what makes you think that you can cop out and meet the gods out the window?

"You must meet yourselves as you intersect in the flesh and the seasons. You must know yourselves as you are, and understand the beauty and uniqueness of your own being. Using that as a threshold, you will understand your own spirituality. But denying your creaturehood, you will never fully comprehend either creaturehood *or* spirituality! *Denying the beast will not show you the gods!*

"What we are doing—what you are doing with yourselves—is far more important than you know. To go out of body is *not* to deny your flesh. It *is* to allow you to mix the wisdom—the corporeal wisdom of your being—with the spirituality of your being. It is quite natural to leave your body, and you do it all the time. But when you do so in life, you are also connected with the physical body that you know; and you use that, in your terms, as a launching pad.

"When you are out-of-body, in this life, you still use the attributes of the brain. When you come back to your body, you must interpret the knowledge that you have received *through the brain.* You *think,* even out-of-body, in human terms. When you leave your body, in your terms, for good—when you are operating outside of it—then you do not even think in terms of passing moments, or time. You live whether you are in the body or out of it, but your corporeal expression is your own. It is for a reason, and the soul expresses itself in flesh in a way it cannot do otherwise. The Earthly experience is entirely different from any other, as all experience is. And the mind is for a reason, and the emotions are for a reason; and together they form the road of your experience.

"You could not dream in the way that you consider dreaming—the peculiar thing called dreaming—*unless you were physical!* There are chemical releases within your body, and many interactions that result in the thing you call dreaming."

"Yes," Rudy Storch chimed in, "then right *here*—right here!—is where the knowledge is that we're looking for. We don't have to look in other dimensions."

"It is indeed," Seth answered. "It is in your living, in all of its aspects, and there is no difference: You are as physical when you are dreaming as when you are awake. You are as spiritual when you are awake as you are dreaming. You have the 'truth' whether you are sleeping or awake.

"You may look at the animals and envy them their great and knowing ease. Yet, you perform far more activities with the same bodily grace—and the answers are within your own consciousness.

"You have been told for so long that the answers are beyond you that many of you still refuse to realize that *you have* the answers. That is why you ask the questions! Creation always comes from within, and from that portion of All-That-Is that *is* within you.

"Dreams are a characteristic of your creaturehood! Now . . . cats dream. Monkeys dream. And—*you* dream. In their own way, in the dreams of animals, they explore and expand the dimension that they know. And they reach—in your terms only, now—toward other dimensions of actuality, but through their creaturehood. And so, in your way, through your creaturehood, you do the same and you step up through those levels of actuality, again now in your terms—and actualize them. But do not forget that the animals dream, and they are also creative; and from their creaturehood springs experience that you do not understand—experience that has its own biological spirituality.

"I wanted to tell you that I am returning you to the *sanity* of the animals from which, in your terms, your journey began. That journey still continues, but not by denying your heritage—but by building upon it; by becoming *more* what you already *are*, and not by trying to deny your reality. You cannot find one reality by denying another. You end up by denying all realities.

"*You* are the spirits that roam the Earth, and haunt the centuries, as much as I am. Yours are the voices that you hear as much as my voice is. I am an echo of your creaturehood; of gods couched in flesh. And within you, through your own creaturehood, are your own questions and your own answers, and the unique journey into reality that belongs to each of you and to no other."

NOTES FOR CHAPTER FIFTEEN

1. This was several years *before* Eddie and his wife started the New York City restaurant known as Arnold's Turtle—an interesting connection.

2. A reference to the City, or 'Sumari City,' Seth refers to in Chapter 10, Volume 1 of *Conversations;* he challenged class members to "build" an Inner City—and thus discover the reality of mental events.

3. I wasn't really sure if I wanted to "know," either, when in August, 1979, I asked for a TD/GH that would tell me—no holds barred— the reasons behind my lifelong struggles with weight gain/loss/gain (the infamous "yo-yo" syndrome). The ensuing night's dream series was simple, direct—and utterly terrifying. I've included excerpts, along with some interpretation, to illustrate the beauty of dream response in times of need—and how that response is couched in symbolism precisely to the degree we must have, for comfort's sake.

a). I am with a date at a dinner party. We are sitting with another couple, who turn out to be hard-line religious fanatics. They never quite get into a recitation of their beliefs, but the unspoken—though heavily implied—attitudes make me extremely nervous. I am sick with terror that they will say something with which I disagree so strongly *that I will get mad and ruin the evening for everybody*.

b). I find myself on an island in Keuka Lake [*one of New York State's Finger Lakes*] with Cynthia S. There is a bear on the island, too—we know he's dangerous. Cynthia and I find an old leaky rowboat and get away, to a cottage on the shore owned by John H., an old friend of my father's. But the bear has caught up with us—only here, he's "civilized," and walks around commenting on paintings and latest movies—innocuous conversation, I think cynically.

c). Suddenly, another scene of great threat. Women are walking into the lobby of a hotel—into atmosphere of terrible danger. A minotaur is standing by the elevators, like a doorman. I see him as though I'm looking through a zoom-lens—my eyes come very close to his face, and stay there, watching him. His expression is bland and bored. I see his horns and animal-like facial hair: he is handsome and sexual, but—threatening. Even though he's acting as a doorman in this place, I can sense some great unspeakable force of violence beneath this smooth veneer.

Interpretation: All three of these dreams seemed basically to be addressing themselves to my feelings about womanhood and—behind those feelings—to my basic fears about my self's position in the world. So: universal, yet personal, answers were given. In (a), I am terrified of my own beliefs and opinions; terrified that any "trouble" or unpleasantness that arises will be because of *my* beliefs—this in spite of the fact that the other couple seems to feel no qualms about basking in the aura of *their* beliefs. Better to not have any beliefs at all than be troubled with confrontation? Better to just shut up and eat?

(Humorously, this dream really happened, nearly two years later—and I recognized the scene instantly. A friend—the one named in the dream—and I happened to meet another couple at a restaurant. We sat together during dinner—and the other man started spouting ideas that immediately made me furious. I held back, thinking that I didn't want to start an argument and spoil a pleasant evening—and then remembered the implied message of this dream. Mentally, I backed away from the scene a bit, saw the fellow as a character in his own right who was, after all, no threat to *me*—and we both ended up de-fusing the conversation by treating the whole thing *playfully).*

In (b), the elements of these dreams are taken one step further. Cynthia S., a women about my age, grew up in a family where there was often not enough to eat—they were lucky, she once told me, if there was meat on the table more than one day a week. She is on an island with me in the middle of a once-wild lake—a lake that was in the once vast, "uncivilized" territory of the Iroquois Nation. The dangerous (or untamed) bear is also, of course, "*bare*"—my own body?—dangerous in its "untamed" state; in its "natural" uninhibited physical glory, filled with the dangers of my impulses and beliefs. By the time Cynthia and I escape to the cottage—which in reality is owned by a rather well-to-do *male*—the bear is "civilized." In the midst of opulence,—including physical opulence, or bigness? (as opposed to "wild" thinness)—the "animal" is rendered harmless—*but dull.* Interestingly, throughout this dream, I thought of this bear as"he."

By dream (c), the symbolic messages are blatant. The women are entering a hotel—a place of sexual encounter—*and great danger.* Standing in wait is a male animal of the most sexual demeanor yet—a minotaur. And a *bored* minotaur, at that, holding in bland control unimaginable depths of uncontrollable rage, destruction—and sexual power (all, apparently, the same thing to me). Not only that—here are all these women walking into his hotel, and he's *bored!* He doesn't bother himself with the women as individuals—as civilized individuals (even though his own civilized disguise is a thin one). They are to be taken upstairs for the thing they are obviously here for—what else? The attractive female body, then, not only betrays the female mind, but calls destruction down upon itself in the form of "untamed" impulses, either from within or from without . . .

I've left out much of the interpretation, but the reader can discern other meanings, and perhaps apply them. I can say truthfully, though, that the information given to me in these dreams did more than bring together the divided portions of my self—it smacked me over the head with them! And it's information that I've been able to use, successfully, in a variety of situations ever since.

4. Some examples of these "random thoughts" that I noted at the time include one that passed through my mind while eating supper not long after this class. The thought was: "I am to class as the squash plants are to the garden." Pretty silly, but then I considered how I regard squash: as sturdy, irrepressible, dependable, the best and easiest to grow of all gar-

den plants; even humorous—left in the wild, they form strange shapes and weird new calabash crosses.

       The other thought, one that I've considered many times since it first came to me, asked how people would relate to my mother—and how she might relate to herself in a different way—if her nickname were "Betty" instead of "Liz" (though I once heard someone call her "Betty," and she seemed to be almost offended by it).

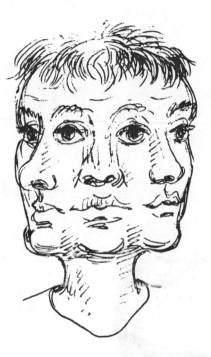

CHAPTER SIXTEEN:

Roads Not Taken: Probable Systems
and Possible Selves

Somewhere
  do cat people
Feed us pet food
  and write books
On people-care?
And do they wonder
  if people dream?

    — Christmas card drawing and
      poem by Jane Roberts, 1979

"If there was one thing I never thought my reading audience would relate to, it was probabilities," Jane says. "Somehow, I just didn't think that people would take to that in an everyday, practical way. But they surprised me, they really did! Our mail is full of letters from people who *instantly* caught on to probabilities, and with deep intuitive understanding."

If Jane's readers responded easily to the concept of probabilities, class—oddly—often treated the whole idea with a mixture of oppressed fascination and worry. "But which probable self am I?" someone would frequently wail. "Do probabilities mean that you never make a decision?" Allan Demming once asked angrily.

"I just can't figure this out," someone else sighed during a probability discussion. "It seems as though it doesn't matter what I do—because no matter what I do, I *don't* do it; or if I don't do it, then somewhere or other, I did it anyway! Why bother?"

"You, the focus personality, are always yourself, and no other," Seth commented dryly. But the possibility of probabilities seemed to make many class members doubt that *anything* definite could be said about who any of us thought we were.

Although not an entirely new concept—for decades, scientists (and science-fiction writers) have theorized the existence of probable systems of reality—probabilities were explored in class as more than conceptual rhetoric. During alteration-of-consciousness exercises, dreams, and in other kinds of encounters, members glimpsed the reality of probabilities and their magical intersection with the moment-by-moment world. Jane's class, then, was *probably* the first place where the boundaries of identity were stretched far enough to admit probable selves and systems as *practical* portions of existence.

Jane and Rob were introduced to the idea of probabilities in June of 1969, when, as Jane recalls in *The Seth Material*,[1] Seth announced that one of Rob's probable selves, a medical doctor in another system of reality, was attempting to contact Rob. In the doctor's universe, according to Seth, the exploration of consciousness was more advanced than in ours, and Dr. Pietra, Rob's probable self, was experimenting with consciousness projection in drug-induced trance states.[2]

Interestingly, as Jane notes, Rob had once done medical artwork[3] and "was amazed at his proficiency at it, and with the medical procedures and terminology, which were quite unfamiliar to him when he began."[4] In a wry turnabout of probabilities, Seth said that Dr. Pietra *paints* as a hobby.

"There are, in fact, infinite varieties of matter, existing in what *you* would call one space framework," Seth said in these first explanations of probable realities. "Action is action whether or not you perceive it, and probable events are events whether or not you perceive them. Thoughts are also events; as are wishes and desires. The human system responds as fully to these as it does to physical events. In dreams, often portions of probable events are experienced in a semiconscious manner. . . . A portion of your whole self is quite involved in these probable events, however. The 'I' of your dreams can be legitimately compared to the self that experienced probable events. [That 'I' would consider itself fully conscious and view the waking 'I' as the probable self.]

"Let us consider the following. An individual finds himself with a choice of three actions. He chooses one and experiences it. The other two actions are experienced also, by the inner ego, but not in physical reality. . . . The results are then checked by the inner ego as an aid in other decision-making. The probable actions were definitely experienced, however, and such experience makes up the existence of the 'probable selves' just as dream actions make up the experience of the dreaming self. . . .

"There is a constant subconscious interchange of information between all layers of the whole self. . . . The package of experience upon which you can focus is indeed composed of many small packages, but the whole package of reality is much larger than this. A portion of the self can and does experience events in an entirely different fashion [than the ego does], and this portion goes off on a different tangent. For when your conscious self perceives Event X, this other part of the self branches off, so to speak, into all the other probable events that could have been experienced by the ego."[5]

Although Rob didn't consciously perceive Dr. Pietra during this time, probabilities became one of Jane and Rob's chief fascinations. Discussions and experiments began in class—with one mobility-of-consciousness "trip" pulling the reality of probabilities right into the room with us. As Jane describes it in Chapter 4 of *Adventures in Consciousness*, Seth had suggested that evening that it might be possible for us to tune in on a "probable" ESP class—of ours—that was, he said, simultaneously dabbling in an effort to perceive probable classes.

We closed our eyes, following Seth's directions to "climb the vowels and syllables of this voice as if they were indeed a ladder, and let them carry you into dimensions that are native to you, dimensions that are yours by right, that are your heritage; dimensions of awareness that you carry within you both day and night, beneath the level of your ordinary days . . . and I want you to sense that identity that is your own and the purposes that are yours, the joy that is a part of your being; and hold that feeling of exhilaration and experience, hold it and remember it to the end of your days. . . . "

As Jane recalls in *Adventures,* the results of this experiment were immediately, chaotically real for nearly everyone. As we opened our eyes, several of us had the impression that one student's face was changing, or *sliding,* in and out of its familiar form, as if it didn't know which place it was supposed to be in; at the same time, the woman remarked that her face seemed to be "made of rubber." Helen Van Dyce, usually a serious, dour person, suddenly started giggling and singing. "I feel just like dancing!" she called out, coming rather completely out of character.

During Seth's monologue, I'd felt a long, cone-shaped figure tugging at the back of my head—similar to the image Jane had mentioned at the start of the class. Mentally, I plunged backwards, down the length of this figure, seeming to travel faster and faster toward a dot of light at its far end. As the dot grew bigger, I could see "myself"—*another Sue*—sitting in the "same" blue chair in Jane's living room, eyes closed, and a cone-shape pulling out of the back of *her* head, rushing up to meet *me.* At the instant the two cones met, I felt a brief, lightning-like exchange of information—more like an exchange of self-sense. Abruptly, the experience ended; I was sitting in the chair, my eyes wide open, feeling as though I'd just jolted awake from a dream. *Had* I fallen asleep? Did it matter if I had? Because in those brief seconds, I'd experienced a sense of myself gone a different direction, a Sue who was (or is) highly proficient in mathematics (which I'm most assuredly not) and the physical sciences. I also knew that *she* had sensed *my* world, abilities, and purposes. In addition, I'd felt (as had others in class) a tingling, evocative hint of what *that* class was like, and how different versions of ourselves formed it.

They, of course, would consider our class the "probable" one.[6]

If all that we did in that class was exercise our collective imaginations, then it served as a good demonstration of how "imagination" can affect one's life. Helen never forgot the sense of fun she'd picked up that night; another student found it much easier to express herself after sensing that probable ability; others had experienced a mental agility that surprised them. As for myself, I'd felt my own form of "math anxiety" as the psychological belief-barrier that it was: a method of disdaining what I thought of as the rational, logical, "male-oriented" world. In objective terms, of course, our physical room was the same: flower vases and tables hadn't slipped around corners; no strangers had mysteriously appeared in our midst. But subjectively, something *had* happened to the characteristics we called ours; something more substantial than chairs had whirled through the substance of space; and how consistent *was* our physical universe from one moment to the next?

Again, it was another step in our reconsiderations of subjectivity. And probabilites were definitely coming alive for all of us: hardly a week went by without someone reporting a dream "about a probable self who'd become the teacher I thought I wanted to be," or a dream "in which I saw what would happen if I decided to take that job offer."

In August of 1973, probabilities took class by surprise when Matt Adams showed up for one of his infrequent visits. Although I'd known Matt for several years by then, he'd walked into Jane's living room, greeted everybody, and gotten halfway to the sofa before I recognized him at all. *Wha-a-at??* I asked myself, astonished.

"Is that Matt Adams?" Harold Wiles hissed at me in a loud stage whisper. So—it wasn't just me having this vertigo. What *was* it about Matt that was . . . different? More than different. Was he thinner? Well, maybe, but . . . was it just because he'd shaved off his moustache? Well, maybe, but . . .

"Boy, has he changed!" I heard Camille Atkinson say to Harold. Oh, well—people just change, I shrugged. But swiftly, Seth had appeared and was in a lively conversation with Matt about his editing job.

"I also want to tell you," Seth was saying to Matt, "not that you do not know it—and to inform class—that what you are seeing—those of you who know Matt, and who have met him before—*is a new probable self!"*

A kind of self-conscious gasp rustled around the room; everybody was staring at Matt, who just smiled at Seth with his usual nonchalant composure.

"Now," Seth went on, "in my books I have said, that often when this occurs, people will say, 'You seem almost, but not quite, like a different person,' or, 'There is something so different about you, and you have changed in a way that I cannot explain.' But the theme is picked up at once!

"Now, approximately—approximately—seven months ago, the change began, and Matt, then, made certain decisions," Seth said to the rest of us. "He decided to embark upon a different road of probabilities. Now, since all selves are one, another Matt, who was the same Matt, decided to do something else. And none of these things has anything to do with physical events—but opaquely, it had to do with growth, directions of growth; directions of vitality and energy."

"I hope in terms that you would approve of," Matt responded, grinning.

"I do indeed, I do indeed," Seth replied, "but then—I knew. Now, part of this . . . had to do also . . with new probabilities embarked upon by our friend the Seagull, Richard Bach, and by Ruburt, and you, and Joseph, in the approximate same period of time, in your terms.[7] And various affiliations came about. There were probable intersections; in various realities, other events are occurring. But in this reality, new probable selves blossomed!"

"Throughout that class," Matt remembers, "I kept trying to recall any significant, ground-breaking decisions I'd made six or seven months before. To my disappointment, I simply couldn't think of any. At the time, I figured that Seth had vastly exaggerated the importance of some idle whim I'd once entertained, then promptly forgotten.

"Now, however, I suspect that any major shift between probabilities *usually* appears seamless, 'natural,' and inconsequential. Of course, everbody can recall certain dramatic 'chance' events that led to a new job, say, or a dramatic and sudden love affair. In those cases, the intersection of two probabilities is obvious, especially in retrospect—we can see just where the graft occurred. But for the most part, I think, probabilities blend and flow into one another with much more ease and grace, just as one season progresses into the next. And it makes sense that any 'strong' probability should *naturally* create a corresponding probable past from which it 'logically' and 'inevitably' sprang.

"About a year ago, I read in *Science News* that paleontology had been forced to revise its reconstruction of the brontosaurus. Apparently the first nineteenth-century scientist who tried to assemble a complete brontosaurus skeleton used the skull of a different species by mistake. The 'real' brontosaurus had pencil-like teeth and a flatter head than the beast we've seen depicted in those murals and sci-fi movies.

"But did that scientist *really* make an error? Could it be that a probable Jurassic dinosaur came into being just last year? Of course, our beliefs simply don't permit the past to re-arrange itself spontaneously. And so that nineteenth-century academic error may be just a convenient alibi—a classic example of how an emergent probability covers its tracks and makes itself appear legitimate."

Indeed, in *The Nature of Personal Reality*, Seth treats probabilities as the *basis* of choice and action—as the bones upon which the flesh of the moment is grown. "There is creativity in your past waiting for you even as there is in your future," Seth says of the process of changing your daily reality. "To utilize such experience [means that] you must learn to alter your beliefs, and to some degree escape from the particular kind of limited conscious focus that you habitually use. . . .

"The fact remains that there are probable past events that 'can still happen' within your personal previous experience. A new event can literally be born into the past—now!

"On a grand scale *this rarely occurs in such a way that you perceive it*. . . . A new belief in the present, however, can cause changes in the past on a neurological level. You must understand that basically time is simultaneous. Present beliefs can alter the past. In some cases of healing, in the spontaneous disappearance of cancer, for instance, or of any other disease, certain alterations are made that affect cellular memory, genetic codes, or neurological patterns in the past . . . [8]

"All of your present experience was drawn from probable reality. During your life, any event must come through your creaturehood, with the built-in time recognition that is so largely a part of your neurological structure. . . . In a manner of speaking, each belief can be seen as a powerful station, pulling to it from fields of probabilities only those signals to which it is attuned, and blocking out all others . . . Each condition is as real or unreal as the other. Which you? Which world? You have your choice . . . "[9]

Probabilities, and the choices within them, are thoroughly explored in *The "Unknown" Reality* on both a mass and personal scale, particularly in the coincidences that Jane and Rob encountered during their house-hunting expedition in 1974. But for Jane and Rob, and ultimately for me, the most personal and electrifying sense of probabilities sprang from the episode of the York Beach couple.

"In late 1963," Jane explains in *The Seth Material*,[10] "some months before our sessions began, we'd taken a vacation in York Beach, Maine, hoping that a change of environment would improve Rob's [*bad back*] . . .

"On the night in question, we went to a nightclub in search of a festive atmosphere. Rob was in constant pain, and though he didn't complain, he couldn't hide the sudden spasms. Then I noticed an older couple sitting across the room from us. They really frightened me by their uncanny resemblance to Rob and myself. Did we look like that — aloof, bitter — only younger? I couldn't take my eyes off them, and finally I pointed them out to Rob. . . .

"Rob looked over at the couple and groaned with another back spasm. Then something happened that neither of us had been able to explain. To my complete amazement Rob stood up, grabbed my arm, and insisted that we dance. A minute earlier, he'd hardly been able to walk . . . We danced for the rest of the evening, and from that point on his physical condition improved remarkably. His whole outlook on life seemed brighter as of that moment."

According to Seth's earliest sessions, the mysterious "York Beach couple" represented a *common phenomenon*: " . . . fragments of yourselves [*Jane and Rob*], thrown-off materializations of your own negative and aggressive feelings . . . The images were formed by the culminating energy of your destructive energies at the time.

"While you did not recognize them consciously," Seth continued, "unconsciously you knew them well. Unconsciously you saw the images of your destructive tendencies, and these images themselves roused you to combat them . . . Your dancing represented the first move away from what those images meant . . . a subtle transformation could have taken place in which you [*Rob*] and Jane transferred the bulk of your personalities into the fragments you had yourselves created."[11]

If they *had* "transferred the bulk" of their personalities into that couple, Rob asked, what would have happened? "If you had accepted them, you would have ended up as replicas as you transferred into the images," Seth told him. "You would be recognizable to friends, but changes would be noted. The remark would be made that perhaps you didn't seem the same, and with good reason."[12] Again, Seth emphasized that the York Beach incident represented a common occurrence.[13] Jane and Rob thought about people *they* knew who'd suddenly seemed "different" — and wondered: psychological symbolism? Probably. Practical truth? Well—maybe.

I'd always been fascinated with the account of the York Beach couple and had discussed them many times with Jane and Rob. By 1970, I'd also been having numerous vivid dreams and out-of-bodies that dealt with probabilities. In one, I'd floated down the cellar stairs and walked through a doorway that obligingly opened up in one wall for me—and into a "reality" where linear consciousness had developed through the *feline*, rather than the simian, form. It seemed as though hours passed while I walked the streets of a city there, awed at how wide-awake I was, talking with the people—who stood upright and wore clothes, but retained their cat-like oval eyes and soft, compact fur. "I think it sounds like a good science-fiction story," I laughed when I described this one to Jane: yet something about a probability of cat-people was intuitively satisfying to both of us—and why not? Seth was constantly emphasizing that the reality we know represented but one line of development; and that all species, including animals and humankind, had taken other, coexistent directions.*

I was spending that August weekend in 1970 with my parents. Ned was out of town, pleading his Conscientious Objector application before the district draft board in Buffalo. He hadn't harbored many hopes of winning his case, however: Ned was of no particular religious sect, and was basing his CO stand simply on his feelings, without an "acceptable" framework to justify them. It was a position that many young men found themselves in during those years. What Ned would do if he were eventually drafted wasn't really clear in his mind—but then, neither was it clear to him what he'd do if he got his exemption.

It was a difficult time; I slept uneasily. Finally, I drifted off into a light dream of poling a raft down a slow, muddy river. Suddenly, the river turned into a roaring waterfall, and my raft plunged ahead. The faster it traveled, the more alive and vivid the dream details became—although I was fully aware that I was dreaming and could feel myself coming more and more "awake" within the dream state. Then the waterfall unceremoniously dropped me on a sidewalk, in what I could see was a small town, not unlike Elmira. I was fully conscious and aware that this was an extraordinary dream, or an extraordinarily lucid state of attention on my part, at least.

From my notes:

"I walk along the town's streets and enter a pavilion-like outdoor restaurant set in a municipal park; grass and trees are all

* See Appendix Five: "A Waking Dream: The Probability of Eyau."

around. I notice all the details—even the salt and pepper shakers on the large common picnic table in the middle of this building. I'm fascinated by my own state—there is no strain to stay here at all.

"Then I see, to my surprise and joy, that Jane and Rob Butts are sitting at the other end of this table, talking to some other people. Or *are* they Jane and Rob? I stare at them. They are older-looking and they're both acting very cynical about whatever it is they're discussing. I wonder if this town is Sayre, Pennsylvania (where Rob grew up), and if we're "really" there, in a physical park. The other people go away, and I sit down next to Jane. To my complete surprise, they do not recognize or acknowledge me at all.

George Rhoads's drawing of
a probable Rob

"Are they just my own dream materializations? I concentrate on getting a clear focus—but there they sit, as three-dimensional as they were last Tuesday in their living room. Then all at once, I'm struck with the knowledge that I've entered a probable system of reality—that these are probable selves of Jane and Rob's. In a rush of excitement, I say, 'My name is Sue Watkins, and my husband's name is Ned.' They give me a rather nasty *so-what?* look.

"I look up and notice that an older, short, stout man in a dark robe is sitting across the table from us—and realize that it's *Seth*. 'Hey—do you know *him?*' I say, pointing. Jane laughs. 'You mean old Saint Nick over there?' she says derisively.

"I then observe how haggard they look. Jane is much heavier; her hair is quite gray. Rob looks extremely tired and is sitting in a slouch; his face is not fat but *fleshy*—almost dissipated. He is smoking one cigarette after another. They both look bitter; not happy at all.

"Now I feel very protective toward them. In whatever probability we might meet, Jane and Rob are still my friends. Somehow, I start a halting conversation with them about Seth's ideas on the nature of physical reality, etc. To my amazement, Jane tells me that a few years before, they'd received 'some strange messages' through her, 'from someone claiming to be a dead spirit.

"'But it was ridiculous,' Jane says, 'so we dropped it.'

"'Look,' I say, hardly knowing where to start, 'look around you. You two and I are in the dream state. I am from another probability system. You know me there. In that system, you kept on with the "messages" and found—' I glance at Seth, who is smiling, rather indulgently '—and found that they were from *him*, and you went on to discover fantastic things about life.'

"They seem to be listening. I plunge ahead. 'In that probability, you, Rob, are a professional artist and Jane had published a bunch of short stories, a novel, and poetry before all of this other stuff even got started. Is this your work now?'

"Jane and Rob glance at each other and laugh—a nasty, bitter laugh. 'She still works all day at the taxi company,' Rob says, 'and I work too. Want to come see some of the paintings I've done?'

"We walk out of the pavilion—Seth trailing along behind—down a quiet, shaded street to a large white house with a screened one-story porch. There is a large tree to the left of the porch, and a weedy driveway leads back to a large white barn or garage with double top-hinged doors. We go up a set of outside stairs and into a second-floor apartment. Rob is about to haul some paintings out into the large living room when he groans in pain—'from a bad back,' Jane says. He lies down on the floor. I try to suggest some exercises to him, but he brushes me off.

"At this point, I hear a chorus of voices calling my name. At first I think they're outside the house, out in the yard; but then I realize they're calling from within *me*. Instantly, I wake up in a strange room. This is a 'false awakening,' I realize, and I'm filled with the urge to wake up and write this whole experience down. I close my eyes and concentrate on my own bedroom—and finally wake up, for real, in it . . . "[14]

That morning, I called Jane and described this dream— or whatever. "I've got the feeling that I was in contact with the York Beach couple," I said, "but what does *that* mean? Why should

I—instead of one of you two—stumble across probable selves of *yours?*" Later that evening, Seth brought up the experience in their private session, and his comments on those questions, and on the nature of probabilities in general—along with Rob's notes—were so evocative that I've included excerpts from it here; they also shed light on some of the probability experiments we'd done in class.

"The experience of your friend Sue Watkins, and its connection with the probable universe . . . was quite legitimate," Seth began. "It was meant as a lesson on many levels.

"First of all, it is apparent that there *is* communication between various systems of probabilities, and that actions in one system can and do affect the other. The couple [*of my dream*] do exist, probable selves of your own in a different system. [Sue], in developing her abilities, has become involved with activities in probable fields and was drawn to the couple emotionally because of her emotional connection with you in *this* system.

"The couple involved will recall portions of the experience, and it will serve to remind them forcibly of abilities that they are not using; acting therefore as a stimulus in that system, coming however from this one, and through the agency of a friend. The affair is also a lesson to *you* when you think negatively, showing you the results of such negative thoughts, followed without letup, and in fact followed in spite of redeeming actions that would change events. The other couple, for example, ignored the contact with me [*through Jane*]. The negative and bitter qualities of personality came fully to the fore [*in that couple*], uncompromised and unredeemed by the fulfilling and creative functions that they had also smothered.

"They, you see, quite envy you. They were, however, unable to take advantage of *your* knowledge because of the condition of their own psyches. The affair served to remind them once more of my contact with them [*which the probable Jane mentioned as 'ridiculous'*], to make them think twice; and it also serves as a new stimulus for further contact."

("Seth gestured humorously enough," Rob's notes state, "but then quieted and leaned forward in a mood of emphatic seriousness.")

"We attempt to save even the shadows of ourselves," Seth continued, "and we create light in even the darkest recesses of our own hidden fragments. To that extent, and in those terms, we are our own redeemers.

"To a large extent, also, you see, you and Ruburt were responsible for the contact, for were it not for your own present experiences, your relationship with me, and your friendship with [Sue], the help would not have been given to those probable selves of yours. So one portion of the self lends a helping hand to another, in the same way that I give you a helping hand.

"What I want you to see here is that the communications do not just operate in a vertical, ascending or descending fashion, but horizontally, in those terms.

"At the same time, the experience was meant as a moral lesson to your Sue Watkins. She sees you in physical reality as people she respects and admires. Through the probable experience, she was able to see what could have happened to you in *this* system, had you given in to negative thoughts and feelings and had not been persistent in your work and efforts. By comparing the two couples, therefore, she receives an object lesson both for herself and her husband. More than this, however, all of you through the experience learned that help is extended from one system to the other. The other couple, the probable couple, have also helped you and [Sue], though quite unknowingly at conscious levels, by serving as such object lessons.

"Now, Ruburt has also done the same service for a probable Sue in *another* system of reality, though in an entirely different way. And you [*to Rob*], incidentally, have helped a probable Ned in the same manner—[to use] his creative abilities. The probable Ned, in other words, has strong creative abilities, and you have helped him understand this.

"The experience brings up several points that have not been discussed in connection with probabilities. Because you are physically born into this system, you take it for granted without thinking about it that you are born in the same manner into other systems. This may or may not apply, but it is definitely not applicable to the systems of probabilities as a whole.

"The couple, the probable Robert and Jane Butts, came into being *at* York Beach, as given in earlier material. They disappeared from your view, but energy created in such a fashion, as you know, cannot be negated, but must continue along its own lines of development. From *this* standpoint, these are 'fragment' personalities, therefore. They have your memories up to that point of their initiation, and they continued on from there. They were seen by you as far older—as you interpreted, created, and then perceived bitterness and negative attitudes. To them, however, they were the age that you were at the point of their breakoff. Such personalities can be created, and are created, under too many varying circumstances to enumerate.

"In this case, however, you both sensed your lives at a period of crisis, and projected your fears outward into the formation of the images."

("You mean at York Beach originally?" Rob asked.)

"At York Beach originally," Seth replied. "They contained, therefore, all of your fears, for you foresaw that in this system you could become such people—not that this was inevitable, but definitely probable—and more than possible.

"At the same time, however, you must understand that these probable selves were also created because of your own great hopes—hopes you felt you could fall far short of; so they were 'born' with the same hopes that you had at that time, but they were personalities that were overburdened with fears.

"Having created them, *because* of your abilities you then perceived them as objectified apparitions in physical reality, when Ruburt immediately made the conscious comparison, and resolved that you should never end up looking like them, or filled with the bitterness that was written in their faces. The conscious notice, therefore, was all you knew of the deep unconscious creative endeavor and psychological mechanism that brought them into existence."

("Even today, we remember these images well," Rob noted. "The scene was a smallish dancing room, with a band, in the Driftwood Hotel in York Beach, Maine. The room was filled with smoke and active bodies; all the tables were full; the band blared. The twist was the rage then. Jane and I had never danced it, but after we sighted the images, I suddenly had the urge to dance—I dragged a protesting Jane onto the floor, and we danced the rest of the night.

("Jane noticed the older couple first. They were like bloated copies of us at a later age. The woman was much fatter, but bore a striking resemblance to Jane. The man was thinner, I believe, but looked enough like me to be my brother, or father—or myself. His hair was snow white. The couple didn't smile during the time we observed them, nor do I recall them speaking to anybody, or each other. I couldn't swear to this last statement, however.

("Jane was fascinated by them, I remember, and kept calling my attention to them. I believe I was somewhat reluctant and embarrassed to stare at them as openly as she did. I remember that when we started dancing in the noisy, hot, crowded room, we were very close to their table at times, possibly even brushing against it . . . ")

"Even weighed down by fears and negative attitudes, they [*the York Beach couple*] retained their own close relationship," Seth said, "but they were not able to help each other, and were united by bitterness against the world as much as by love for each other.

"That Robert Butts did not continue his painting with any purpose, trying to be 'objective' and 'sensible'; lacking the understanding of his parents that you have achieved through sessions, he put security in financial terms above everything, took no chances at all along those lines, and despite this, of course, is not making much money because his heart was with the painting most largely abandoned.

"Ruburt's creative ability quickly deteriorated, for bitter attitudes shriveled up the source of the creativity. In that reality, you returned from York Beach, gave up your apartment in Elmira [*on West Water Street, where Jane and Rob were living at the time of this session*], returned to Sayre, lived for some time with your parents, *commuted* to your Elmira job [*in a greeting-card company*] to save money.

"You had planned for this as a temporary arrangement — six months at most to save money; then you were going to paint full-time. Instead, however, . . . you stayed, supposedly to aid your parents, but this was largely an excuse because you were afraid to take the chance and paint full time . . .

"There is no need to go further into their history, but I assure you that it was in keeping with the characteristics that you gave them — and remember, these were your own strongest fears. With all this . . . they had your potential. I was able to make an inadequate but definite contact, and their existence can still be changed and altered, for they have free will, as you do.

"Unconsciously, you are aware of their progress, as unconsciously, they are aware of yours. You saw to it that they would be helped. Remember that regardless of anything, you gave them existence and consciousness, a gift of creativity, and potentials that they will try in their own way to fulfill. Their experiences have been different from yours. Their fulfillment, when they achieve it, will therefore be of a different nature, bringing out facets of activity that will not exist in your circumstances — their meeting with your friend [Sue], for example.

"Now. In the life of each personality there are, of course, moments of deep crisis and decision, where a personality decides upon one of various possible choices. These moments are not necessarily conscious at all, and the choices are not *necessarily* conscious, though often they rise to consciousness. But by then the inner work and decision has been done.

"The two of you were therefore freed largely of the most volatile of your bitter attitudes and tendencies when you thrust them out from you in such a way. You [*Rob*] began your [physical] improvement from that point. You got rid of a dangerous accumulation of explosive negative energy, and freed yourselves to that extent. You had not learned to change your attitudes, however, nor learned how to prevent a new buildup, you see.

"This was your next line of your development, however. You cleared away debris. You gave yourselves psychic breathing space so that your creative abilities could arise, and saw that the way was open for our sessions to begin.

"The sessions quickened your development, gave you much more flexible attitudes and made you conscious not only of psychic reality, but of your physical personalities, which you then began to change . . . "[15]

During the next several months, I dreamed many times of this York Beach couple, but none of these had the quality of clarity and immediacy inherent in that first one. In my last dream of them, we sat around a large table in the West Water Street apartment, which they'd obviously just moved into—or *back* into, as they indicated. They seemed much more jovial than before; several stacks of Rob's paintings were there in special moving crates and Jane—*that* Jane—showed me some short story manuscripts based on these dreams with me! Reluctantly, not wanting to discuss it, *that* Jane admitted that they'd "had contact from this Seth business," but she wouldn't elaborate.

"My feeling this time was that they'd somehow become more conscious of the activities of *this* Jane and Rob," I said in class, after explaining the dream. "They should, anyway—since I told them a dozen times that I was from another probability!"

Jane had been listening, grinning at my enthusiasm, a cigarette in her slender fingers; but swiftly, Seth's "*Now!*" rang out.

"You did a very good job indeed!" Seth exclaimed, waving Jane's glasses in my direction. "There is of course a bleed-through. No system of consciousness is ever closed! Only *you* pretend that they are closed."

Seth turned his gaze to the class. "Now, personality has no limits," he began, softly. "Each of you, in this reality, have decided upon emphasizing certain charactcristics and forgetting others. You

have allowed, therefore, certain characteristics to come to the surface and you are aware of them and you use them—and you think,
'These characteristics are myself.'

"The ego is a king with a very precarious crown, and you
think you are what your ego is. It does not occur to you, however,
that there are literally countless, countless probable egos within
yourself; numberless abilities that could come to the foremost of
your consciousness to be latched upon and used. You are unaware of
these buried selves; these buried abilities; these buried creative functions and combinations; and yet in other layers of reality, these come
to the forefront and you allow these their play; and the characteristics that you think of now so securely as your own are buried.

"But while they are buried, they are not unaware; they
are in trance, and you *can* become aware of them."

Seth learned forward, placing Jane's glasses on the coffee
table, and her cigarette in the pearly abalone ashtray. "Within the
self that you know are countless combinations of selves that you do
not admit," he continued smoothly. "In other layers of probable
realities, these selves have their say and live out their potential. They
are sleeping within you in this reality, but in those realities, *you* are
sleeping within *them* as latent potential.

"The trees that you see outside the window you see simply
as trees because you perceive them only through the physical viewpoint; and yet even these trees have potential abilities and potential
combinations of consciousness that you do not perceive and that exist in other probable realities."

Seth turned again to me. "Within you, for example—and
everyone in the room—there is an unlimited amount of what you
would call identity. Now, all you do when you have an identity, and
focus upon it, is grab out of your own bank of potentials a *group* of
potentials and say, 'These are the ones I will settle upon for now,
and these I will call my identity and so I will use these and I will ignore anything else.'

"But another portion of the self says, 'Ah-hah! *These* potentials are not used—they are free-wheeling, and I will adapt these,
and these will be those potentials with which I will work.'

"There are no potentials within you that are not being
realized, and no creative abilities that are not being used . . . This
does not mean that you need not use [your abilities] . . . and . . .
say, 'Ah-hah, well, they are being used in another period of reality!'

"Now, development is a journey within creativity," Seth said during another class discussion on probabilities. "You have at your command literally infinite amounts of energy. In your terms you are, if you prefer, latent gods. You must learn to handle and use this energy . . . as mentioned earlier this evening, you will create. You cannot help creating any more than you can help breathing; and when you breathe no longer, you still create.

"You cannot escape your own creations. It is not death any of you have to worry about—it is your own creations, and you cannot blame your own creations upon any god or any 'fact' or any predestination! If you want to speak in terms of God, then from that infinite gestalt you receive the energy to create. But because you have free will, you create what you choose and you learn through experience . . . If, however, one portion of your personality has not learned from the experience, other portions may well learn . . .

"I want you to understand a few points along [the lines of probabilities]. First of all . . . as I have said, you are not tied to a neurosis from a past life; but also I wanted you to know that your present thoughts, feelings, and emotions not only affect you, but affect your probable selves. And yet—*no probable self is at the mercy of negative thoughts of yours!*"

As he made this last remark, Seth stared directly at me. Earlier, I'd been wondering if somewhere there were a whole *universe* populated by the offshoots of pent-up fears and angers. "Think how they must picture *their* gods!" I'd groaned, only half-joking.

"Each consciousness," Seth continued, "has its own responsibility for those thoughts and emotions. The [probable] personality in its entirety includes, therefore, probable selves of which you are presently unaware.

"This does nothing to negate the validity and integrity of the self that you know. The divisions are illusions, and when you wake up to yourself—to your *true self*—then you are aware of these other portions of your personality.

"Now," Seth boomed out, grinning all the while, "in terms of growth and development, and speaking, now, simply, to get the idea across—theoretically, you are working toward a time when the 'you' that you now know will be aware of the entire personality and accept it as your identity! The whole personality is not like some super-self in which you are lost; in which the identity that you know is gone. You must simply accept the fact for now, until your

experience begins to prove it more and more, that the inner identity
. . . is far more than you presently realize, and the best way to work
toward such realization is to accept the self that you are now, *as* you
are; to feel the movement of the spontaneous self."

"Is each personality aware of itself and the other selves
also, at the same time?" asked Pete.

"Time is basically meaningless, so that the question cannot be answered in the framework in which you asked it," Seth told
him. "Each personality to itself has continuous consciousness. Its
consciousness is continuous, and it knows who it is and it experiences
no lapses. Do you follow me?"

Arnold Pearson, who had earlier been talking about the
pulsating nature of Seth's EE units,[16] spoke up. "Either I misunder-
stood before, or I am misunderstanding now, but I thought each
personality, each portion of a whole self, went through pulses," he
said.

Seth nodded. "To explain [probable selves], that is what I
used; but the *feeling* of continuity is continuous. Now, it is also true
that for each moment that you exist, in this universe, you do not exist in it. This is *not* an analogy, but for you there is a continuity of
experience. You only accept as 'real' those moments in which you
are aware within physical reality."

"Yes," Arnold said, thoughtfully. "I understand the feeling of continuity, certainly."

Nadine Renard raised her hand shyly, like a schoolgirl.
"Seth? Is it possible to experience some of these personalities while
you are still conscious of the personality you have at the moment?"

"It is," Seth answered dryly. "When you are doing Psy-
Time[17] and when you relax your ego enough, and when you are
spontaneous enough, and when you realize that these other realities
do indeed exist—then it is."

"Well," Nadine pursued, "how can we tell probable selves
from past reincarnational selves?"

Seth stared at Nadine, an impish grin on Jane's face.
"Now, I knew that sooner or later *someone* would bring up *that*
bugaboo!" he roared gleefully. "It has taken me some time to get the
idea of probable realities through your heads, and I knew that someone at some time would ask me about reincarnational selves, and so
I suppose it behooves me to try to give you an answer, and it is this:

"You are presently within one system of reality; one probable reality, the reality that you now know and form physically. Now
within that one reality, you have reincarnational selves. They belong
within the concept of that existence. All probable systems do not

have reincarnational existences. Some do and some do not, so that these exist only here, as far as you are concerned for the moment. And I know I am only going to confuse you, but if you have probable selves, then you know there are probable universes and probable earths and probable histories of your earth; and you see what this is going to do to your concept of reincarnation as you hold it!

"So within the system that you know, you also have probable reincarnational selves within those probable historical earths.[18] Now, this does nothing to deny the basic integrity or validity of what you may prefer to call the soul. It simply means that the inner self is far more creative, far richer, and far more varied—and much different—than you originally supposed. Some of you could meet yourselves coming down the street and not even say hello!"[19]

Seth looked around at all of us, sitting in somewhat boggled silence. "You stand, or you sit, in the middle of forces that are a part of you," he said, softly. "These are not alien forces of which we speak; these are not things that happen *to* you. These are forces that emanate from your own being and you can, to some extent, become aware of them. The methods have been given, not only by me, but by others through the centuries. You are not nearly as lonely within yourselves as you suppose that you are. You have only shut out the other messages that come to you all the time. You are not divided from your fellow man unless you choose to be.

"Remember, you call this your universe and your reality, and it is indeed, for you form it; and yet within you is also the knowledge of other great experiments that are being tried, and other probable systems are aware of the experiments that *you* are trying. In your terms, and I am speaking now in your terms only—which to some extent means that I am hedging the fence—other civilizations have gone your route. Some have failed. In your terms, the inhabitants of some earths, however, have succeeded very well, and your future, in your terms, is not set.

"You can follow any road that you choose, but until each individual realizes that he *practically* forms his own personal life and has a part in the mass formation of reality that you know, then there is much learning ahead, for this is a lesson you are meant to learn within physical reality. You are meant to judge physical reality. You are meant to realize that physical reality is a materialization of your thoughts and feelings and images. You are meant to realize that the inner self forms that world.

"You cannot be allowed, in your terms, to go into other dimensions until you understand the power of your thought and subjective feelings!"

Seth leaned back in Jane's chair and closed her eyes. "And so even when you think you destroy, you destroy nothing. And when you think that you kill, you kill nothing. And when you imagine that you can destroy a reality, you can only destroy a reality *as you know it*. The reality itself will continue to exist.

"You think a thought and because you cannot follow it, you think it disappears, and you wonder where it has gone: Has it fallen over some invisible cliff within your mind? But because you cannot follow the thought, and no longer perceive it; because you can no longer hold it in consciousness, does not mean that that thought no longer exists and does not have a reality of its own—for it does indeed.

"And if a world escapes you and you cannot follow it and you think it has been destroyed—then the same thing applies to the world as to the thought. It continues to exist. And what I have said should inspire questions within you.

"I bid you all a fond good evening, and—" here, Seth opened Jane's dark eyes and turned directly to Joel Hess "—if you cannot follow where I am, then you have trouble following where *you* are, and when you find out where you are, you will not need to ask where *I* am! And what blessings I have to give, I give to you," Seth finished in his usual fashion.

"I accept them with gratitude," Joel replied, "and such blessings as *I* have to give, I give to *you*."

Seth grinned. "And those *I* do not have," he answered humorously, "I must, of necessity, withhold!"

NOTES FOR CHAPTER SIXTEEN

1. In Chapter 15 of *The Seth Material*, "Probable Selves and Probable Systems of Reality."

2. See more on Dr. Pietra and Rob, and connections with the counterpart concept, in Chapter 18 of this book.

3. As did George Rhoads, also a professional artist and, according to Seth, Rob's counterpart. See Chapter 18 of this book.

4. Chapter 15, *The Seth Material*, p.195.

5. *Ibid.*, pp. 200-203.

6. For a note on how we may have tuned in on a probable ESP class during another mobility-of-consciousness experiment, see Chapter 3 in Volume 1 of *Conversations*.

7. Richard Bach, author of the best-selling *Jonathan Livingston Seagull,* had visited Jane's class the week before.

8. *The Nature of Personal Reality,* Chapter 14.

9. *Ibid.,* Chapter 15.

10. *The Seth Material,* Chapter 2, "The York Beach Images—'Fragment' Personalities," pp. 25–26

11. *Ibid.,* p. 26

12. *Ibid.,* p. 28

13. The idea of fragment personalities and projections is discussed throughout Seth and Jane's work; in *The Seth Material,* pp. 28–29, for instance, Seth specifically mentions a "fragment playmate" that Rob materialized as a child; this phenomenon, as Seth puts it, is a common occurrence in childhood years. In this category, I would have to place, for instance, the animals I frequently saw around me during my childhood and teen years—and still do, on rare occasion. Many people would be able to think of examples: Betty DiAngelo's little girl by the library steps, for instance, or anyone's "imaginary" playmate.

14. I've never been to Sayre, Pennsylvania, not even at this date in 1981, although Jane and Rob and I once talked about driving through that town to check on the details of this dream. In 1970, at the time of the dream, I also didn't know that Rob had once been a chain-smoker. By the time we met in 1968, he'd quit.

Jane and Rob moved from Sayre to their Elmira apartment in 1960. According to them, there is a small central park in Sayre with a tiny open bandstand in the middle—a feature of many small towns. "We used to go there often; it was near were we lived," Jane says. "There was also a place on a hill outside of town where there was a big old deserted park with picnic tables; we used to go there, too." Their apartment in Sayre was in an old house on a shaded street of old houses—most of which had barns or large garages behind them. They lived on the second floor and also used part of the attic for living and storage space. "I think the house next door had a screened-in porch," Jane recalls, "but our house was green." There was also a taxi company in Sayre, although the Jane I know never worked there . . .

15. It's interesting to speculate on the multilayered reasons for my dream-contact with the probable Jane and Rob at this time in my life. As I've indicated, there were many pressures of a personal nature, not the least of which was the care of a ten-month-old child. I'd barely begun to learn how to recognize and release pent-up angers and anxieties; and the numerous beliefs and skirmishes involving marriage, motherhood, and the nourishment of my developing abilities were boiling to the fore almost daily. Certainly none of these contents of my life then were much different from most daily lives; but once again, as these two volumes have constantly shown, the psyche rises up to meet one's needs in astounding ways—ways that most of us are systematically trained to ignore.

"You contact them [*the York Beach couple*] in a state which is not waking or dreaming," Seth told me in class when I asked if that Jane and Rob were dreaming of *me*. "You are familiar, to some degree, with your own state of consciousness, but you do not examine these too closely. You assume you are awake under certain conditions, and you assume that you are asleep under certain conditions. Now, there is what I can describe as a *mean* of consciousness that is a *constant* between the waking and sleep states. It is yours whether you are awake or asleep, and this is the state you are reaching them in."

16. Seth first mentioned these EE (electromagnetic energy) units in 1969 and includes information on them in *The Seth Material* and *Seth Speaks*. According to this material, EE units "exist just below the range of physical matter and accrete in response to emotional intensity," eventually forming physical matter, as Rob notes throughout the two volumes of *"Unknown" Reality*.

17. "Psy-Time," as members of Jane's class referred to it, is simply a form of meditation or relaxation in which we attempted to remain lucid while falling down through various stages of consciousness. It was often the state that induced out-of-body projections, clairvoyant experiences, and the like. See Appendix 2 of Volume 1 of *Conversations* for Theodore Muldoon's notes on "The Great Hall," a series of inner journeys taken largely during Psy-Time.

18. An example of a "probable historical" earth-person, according to Seth, would be the image of my grandfather that I used to see during my early teen years. See Chapter 6 and Appendix 3 of Volume 1 of *Conversations*.

19. Seth explores in great detail the relationship, or more accurately, the lack of divisions, among probable selves, reincarnational selves, and counterparts, in both volumes of *The "Unknown" Reality*.

CHAPTER SEVENTEEN

Them As Us: Characters Who Passed
Through Class

Caught Up With

Sometimes we have to wait
for trees and sparkling waters
to catch up with us—
It takes a sudden windy blast
to place us in the sites of Here—
this trembling scene of earth
and shaken wind-blown light.
And then it comes so fast
we're thrown upon the ground
and there we're met face up with
leaves that have blown away;

a mushroom that's about to burst
above the surface of the sand.
Two dragonflies arrive and compass
point an eastern and a western
hand and knee.
And finally you're caught up
              with.
Your world again has come to be.
But that's what it takes sometimes to
              see.

                    —*Dan Stimmerman, 1976*

"The cannibals," Seth was telling us, "in one way were far more discerning, far more religious, and far more sacred in their attitude than many of you here in this room."

"Ulp!" mumbled the enormous woman visiting class that November night in 1970.

"They ate, for example, both human beings and animals, but they did not eat indiscriminately; nor did they eat without a knowledge of what they did," Seth elaborated. "They realized that their life was a portion of all this life . . . they gave thanks to the body that they consumed; they hastened the spirit that had been in the body on its way with thanks . . . many of them, in their own environment, knew that those who were not eaten by them—for example, other warriors—would die of hunger in any case. They ate them, then, with thanksgiving and joy."

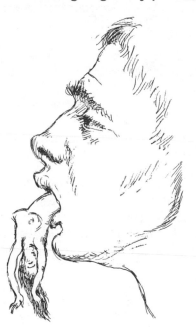

The woman, wedged firmly in her chair, was suddenly dripping with sweat. "UGH," she said aloud. The poor lady must have weighed 350 pounds; when she first arrived in class, Jane had gently directed her to the sturdy armchair by the kitchen door—and with good reason. The old chair's legs were now sunk into the rug. How had we gotten onto the subject of *eating* things? A minute ago we'd been talking about the evolution of the dinosaurs . . .

"You, however, eat indiscriminately, with no thought of the living animal that you consume!" Seth was saying, rather pointedly in this woman's direction. "Now, as you consume the animals, so one day will your physical body return to the earth and help form other animals. And portions of the atoms themselves that compose your body will run across the fields in Iowa a hundred years from now, changed . . . but remembering their backgrounds." Seth stared directly at the woman with his penetrating gaze.

"There is a sacrament here that you do not understand," he said, "and when you gobble down food indiscriminately, and when you do not give silent recognition to the fact that what you eat once lived, then you lose part of a cycle in which you rightly, as physical creatures, and as spiritual creatures, have a part."

"Oh-h-h-ggghh," the woman gurgled.

"Is this not true whether we eat meat or vegetables?" Arnold Pearson asked.

"It is, indeed," Seth answered.

"Then," Grant Sayles spoke up, "should people get a pleasure out of killing, like people do for sport, instead of killing for food?"

"In your terms and in the way you are asking the question, the answer is that no, they should not; and that they will have to deal with this," Seth replied.

"In what way will they have to deal with it?" Grant pursued.

"It is a lack of development, spiritual development, and so it will automatically lead them into trials that they will have to face—not in terms of punishment, but in terms of understanding. The ignorance will cause them sorrow until they learn to rid themselves of it."

"This would be the same thing as if I went out and chopped down a tree for no reason at all," Grant stated.

"It is, indeed," Seth agreed. For a moment, Seth stared again at the woman, who was now sweating profusely, her eyes bulging as she gasped for air.

"Well, *I* don't think it sounds like the cannibals were very religious," Florence MacIntyre remarked from the sofa. Florence, who had a weight problem of her own, was dwarfed by this woman tonight.

"You were never a cannibal!" Seth answered. "The cannibals knew this sacrament subconsciously [and] it was built around a religious ritual. Their rituals were as strict as they are in your church, and they were as religious as they followed them.

"They ate the brave and the strong. Now, some tribes ate the elders. When the old could not care for themselves, if they were very wise and brave men, then they had a dance around them, and this was known by all involved. Then they killed and ate the wise elders . . . Both as a method of ending their lives, in a quiet manner, for they killed them easily, when they were too old to run from jungle animals or from hunters or from warriors from other tribes; [and] so that the wisdom could become a part [of the tribe] . . . In one way, immortality could be achieved, in that the elders would then feel that they were a part . . . of the flesh and the blood of the tribe, and this was believed by all and not feared by the elders. The elders preferred it rather than to be banished and left the prey of animals or to die of starvation or slow death outside of the tribe."

The huge woman covered her face with her hands. "I need a drink of water," she groaned. Jane came out of trance just in time to see her guest heave herself up out of the chair and stagger toward the closet-sized kitchen.

"Uh—" Jane said. "Well, I guess it's time for a break, unless somebody wants to fill me in on—"

CRASH!!

The room shook with the sudden impact: glasses rattled on tables; Rob's paintings flapped in place against the wall. Willy, Jane's cat, shot wild-eyed out of the closet and scrabbled for the safety of the bathroom.

"Oh, my God!" Sally Benson wailed. "That woman's fainted dead away in there!"

Joel Hess, who had some first-aid training, ran into the kitchen ahead of several others. The woman had indeed passed out, and was stuck good and tight in the tiny space between the refrigerator and stove. Her short, thick arms were caught up over her head. Her face was purple.

Joel grabbed a glass and filled it with cold water. "Here! Drink this! Drink this!" he yelled, waving it under the woman's nose.

"Joel, you jerk, she's out cold!" I pointed out. "Slap her wrists or something."

"That's not going to help her now!" someone said from behind me. "How are you going to get her out of there?"

"We'll just have to move the stove out," Joel offered dramatically.

The woman's eyelids fluttered. "Oh, sweet Jesus," she mumbled. She looked up at Joel, still standing there with the glass in his hand. "Get me out of here!" she wailed, panic pushing at her voice.

"Now, now, don't worry; it's okay, we'll help you," Joel soothed. He looked the situation up and down and made helpless gestures. There was hardly enough room in the kitchen for any one of us, let alone enough people to help her. I started to shake with repressed laughter. This was awful—the poor woman must be utterly humiliated, as I certainly would have been, and here I was suffocating with stopped-up giggles.

I left the kitchen. Arnold Pearson replaced me, and there was a lot of grunting. Something ripped. The oven door banged open and slammed shut. Finally, the woman emerged into the living room and walked straight out the door, muttering something in passing about having to get home early. We never saw her again, which isn't surprising. Jane explained that the woman had told her on the phone that afternoon that she wanted to come to class for some insights on how to lose weight.

"And Seth goes and talks about *cannibals??*" Jane groaned, rolling her eyes toward Heaven. We really felt like dogs—the lady must have been devastated. Had Seth gone too far? Yet, his remarks on food and "indiscriminate" eating had sprung from our own conversation, and were certainly applicable to all of us. Obviously, they'd hit home for that woman—and we sincerely hoped she would find some help through them. But from then on, whenever someone in class started complaining about a weight problem, we'd remember the lady who fainted in the kitchen over the carnivorous habits of the cannibals.

"I remember so many incidences with people who came to class that demonstrated the nature of beliefs," Betty DiAngelo says. "There was the guy who wanted Seth to do card tricks: we were seeing extreme and rigid ideas [and] it was pretty obvious that he wouldn't have trusted the outcome of the tests anyway, as he really didn't trust himself. I suppose we've all done this in some area; I was almost embarrassed for the guy . . . and yet he was being completely himself. I remember Margaret, who wanted to help someone, [even though] that person did not want Margaret's help . . I know I recognized my own tendencies in these kinds of incidents and while I may not have been able to recognize them [in myself] if someone pointed them out to me, I recognized them or saw their reflection in others. And experiencing others creating their reality in a particular area and the beliefs involved, pointed out the way to me to examine my own beliefs."

Martin Crocker

Indeed, some people who came to class wanted Seth to be a new god; and when class overreacted to these ideas, Seth would point out (sometimes none too gently) that we were seeing in them our own hidden desires to set him up as a new comfort blanket—"but I take your comfort blankets away," he would tell us. There was Martin Crocker, the gentleman spiritualist,[1] who said he'd seen cups fly through the air during seances, and who insisted on set definitions for all experience—including the Seth phenomenon, which he saw as the perfect example of a "spirit guide" in action. I was furious with the man and cowed by his expectation of "respect" for being older—and male. Yet how often had I yearned for well-defined answers to all *my* problems, perhaps whispered in my ear by spirits dancing through the room? And there was the young student of Eastern religions who sat with a never-changing smile glazed on his face the whole evening; whose only comment (repeated several times) wound through hopelessly sugared Zen-isms of non-thought: yes, Seth was bliss; *all* was bliss; bliss was Be-ing; all we had to do was *Be*. I was infuriated that time, too—yet how easily in the past had I passed off the implications of my own experience in favor of words from Jane or Seth that might show me how to find . . . bliss?

Then there was Don the parapsychologist: the scientist come to analyze the medium.

Don was a trained parapsychologist who claimed to have studied under Dr. J. B. Rhine at Duke University,[2] and who wanted to add an investigation of Jane's psychic abilities to his record, he told us. Ironically, Don admitted to several startling subjective experiences of his own, including an out-of-body that he said had cost him a government research grant. According to Don, he'd made the suggestion one night that he could "travel" to the federal office that would handle his grant request; he thought that a description of a room that he couldn't possibly have seen physically would give his psychic research proposal more "punch." To his own surprise, Don said, he'd found himself in the out-of-body state, standing in front of an office desk piled with official-looking files and folders. In his grant proposal, Don described these folders with some precision. Within days of its receipt, Don's request was rejected without explanation, and he was told to abandon his project immediately—no questions asked!

But in spite of this kind of personal experience, Don tried hard in class to be impersonal and uninvolved, so that he could discover the truth—or non-truth—of Jane, Seth, and I suppose, the rest of us. One night, though, class got out a couple of end tables and started some riotous table-tipping—yelling and laughing and dodging each other as the tables danced around the room. Finally losing his carefully honed air of detachment, Don stopped his note-taking and left his chair to join the five or six of us with fingertips on Jane's little green lampstand, which was happily thumping back and forth on the rug.

Don placed his fingers on the table with great care. "None of you've got your thumbs underneath this, do you?" he joked loudly. He was really trying to enter in the fun of it all, but the instant he touched the little table, it began tipping violently around on its legs, from one side to the other, crashing down dangerously close to our toes.

"Jesus!" Don shouted, jumping back. The table stopped dead, thumping down on all four of its legs. Carefully, Don touched it again—and immediately, the table was tapping around in a circle so quickly that we could hardly keep in contact with it. And then, just to polish it all off, the little table seemed to leap at Don, whumping right up against his legs so that he hopped backwards in self-defense. Almost gleefully, the table tapped forward again, nudging Don's thighs with firm, continuous shoves. Our fingertips brushed its surface lightly, but stayed in touch.

"Hey!" Don wailed. "The goddamn thing's chasing me!"

"Whoopee!" Dan MacIntyre whooped. The table seemed to leap forward in a fresh burst of energy—and pinned Don right up against the bookcase, a thud! rattling the books and vases as Don's backside hit the shelf. With that, Don yanked his fingers away, pushed the table aside, and sat back down in his chair.

Immediately, the little table lamp next to him blinked off.

"What the hell . . . !" Don stammered, staring at it. As if in answer, the lamp blinked back on.

"Sorry about that," Jane said, with a straight face. Everyone in class knew that the lamp was defective, but Jane liked Don and couldn't help teasing his serious demeanor a little. "That thing just doesn't have any manners at all. Lamp, you stop that."

Smoothly, the lamp blinked off again.

Don gaped at it in shock, apparently so devastated by the marauding table that he'd forgotten the jungle of electric plugs jammed in the loose wall socket behind his chair, and how suspiciously the plugs jiggled when anyone sat down near it.

Another group continued to tip a three-legged table on the other side of the room. Don just sat in his chair, nervously rubbing his hands together. Eventually, when everyone quieted down a little and put the tables back in the closet, Jane said, "I think someone has something to say to our scientist," and removed her glasses.

"You must realize the vitality that is within each of you and not be afraid of it—as you are," Seth said, turning to Don. "Now you are controlling it and disciplining it, but you are also afraid of it. You simply bottled it up out of fear of your abilities and of the power that resides within you." Seth also told Don that there was a great contrast in his attitudes toward such phenomena as the table demonstrations: "On the one hand [you have] the determination to show up all fraud, and on the other hand, the fear underneath that your own experiences could somehow be fraudulent. Therefore, you could not trust yourself."

Jane came out of trance and asked Don to explain what Seth had said. "He was talking about my underlying fear of psychic matters," Don began—just as the table lamp beside him snapped back on. Don stopped in mid-sentence. Soon thereafter, he left—and never came back.

It would be easy to poke fun at Don and his "scientific" approach to Jane's class—if it weren't for all the times that any of us have trusted a set of definitions more than our own experience. And how many times have we been scandalized by irreverence, confusing what is "serious" with what is "true"?

The ideal balance in class, achieved under Jane's watchful eye, was one of its principal lessons: how to combine the intuitions, emotions, and intellect as we were naturally meant to do. I say "ideal" because it didn't always happen that way. We were groping for something, without really understanding what it was. And the characters who appeared in class (often at weirdly appropriate moments) acted as living illustrations of what we were exploring—usually by showing us our own extremes.

In May of 1971, after several hours of class debate on good versus evil and the psychological origins of heaven and hell, Seth abruptly announced that one of his physical lives had been spent as a "minor Pope" in 300 A.D.; therefore, there was an "authority" present on the subject of heaven and hell. Amidst the chaotic reaction to this statement, Seth went on to explain that " . . . the rigorous concepts of good and evil are themselves highly distorted, and when you find such a dilemma where goodness is one thing and evil another, and both contrary and separate, then you automatically separate them in your minds and in your feelings and in your fantasies.

"You do not seem at this point able to realize that what you call evil works for what you call good," Seth told a somewhat incredulous class. "Both are a part of energy and . . . you are using energy to form your reality, both now and after this life. This is because you deal with effects physically, as you see them. And until you divest yourself of such psychological behavior, it will always seem to you that good and evil are opposites and you will treat them as such in your feelings and in your concepts and in your myths."

At this point, Ron Labadee (the intensely "intellectual" fellow described in Chapter 3's playing-card incident) sat forward in his chair and interrupted Arnold Pearson in mid-question. "Is it ever justified to do evil for the sake of good?" Ron asked.

"In the terms in which you ask the question, the answer is no," Seth answered benignly.

"In other words," Ron continued, "in this reality, we are faced with decisions. In that context, is it true that our decisions can be only constructive and good, or destructive and evil?"

"Only in the terms in which you ask the question," Seth said. "In larger terms, there is no such thing as destruction; and your second question does not follow logically from the first one. If you will look at the script when you receive it [*the following week*], you will see what I mean. You ask questions without considering the answers that have been given. Think of the answers before you form your next question."

"Yes, but I don't necessarily agree with the logic of your answers," Ron said.

"I do not *need* you to agree with my logic," Seth replied. "I need you to understand the faulty quality in your own logic, and that must come from yourself and not from me."

"Yes, but—"

"Now, wait," Seth said. "Part of this is due to the fact that you form questions before you comprehend the nature of the answers that you have received. Read the script. Find out the answers I have given you, and then form your questions."

"Well, I have a question that I know I'm going to form after I read the script," Ron said, oblivious to the glares and groans from those around him. "It is that *your* response was that *my* question was only meaningful in the terms that *I* use; so what I'm asking is how do *you* conceive of good and evil in *your* own reality?"

"There is no destruction, and there is no evil," Seth answered emphatically. "*But while you believe that there is, then you must act accordingly!* While you believe that to murder a man is to destroy his consciousness forever, then you cannot murder, and in your terms it is an evil."

"Well, Hitler could have used that justification for wiping out six million Jews!" Ron cried.

"He could have indeed," Seth agreed.

Ron was beaming with satisfaction. "Well, then, I disagree with you—I think that even in the way we look at it now there is destruction, which is evil."

"I *know* that you do!" Seth roared. "You live within that reality and while you live within it, you must deal with it—and so you are!"

"So . . . " Ron mused, coiling for another pounce, "is there such a thing as a moral decision for someone who exists in the next plane of existence?"

As Seth, Jane sipped some wine and placidly returned Ron's gaze. "There are *always* moral decisions," Seth stated. "They involve the use of creativity and development. They involve the use of spontaneity."

"What system of values do you use to choose in your moral decisions?"

"I have told you. My last answer implies that answer."

"In your words, it would be whatever is the most creative in terms of what you want to do."

"We will ignore the last part of your sentence and agree with the first part," Seth answered, grinning impishly. "And I shall certainly see to it, if I have any abilities to do so, that in your next life you are put in the position of answering someone whose mind works exactly as yours does!"

"I feel like I've made contact with you very well," Ron said. Irritation among other class members, with whom Ron rarely talked about anything, was turning the air sharp as daggers.

"You have indeed," Seth answered dryly. "However, the intuitive rapport that you need to contact others within your environment is at least to some extent lacking. Reach out to them with feeling rather than with the guise of probing words."

"I don't necessarily deal with physical entities the same way I'm dealing with you right now," Ron said, rather loftily.

"You should learn to!" Seth replied. "I egg—listen to me—I egg you on. It is good for you and good for the class and very good for this one over here—" Seth waved Jane's hand at Florence MacIntyre—"because you ask questions that she is already thinking of, and for some reason she has suddenly grown timid about her questions! Now, continue."

"Well, I was just going to say that no evil can be justified on the basis of the greater good," Ron said.

"That is what I told you operates in your reality, and you did not listen to my answer. When you read the text, it will be simply clarified. In your reality, the stance that you adopt is a necessary one, and you must hold to it. The fact that it *does* apply only to your system need not presently concern you."

"Hmmm." Ron placed his hands in front of his face, fingertips touching. "Are there instances in which a spirit from another reality would intervene in this reality, and we would call that a destructive act but the spirit would say it was creative?" he asked suggestively, a thin hint of a smile on his lips.

"Oh, for the love of God!" Arnold exploded, but Seth merely answered, "I do not like your term. Any such intervention would occur only on the part of a personality who was, for the present time, physical; as the villain in a religious drama would be a creative figure. But he would exist historically in your time and not, for example, be a ghost whispering in the night. There are no creatures whispering evil in your ear."

"There are no intervening entities?" Ron repeated.

"Not in those terms."

"But in the terms that we are all spirits acting out our own inner drama, the term 'spirit' has some meaning?" Ron probed, with one of his few smiles ever.

"Sometimes—but only occasionally—I think you are catching on!" Seth yukked. "There are no forces outside of yourselves that in your terms cause you to do evil. Unfortunately, what you think of as good and evil reside within yourselves and you cannot blame an evil force for the destruction that runs rampant across the earth.

"Again, in these terms, these are your problems, and no god or devil put them upon you; and there is no one to blame but yourselves," Seth said to the rest of the class. "On the other hand, for the seasons and the [flowers], you have yourselves to thank. You are learning to use the creative energy of which you are a part, and you are indeed quite isolated, so you cannot do much harm, in your terms! And so that the evil that you think you do is an illusion. . . . And if you destroy your planet, you will have others to work with, and those that are destroyed are not destroyed. You are in a training system. The mistakes in the long run, and in your terms, will not count, but they are very real to you at this time."[3]

Ron stayed in class for about six months, but without participating, holding his presence to himself like a weapon, relentlessly following Seth's words through every twist and turn of logic, picking up truths and casting them down like imperfect artifacts. And it was here that Ron lost the real experience of Jane's class. Ron wanted answers on a platter, according to *his* definitions; answers that would answer all the questions ever asked and that would erase all the doubts of human existence. And for that, who could fault him? Who had not wished for the same? Yet, as Ron sat there, cold and severe as a brittle wind, you could see that such demands would not work. You would only ask and ask and probe and discard in your serious scientific garb until you dried up trying. You had to *feel* your answers, and the feelings had to rise up out of your own experience, and fall back into it with warmth and joy and acknowledgment. But Ron's posture of intellectual criticism was crushing the other portions of his psyche.

On the other hand, whatever obstacles Ron manufactured for himself in the name of intellectual probing seemed like *nothing* compared to the messes people got themselves into as a result of credulousness—if only because it was more fashionable to be cynical.

Allan Demming started coming to class in 1974, during his student years at a nearby law school. He was soft-spoken and discoursed with reason and compassion; just what you'd expect in a budding lawyer. What nobody would have suspected at all (particularly, perhaps, of someone in Allan's career field) was the reason he gave one night for coming to class in the first place: an occult group he'd once joined in California had told Allan that in a past life, he'd traded away his spiritual freedom while under the influence of hypnosis. This West Coast group's leader, Allan said, had given him the procedure that he had to follow in order to negate this trade-off and get on with the business of "uplifting his Karma." With a complete lack of embarrassment, Allan concluded this story by saying that he hoped that Seth could fill him in sometime on how he was doing with his renegotiations.

Sighing bravely, Allan raised his eyes to Jane.

"*AL-L-L-A-A-A-NN!*" Jane screamed in outrage, nearly leaping right out of her chair. "Wha—how—you mean—*ALLAN!!!*" She stopped to catch the words. Giggles drifted around the room, but Allan sat quietly, proudly. "Allan, for chrissakes, you can't trade away your freedom, spiritual or otherwise!" Jane sputtered.

Allan frowned, puzzled. "But it explains things, problems I've had for so long," he said. "The guru out there gave me methods to destroy these psychic structures that they said have been confining me in this lifetime—and that once I do that, I can get out of . . . ah . . . " but Jane's glasses were tossed on the rug.

"Oh-oh, here goes!" someone said, and with his wide, dark eyes close to Allan's, his voice low and intimate, Seth began.

"Now, before they can give you a method for destroying psychic structures, they must con you into believing that they exist in the terms of their school!" Seth told him. "Now, you do not believe in Original Sin, in conventional terms. So you simply switched your beliefs into another area of activity!

"When anyone tells you that your power is not your own, and you are not your own person, then run! This has been done through the centuries."

Allan straightened his own dark-rimmed glasses and shook his head; he was plainly confused. "But Seth, you're saying that . . . I mean, uh, are you *familiar* with these people out in San Francisco?"

"I am familiar with those people, and with all people, who tell you that you can trade your soul, or your energy, or your free will; or that another can take it from you," Seth said. "People who then give you a code that will enable you to regain the self that you have never lost; who lead you into a system of beliefs that appears quite valid, once you accept the basic precepts."

"Then, I mean, uh, you're saying that—" Allan stammered.

"I am saying that you are free!" Seth replied loudly. "That you have *always* been free, and that no one can hypnotize you against your will; that any 'deals' you make in this world, or any other, you make of your own free will, and can break of your own free will!

"You need to use the common sense that is yours as a human being—and this applies to each of you, to whatever system of beliefs you have allowed to use you!"

Allan sat quietly, considering these words.

"Now, in a great display, I could—though I will not—frighten you out of your beliefs, or snap my fingers and say, 'Oh, thou demons be gone, and set our Allan free! Let whatever evil possesses him go on its way!' But I give you a greater truth. There never was any evil that possessed you, and you never sold that which you cannot give away!

"You are free, as you have always been free, and that also means that you cannot blame anyone else for anything. So accept that freedom!"

Seth withdrew, and Jane blinked back into the living room. "What was this?" she asked Allan.

"Why," Allan said, his voice filled with wonder, "why, Seth said that . . . that I'm free! That I never traded away my freedom at all!" He was wide-eyed with amazement. "It just must be a lot of negative beliefs that I've got that cause me all the trouble," he concluded.

And you knew that Allan was discarding the San Francisco system for the Sethian Technique, right in front of us, with as little thought given to one as the other . . . well, at least here, Allan might learn to start using his lawyer's head. Unfortunately, Ron Labadee had left class by then; the two of them might have helped one another out. But nobody put Allan down too hard, because obvious as his form of idiocy was, it haunted more old closets than Ron's belligerent attempts at scientific cunning. How many of us had found it easier, at least for a while, to declare ourselves as weak, sinful, or fat, as failures of the flesh or victims of society, and so placed our power in the hands of the rigors of confession, diets, drugs, astrology, or religious dictates that denied fun, desire, and eclecticism in the name of salvation from the physical world?

There was Ira's guru for instance; the whipping that Ira had endured to be "cleansed" of his existence in flesh. Even though Ira's search for the esoteric had apparently strained his common sense at that point, what he'd submitted to wasn't overwhelmingly different from any other system that reflected beliefs of worthlessness. But when Ira first described his guru initiation, I had to laugh at myself: a year before his trip to India, Ira had shown up unannounced in Jane and Rob's living room one Friday night, a complete stranger to all of us. Immediately, he'd unsheathed his guitar and started singing religious hymns—which he kept up for hours. I'd felt like whacking him one myself; for one thing, underneath his veneer of happy spirituality, he was so damn deadly serious—pinning us to our chairs with Jesus! But at the time, it seemed too ungracious to tell him to knock it off—even humorously.

In class, however, the pitfalls inherent in rigid seriousness were probably best illustrated through a group of people who for a year or two regularly flew to Elmira on Tuesdays from another part of the state. These five or six likeable, good-hearted men and women lived in a community dedicated to the philosophy of G. J. Gurdjieff.[4] They'd started attending Jane's class with the permission of their community leader, Eugene Nyland; and their pursuit, as they saw it, of Truth, was a serious endeavor indeed. In 1973, Nyland himself, by then an elderly man, arranged to have some of his students drive him to class.

"That group was so ungodly serious!" Jane recalls. "Nyland had known Gurdjieff personally, it seems—I think he was one of the national directors of these study groups. To Rob and me, the funny thing about it was that when Nyland came up to talk to us the day before that class, he made the student who drove him wait in the car! His position was that the 'students' and the 'leaders' didn't discuss things together—that you let only the most advanced ones in on the 'information.'

"But Nyland was a delightful man—sort of European, I guess you'd call it, in terms of expectations of tribute. He wanted to be addressed as 'Mr. Nyland' in class, but I told him that we didn't kowtow to titles here.

"His thing, his group's thing, was that 'The Work' had to be *literally* worked at, like you had to work at 'The Self,' or you'd just fizzle out. It was the complete opposite of spontaneity."

And unknowingly, without an explanation from Nyland of his beliefs or purposes, that class managed to get onto the subject of play, and playful behavior. About halfway through the evening, after several appearances, Seth turned his gaze to Nyland and his group.

"Now, Gurdjieff loved to play," Seth announced to them. "He was a playful man, and what came to him so beautifully and so naturally, and with such brilliance, was his own vision, and he tried to communicate it to others. He expressed what he believed in. To him, however, regardless of his words, there was an easy transparency in what he did—a joy of vitality that no words could destroy—a spontaneity and a great vitality. But many others do not understand that spontaneity or joy. Now, [*to Nyland*] you do, and you have. The trouble is, you see, you want people to play seriously, and want them to work playfully. There is, after all, not that much difference!

"The grasshopper leaps out of the great vitality of his being, but when he tries to tell others how he leaps, others listen and say, 'Aha, yes, I do this!' or, 'I do that!' or, 'But I am not a grasshopper.' Or, they do not understand the miraculous presence and immediacy of a grasshopper; or, more important, a grasshopper mind.

"If you know how to play, you do not need to know how to work; if you know how to play, then you understand what play is, and you know that it is not chaos. You know that games have rules. You know you make the game; and therefore, you make the rules. And you can, like a grasshopper, or like a child playing hopscotch, skip from square to square. Gurdjieff did, in Ruburt's terms, do 'his own thing.' And his message is, 'Do your own thing.' And my message is, 'Do your own thing'—only I make you make up your own rules as you go along, and Gurdjieff gives you more help!

"If there is one thing Gurdjieff did, however, that many have not done [was to work] with the mobility of the intellect and of the mind, and not ignore it. And this also I want you to do—but playfully! For . . . *the only real work is done in play*, and if you realize that, all 'work' is done, and you do it."

"I was wondering," asked Jerry, one of the New York Boys, "is it true that rules were made to be broken?"

"Rules are made to be made, to be followed and broken,"

Seth told him. "Rules are made to be rules. When you need them, you make them. When you want a new set, you find a new set, but always you should follow your own inner dictates.

"Now, let us clear up a point—occult point—for some of you do not understand something that is important," Seth said, turning again to Nyland. "Ruburt understands that work is play, because for him, writing—which is work—is also play.

"When you think of work, you think of something that you must do that you do not want to do, and therefore imagine a great resistance. We are speaking [now] of the situation where work and play are one, and that is the nature of creativity. You are not doing something because you must do it, or because it is the right thing to do, but because it is a part of your nature. It may require, in your terms now, certain framing. It may involve many things. But it is play to you because it is so natural, and 'The Work' does not involve the same kind of resistance that you encounter when, say, you think of going to a job that you dislike, or tackling a chore that is beyond you. You may think of work-play or play-work, but it is a creativity in which there is a birth of spontaneity and inner structure that goes so in hand that it is impossible to separate one from the other."

Margaret, one of Nyland's students, raised her hand at this point. "Why did Gurdjieff call his methods to teach people to play 'work on one's self'?" she asked.

"He used the terms that he believed made sense in his time and circumstance," Seth answered. "He also believed in the seriousness of high purpose, and so he used the terms that he thought would help others. He also hoped to use the terms, quite trickily, that religious people used. They would play better if they believed they were working harder! He understood that many people with guilt complexes could not be told to play. They would feel too guilty, and so he told them it was work—and it worked!

"Now, you see, I would say that what Gurdjieff wanted *in* was culture. That is, he was fighting against cultural beliefs that still exist, where I do not fight them. I am telling people to play, and through play they will discover their purpose."

"I think they can find out, by play, what is lacking in them," Nyland commented.

"They can, indeed," Seth replied.

"And that is why," Nyland added, "when they wish to play, they must know first what they can play with, in order to reach what they wish to create."

Seth paused, smiling affectionately at Nyland. "Now, it is a matter, first of all, of vocabulary," Seth said after a moment. "Secondly, [it is] that I have perhaps, now, a greater trust in what you are. For I believe your playing, of itself, will lead you to your own answers. You are simply adding a helpful structure, through which people can test themselves, and there is nothing wrong with that. It is a structure that many people need.

"But, from one old gentleman to another, encourage them, then, to show their emotions—to be themselves in that way, and even to lift their heads out of the structure of words," Seth continued. "Gurdjieff understood the structure of words. He gave you words and structures because he understood what structures were; but he wanted you, then, working with structures, to go beyond them—*playfully*—and when you learned what play was, to throw those structures aside and emerge awake, *above* the structures . . .

"Now, excuse this voice which comes through so loudly, simply because energy has its own way," Seth added humorously, in his best booming tones. "So if I sound—though I am sure I do not!—loud, it is because of the mechanisms involved. And what you are witnessing now is playful work and creativity, and a break-through—the kind, incidentally, with which Gurdjieff would have been happy, and he would have jumped up and down with un-holy glee!

"Now, I did not mean that our friend Gurdjieff would be jumping up and down with joy because there was another group with different ideas! What I meant was that the great vitality and joyfulness of Gurdjieff would be happy to see this particular kind of breakthrough, for he would recognize its highly creative nature, and he would recognize it as a breakthrough—a giant grasshopper leap! [But] there is nothing wrong with the physical structure through which all vitality, in your space and time, sings—as Gurdjieff himself did. That spirit, when you think of Gurdjieff, knew itself through corporeal knowledge, and through the joy and the vitality of the atoms and the molecules that compose the body—as you know yourself, *in*, now, *in* this space and time through your corporeal image. You exist independently of it, and you know that."

"Yes," Nyland agreed. "Sometimes concepts of that have to be put in certain words to make you understand. But it does not mean one has to take the words for the concept."

"One should never!" Seth answered. And he and Nyland seemed to come to some meeting of terms. But the following week, Seth once again addressed the Gurdjieff group (who continued to attend class without Nyland). "Did it ever strike you as strange that a man so given to the ideas of play [*Gurdjieff*] should initiate a system that was so concerned with work?" he asked them. "Or, indeed, how playfully was he pulling your serious legs?

"Now, if you take a dead frog, and stimulate it, the dead limb will move. That is what [Gurdjieff] was doing, and you react very well to him. His seriousness of idea and doctrine was like bait that he dropped down to all serious fishes to swallow! But he was a playful fisherman, and he hoped to end up with playful fish! I am not a fisherman, I am a fish—a playful one, swimming through realities that change, in your terms, in every moment; peering down with huge fish eyes at this strange reality that you call your own. And you peer down into your own reality and find it strange!

"Oddly, I play a trickier game than Gurdjieff—though you may think I am so straight, in terms of integrity . . . for I then turn you all back to yourselves, and let you look into the eyes of your own authority, and your own playfulness; and from that seeming dilemma between your own playfulness and your own authority, you come out with fine music [*a reference to Warren's cello rendition of the Sumari 'Song of Creation,' which he'd performed that week*], excellent dreams, some good insights, and the creativity that is your own."

Throughout class years, Seth warned us repeatedly to be alert for the appearance of strangers, both those in our dreams and in waking life; that those who played out dramas before us in either state were connected with us in ways we did not guess. "You choose this place and time for your own reasons and your own challenges . . . and so this planet is not peopled with strangers, but those who are already psychically united, who then come to this planet in your time," he told us in late 1974. "Your world is far more extensive than you realize, and your concepts have limited your experience. So, here, we knock the old concepts down. You knock them down as you encounter your own living psyche." And so, as it developed toward the end of class, strangers and characters who passed through those Tuesday nights were as entwined with us as the symbols of our dreams.

But out of all the unique people who appeared in Jane's apartment (many of whom probably thought *we* were all crazier than hell), the one most "unforgettable character" in my communications with class members was Florence MacIntyre.

Florence was an open, loving woman who took great pride in intellectual achievement. In class, it seemed that she was always at odds with the more liberal viewpoints—and yet she was not a prude: she and her husband once invited the whole roomful of us to their backyard swimming pool for some after-hours skinny-dipping. But while apparently unperturbed at the sight of twenty-five naked people running around her suburban lawn (blocked from the rest of the neighborhood by a seven-foot fence), in Jane's living room, Florence was a consistent and volatile traditionalist.

In October 1972, I told class what I thought was a wickedly humorous story: my three-year-old son had happily yelled, "Lookit that ole fuckin' bug!" at a bee buzzing through my parents' kitchen. In spite of my parents' understandable surprise, I ignored Sean's words, and after a few moments, my parents also shrugged the whole thing off.

An appreciative chuckle rippled through class, but to my dismay, Florence immediately registered strong disapproval.

"You don't know what you're doing!" she admonished. "Sean is going to be in big trouble when he gets to kindergarten and starts using those kinds of words! He should be corrected now, before he gets there—you know, you could give him substitute words, possibly something like 'ding-dong,' so he doesn't cause a problem."

A dozen voices leaped into the fray, abruptly cut off by Seth's swift appearance. "For Sean, the word is not loaded!" he said to Florence. "He will not feel the need to show off to his contemporaries—*in his fucking kindergarten class!*"

Billows of giggles fluttered like nervous birds around the room. Florence scowled, her expression pained. There she was once again, fencing philosophies with Seth.

"Children who will come up with the word in kindergarten class, our dear lady of Florence, are those who have a charge behind the word, and will try it out in front of you to see if your reaction is the same as their mothers'," Seth continued, oblivious to class reactions. "And they will know that 'ding-dong' or 'ding-a-ling' is a safe word for 'fuck'! And they will know that you know . . . but the children who would use the word to shock your class, or to shock you, are not the ones who can use it readily at home and have it pass by unnoticed."

Seth turned to the rest of us, his voice slow and serious. "When will you learn that your bodies are good, and that what they do is good? And that the words to describe the bodies' activities are good? *You have fucking bodies!* It is the method by which you come into this existence! It is a glorious term except when you think that it is wrong. And when you accept from others the *idea* that it is wrong, then when they use it, they use it to be nasty, because they know it will have that effect upon you.

"In this life, you come from the sperm and the womb. You come from the meeting of flesh and flesh, and you come from singing . . . "

Nobody was giggling when Seth finished this time — we all knew how many times we'd used (or thought about using) "Fuck you!" as the ultimate insult. But in the following week's class, the New York Boys again brought up the subject of "forbidden" words — and actions.

Florence

Eddie Feinstein (who'd established a reputation for driving all the way up from New York and snoring all the way through class) recalled the first time he'd used the word "shit" in school: he'd been paddled by the principal. "I suppose I'd been okay if I'd used the word 'doody' instead," Eddie laughed, "but what's the difference? We all know it means that same brown stuff, right?" Florence sat without comment, and looked plainly relieved when Seth came through.

"You can take the word 'Mu,' thinking it, speaking it cautiously when you are sure that children are not present, whispering it behind closed doors," Seth began. "Whenever anyone hears the word, catch yourself short and do not speak it. Before you speak it, look in all directions, and soon, in Florence's kindergarten class, you will have some smart alec say, '*Muuuuuu!* and you'll have to find a new ding-a-ling, or ding-a-long. The *words* are meaningless."

Seth's voice softened as he turned to Florence, his eyes wide and dark. "Now, Florence, our Lady of Florence—and when I use the word 'Lady,' I know what I mean—our Lady of Florence has come to this class longer than any of you, and with much greater yearnings and reservations. With much greater hopes and despairs. And she has tried to translate, in her own way, what I am saying.

"And when she speaks, she speaks your own deepest fears! And you listen to her and sometimes you snicker, and sometimes you laugh, *but they are your fears!* And yet her yearnings are your yearnings also, and do not forget it!

"And so she faces, in a very practical way, the problems of putting the material into daily use. And with all due respects, you [*Florence*] have not always been brave! But you have always been sincere and done as much as you felt you could do at a given time.

"And many of you do not have that impetus. You do not have to! You [*Eddie*] do not have to translate this material in the terms of conventional society, and our Lady of Florence does. And so, what she learns, she learns for all of you. And the fears that she speaks, she speaks for all of you. And the yearnings that she has, she has for all of you.

"You [*to the New York group*] think yourselves apart from the so-called 'Establishment.' And you find, in our Lady of Florence, someone quite ensconced within it. Yet she comes here and tries to translate what she learns into those terms—to change [the Establishment]. *And if you do not communicate with it, you cannot change it!*"

Seth withdrew, and class erupted into a lively debate on what he'd meant by people in the 'so-called Establishment.' Eddie, who was struggling with his new-born New York restaurant,[5] said that he thought this venture had put him at least to some degree in the leagues of the "Establishment."

"I was speaking in terms of people who think that the word 'fuck' is wrong!" Seth responded suddenly.

"Yeah, but I deal with people every day who think that way," Eddie said, defensively.

"You do not so far as your friends are concerned, or the people with whom you are intimately connected," Seth said. "You have a freer lifestyle, and so the translation is not that necessary. They will understand the sacred quality of the word 'fuck,' but

Florence's students—and their parents—do not. Now—do you follow me?"

"Yep," Eddie grinned.

"I am glad!" Seth cheered. "And I do not intend to speak as if I came from a barroom, but a barroom can be more sacred than a church—and none of you forget it!"

None of us did, I'm sure; nor do I think that any of us ever forgot Florence's position on our behalf. And her example will apply to the reader—think of people in your social circle who always seem to contradict the norm, or who bring up viewpoints that you'd really rather not think about. "Our Lady of Florence, very nicely for each of you in class, personifies the feelings that each of you have, to whatever degree, involving your inner self," Seth put it once. "She shows them in an exaggerated fashion for you to look at, and so when she speaks, she speaks not only for herself, but for everyone in this room, including Ruburt." And it says much for the peculiar orientations of class that while Florence and the New York Boys, for example, could disagree so fervently, nobody seemed to confuse the arguments with the individuals. "They always seemed to contribute so much to the class," says Priscilla Lantini of the New York group, "and when they weren't there, it wasn't quite the same. I feel a strange affinity towards them. I had a class dream once in which I went down city streets with the Boys and . . . jumped on Big Jed's shoulders, and he carried me around and they were like my brothers. The feeling of unity between the guys and me was great. I especially had a strong affinity for Lauren [DelMarie], when Seth called him 'Pan.' "

"Most any yarn about class characters," Matt Adams notes, "could illustrate beliefs in action: Often, individuals (me included) were so wrapped up in his/her system of priorities that other wave lengths simply did not get through; clues that others might have picked up immediately were missed completely, often to sad or funny effect.

"My father came to class only one night; it was the same night a new member arrived—she was plump, with black dyed hair and a black dress, bright red lipstick; looked very much like a slightly bloated Pola Negri—or a female impersonator, as someone said later. Anyway, she was extremely interested in attention. She was reading, somewhat dramatically, from a list of beliefs she'd extemporaneously scribbled down, when Jane took off her glasses and Seth began with his characteristic '*Now* . . . ' "Now what?" she asked, misunderstanding, and a trifle miffed at being interrupted.

"Toward the end of the evening, she noticed my father there alone — the New York Boys were far beneath her notice — and she asked him to help her carry a suitcase, typewriter, or something down to her car. Her interest was very evident, though I'm not really sure if she wanted action or just attention. She was very enjoyable, in a kind of garish way, but Jane told me later that she had to have the woman stop coming — she was just not fitting in. Too bad she didn't last for the transvestite class!

"I mention my father because that particular class night, Seth did a quick series of transitions that floored him. Jane was in her rocker, and when Seth departed the first time, Jane's head flew back against the back of the chair with an audible *crack!* Jane came to, rubbing the back of her head, and said into the air at large, 'That was a dirty trick!' Zap, Seth was back, to say, 'Tell Ruburt that there will be no pain in his head.' Seth gone, Jane back. 'Jane, there's no pain in your head,' we dutifully repeated. 'Hunh?' Jane said, with apparently no memory of the intervening episode. 'Boy,' my father remarked later, 'that was really amazing.'

"I also recall a particularly attractive blonde girl and her mother," Matt says, "and was rather disappointed to see that they were totally unresponsive to efforts to have them join in conversation. This must have been the week following the nude class (*see Chapter 9, Volume 1*], since Jane told me later that each woman was having some kind of problem in her marriage, and that the previous week had been the first time either of them had seen penises in a nonconfronting manner; impersonally, as it were. These two women were rather grim and intent, two adjectives that never seemed to characterize other class members. I *do* recall that I had worn clean underwear, just in case.

"My point is that the fewer restrictive, narrowing beliefs there are, the less prejudiced is perception. I try to maintain a 'maybe' shelf in which there is no absolute 'yes' or 'no,' but only degrees of maybe. Using that system, it's easier to accommodate practically *anything* that comes along."

NOTES FOR CHAPTER SEVENTEEN

1. For a complete description of Martin Crocker, see Chapter 3 of *Adventures in Consciousness*, "A Spirit Guide is a Spirit Guide is a . . . ?"

2. This claim was never checked out, however.

3. Nearly two years later, in January of 1973, Seth responded to a remark of Ira's about Hitler's beliefs by saying, "Now any time that you commit a violence, or accept a violence, in what you think of as the defense of good, you are doing what was done in that time [*World War II*], and bear that in your heart. The end does not justify the means in your reality. And, when you are teaching others, hold that in your heart. It is your one and only defense against what happened in Hitler's time, and that answer is within you. And, what is more, you know it!"

4. G. J. Gurdjieff was born in Russia in 1878 and died sixty-nine years later in the United States. Considered a mystic by his followers, Gurdjieff's basic philosophy was centered around 'The Work,' particularly as the means to knowing the Self: that self-knowledge required, and indeed was the fountain of, work. According to Eugene Nyland, Gurdjieff also taught that most of humanity was in a state of half-sleep, and that only this self-work would awaken mankind to its own Existence.

5. Now known as Arnold's Turtle, located in Greenwich Village in New York City.

CHAPTER EIGHTEEN

Who Else Do You Think You Are?
— Counterparts Are Comparatively
Encountered

ON BUILDING FENCE
(Love Poem to A Counterpart)

I am perpendicular,
not plumb,
sticking out awry,
trees gawking branches
at angles impossible
to the sky,
and fence posts letting slip
your animals
through corners meeting
parallel and senseless
to the eye;

For your plumb
depths, I would
have traded sense
of tree-thoughts stranded
in good time,
and mended fences
by your side, content
with playful angles growing
sideways off the hills;

And how we would have
zig-zagged, you
and I:
Across the fields
in fencelines
all practical
in harmonies of wire,
letting slip
our questions in
through corners invisible
to the senses;

But you must mend your fences plumb—
And I must follow angles of no worth—

And we string wires
around the thing
our nature is,

And see the other
as fenced in,
Forgetting
how parallel are the senses,
how playful
are the corners of the Earth.

— *SMW*

Rob started it all, of course.

Rob, the "mystery man" who painted undisturbed in his studio through some of the most riotous class events; whose canvases whispered images of other selves, other times; whose watchful sensibilities led him to spend years perfecting his notes for Jane's books. That it should have been Rob's experiences that begat the counterpart information seems like the natural order of things. And once it was explained, this revolutionary concept of personality also seemed like the natural order of things, couched within our unknowing awareness; its attributes unrecognized in the one-line order of logic.

Rob had been coming to class for several months in late 1974 when, in the fall of that year, he reported a series of altered-perception experiences of what appeared to be other lives.[1] Two of these involved two distinctly separate deaths of two Roman soldiers in the first century A.D.—people who would have lived in the same historical "time" as his Nebene character. A third perception was of a Jamaican woman in the 1800's. Rob told class that his impressions of these people had a validity and brilliance about them that he couldn't deny. Some of the details—including Rob's minute description of the fishermen's long-roped nets that had pulled one of "his" Roman bodies ashore—were corroborated by George Rhoads, who'd lived during the 1940's in a Spanish fishing village, unchanged in many ways since ancient times.

Yet, Rob wondered aloud, was this some kind of contradiction? Or if these personalities had actually lived (or were now living, in terms of simultaneous time), what did it mean? Could several "selves" exist in the same time frame?

"What it *could* mean is a literal revolution in our concept of identity," Rob offered in his quiet way. "It demonstrates again how limited our notions are of personality and how vast the facets of consciousness might be." He went on to describe more of his Jamaican woman impression.

"I get the feeling," Jane said in the uncharacteristic silence that followed Rob's remarks, "that something new is up, you know?" In book dictation for *The "Unknown" Reality,* Seth had explained, Jane said, how Rob had helped the Jamaican woman in her "now"—another example of across-the-board reincarnational oneness, like the Nebene-Shirin encounter between Rob and me three years before.

Jane had brought Seth's most recent *"Unknown"* passages to read to us. "'You live more than one life at a time,'" she began, from Rob's carefully typed session notes. "'You do not experience your century simply from one separate vantage point, and the individuals alive in any given century have far deeper connections than you realize. You do not experience your space-time world, then, from one but from many viewpoints.'"[2]

As Jane finished reading, Seth came through, removing Jane's glasses and placing them—and the session notebook—on the coffee table in front of Rob. In an elaborate congratulations to Rob on perceiving the Jamaican woman, Seth told him, "You are neurologically tuned into one particular field of activity that you recognize. [However], if you could think of a multidimensional body, existing at one time in different realities, and appearing differently within these realities, then you could get a glimpse of what is involved."

Robert F. Butts

Well, we could tell by now that this was all leading up to *something*—we'd learned to understand a certain kind of "cue" in class, and in Seth's words. And the following week, as we were vigorously exchanging ideas on probable selves and their relationship with past lives, Florence remarked that there had to be "some kind of a balance" among what we were still calling "reincarnational selves." Swiftly, Seth was in on the conversation.

"Far be it from me to disturb your ideas of *yin* or *yang*, or Jung, or good and evil, or right and wrong, or good vibrations or bad vibrations!" Seth told us humorously. "What I hope to say is that your world exists in different terms than you recognize, and that reincarnation is indeed a myth and a story that stands for something else entirely!

"Now, you take a part of your world as you understand it, in your time as you understand it, and all of the creatures on the earth—in your terms—in the century, participate. And so each of you works out challenges and possibilities, creativity and fulfillment. And so you are born in different races, in different cultures, with different, but same, desires. And each in his or her own way participates in what you think of as the history of your time."

Seth turned to Florence. "Forgive me . . . I will use you as an example," he said, with affectionate apology. With that, Seth announced that Florence had a counterpart, a living "version" of herself, who was a young man, alive *right now*, in China ". . .who does not weigh even seventy pounds. He has starved for years. He feels very vulnerable. It does not particularly help that young man when our Lady of Florence piles weight up because she feels less vulnerable and more protected from the world.

"On the other hand, our young man dreams of being overweight, and it is one of his most satisfying dreams," Seth continued. "Now, in his own way, those dreams are going to be a help to him, because he is already working on some concepts involving the planting of fields that will help the people within his village.

"In this particular village, the elders believe that there is some merit to being underweight. Our young man hates the Americans. He believes that this is an opulent, luxurious, and wicked society; and yet he yearns for it with all his heart.

"Now, our Florence, in her own way, is working with ideas of good and evil, searching for what she *thinks* of as an aesthetic and moral code that she can rely upon. Her counterpart has that code, and he found that he could not rely upon it. Each in their own way are working on the same series of challenges, but there are also two other counterparts, and between the four of them, the century is being covered . . .

"Now, in your terms only, these other counterparts—and in your terms *only*—these other counterparts are like latent patterns within your mind—echoes. How many of you have actually thought of what the 'unconscious' may *be*? Or, the voices that you hear within your mind or heart—are they 'yours'? To what counterpart do they belong? And yet, you, in your own identity, have the right to do precisely as you wish, and to form your own reality . . . "

Connections began to light up: you could see it in every-body's eyes. "Opposites attract," someone remarked.

"I did not mean to imply that you were on a teeter-totter, with a fat self up here and a thin self down there, or a good self up here and a bad self down there, or a yellow self up here and an orange self down there," Seth replied. "Merely that each of you, in your own way, works out your *ideas* of good and bad, of 'opposites'; that you are working with the same challenges, and that—" here, Seth's voice boomed out—"*there are no opposites!*"

Sitting back in the chair, Seth shut Jane's eyes and tapped her foot on the chair rung. "I will give you [another] example," he said. "There is a member of the class—and I will close my innocent eyes so that I do not give the secret away—but there is a member of the class who is indeed a fine Jesuit . . ."

Several people giggled. Seth had called Warren Atkinson "the fine Jesuit" (as well as "the Cardinal") many times, in reference to his Catholic background.

" . . . working out problems of great weight, dealing with the nature of religion," Seth continued. "Now, there is also a man who has been to this class, a 'renegade' priest, who ran off to the West Coast; who likes to put the boot to theology, and do his own thing."

"Collin," Harold Wiles said, remembering the defrocked priest who'd come to class once and conversed at length with Seth—in Latin.

Seth nodded. "There is also a woman. The woman lives in England, and she is extremely devout. All of these counterparts are working with the nature of religion. They are experiencing versions of religion because it interests them, taking different paths and roads as if, indeed, you had a great, bright red apple, and you bit in here, and here, and here, and you said, 'Aha, it is sweet—oh, no, it is sour over here; and here—I do now know!' But it is the same great, delicious red apple! And that is the only hint I will give you!"

"So," Lauren DelMarie asked, "you're saying that if someone believes in good and evil, or health and sickness, that will be translated not only in individual life but into the different lives?"

"I am saying, my dear friend," Seth answered patiently, "that the attributes of reality that interest you, you will create in your own way. And if you want to experience [for example], your ideas on the nature of religion, and . . . do a good job of it, you must be a skeptic and a believer; and an Indian, and a Jew. Otherwise you will not understand anything at all, and have a very lop-sided picture. And you cannot know what it is to be white in this culture unless you know what it is to be black in this culture, and you cannot really—and [*to a black student*] you may not agree here—understand what it is to be black in this culture, unless you are white in it."

"Question, question!" shouted Rudy, waving his hands to get Seth's attention. "Uh, what happens if you've learned to trust your being, and then you've got a counterpart that mistrusts his being? What then?"

"Your being is your own," Seth replied.

"My being is my own?" Rudy repeated, mystified.

"Your being is your own," Seth answered back. "And your counterpart's being is *its* own. Now, in the dream state, so to speak, you compare notes."

Rudy looked up at the ceiling, down at the floor, back up at Seth. "I don't see how that answers the question," he admitted.

"It answers the question insofar as it is the only answer you are going to get!" Seth said with great ironic humor. "You are here a great, creative group. And because you are, you delight in finding your own answers. And I know precisely, when you ask a question, when you expect an answer and when you do not!"

So: "counterparts"—the word stuck. The concept seemed to explode upon us. It was so natural; yet almost terrifying, too, in its portent: the most *pregnant* idea we'd heard yet, about to give birth endlessly. "First, I got myself to understand that the self wasn't dependent on my physical body for existence," grumbled one slightly exasperated student. "Then there was the idea of re-incarnation and simultaneous time. Okay, okay, I finally caught onto all of that, and the next thing you know, there's the bit about probabilities and all directions not taken existing someplace else. Then probabilities and reincarnation got all tied up together as the same thing. Now there's this idea of counterparts! It gets to be more than I can handle!"

Jane sat quietly, out of trance, her face a combination of fascination and disquiet. Seth's remarks about Florence and her counterpart were certainly astute, but then we all knew that Florence's stepfather had been Chinese. On one hand, this fact fit in with the "logic" of the counterpart information Seth had given to her: she said that it connected with all kinds of personal facts and emotional "correctness." On the other hand, did this mean that every single detail of your life connected in some fashion to other levels of physical activity, with parallels that followed through right down to the mole on your cheek?

During the week, I recorded five or six dreams featuring complementary-type relationships with friends and relatives. In one, I'd published a science-fiction trilogy and was giving copies to the characters that I'd created in the story—yet these characters were people that I knew in daily waking life. I gave Volume I of this trilogy to Joel Hess, who'd stopped coming to class in 1971; by 1974, he'd been editing an Elmira weekly newspaper for a year. I gave Volume II to class member Zelda Graydon, herself a writer and neophyte journalist. Volume III went to Jane. It was crystal-clear in this dream that *I* had created these three people. Yet, of course, I hadn't. What did it mean?

The Tuesday of December 3 was cold and gray. A taste of winter things to come rattled the big bay windows throughout class, as gusts of wind whirled around the dark Elmira streets and dashed against the house. About thirty of us sat, warm and cozy, talking about Seth's latest book, *The "Unknown" Reality,* and this new counterpart thing. Late in the evening, Rob told us that he'd had another experience that week like the Jamaican woman and Roman-captain-in-the-fishing-nets perceptions. This time, Rob said, he'd apparently tuned in on the death of yet another Roman soldier—making this the fourth person that he'd identified as living in the first century A.D. "time" of Nebene.

As Rob spoke, it seemed that corridors were opening up inside my head. For one thing, I recalled Seth's constant warning to be aware of "strangers" in our dreams; and his remarks about our relationships with these strangers, some of whom, he'd said, existed now in other parts of the physical world. Then there was that question I'd pestered Seth with for weeks in early 1971: Could one entity have two personalities alive at the same time?

"I was wondering when you would come up with that question," Seth had answered (maddeningly). "Indeed! I am answering in the affirmative." But at the time, he'd refused to elaborate, and the finer implications of his answer were lost to me in the excitement of possible romantic applications. Love at first sight explained! Soul mates defined! But now, as I listened to Rob, I remembered that old question of mine—and something else.

I'd met George Rhoads on Martha's Vineyard in the summer of 1968. Neither one of us had heard of Seth, but we both habitually recorded our dreams and were aware of paranormal events in our lives. Many were the Vineyard evenings when we'd sit on the

Figure 13. "Here are 2 versions of the tower incident..."

porch of George's Lagoon cabin, eating kelp salad and home-made clam chowder, listening to the call of the whip-poor-wills, and swapping dream events. George's dreams were something like his paintings—in brilliant, super-realistic color. He also experienced, he said, vivid and immediate visions while meditating; and one of these visions had recurred disturbingly often during the past year. It was the death scene of a Roman soldier standing on a high wall, with a round parapet nearby. In this image—strangely absent of color, he said—the soldier was shot or hit in the back of the head and fell backwards, or was pushed, off the wall, to his death on the ground below. George said that the details were perfectly clear—that in the background he could hear a murmur, or low roar of human voices, chanting or wailing. He said that he knew the soldier was himself; the emotions were personal and direct; and yet he seemed somehow to be both victim and assailant: he could also "remember" coming up the steps of the tower to *attack* the soldier. The strange duality was subjectively certain—yet impossible, George acknowledged. He drew two pictures of the scene in pen and ink for me (*see Figure 13*), expressing the scenario's somber quality in sparse, shadowed lines.[3]

Now I listened to Rob tell about his perception of the Roman soldier atop a wall with a parapet nearby, and of how the man fell to his death after being struck or somehow attacked. Rob, too, had sensed the low wailing of thousands of voices; had seen the event in dark and somber tones. Rob had watched the scene from a point *above* the soldier; but again, he said that there was no doubt in his mind that the soldier was himself.

Was this reincarnation in some strange fashion? Or two men of similar mind and bent, unconsciously recalling the same history book they'd read once? And even if you accepted past-life (past-death?) memory—well, lots of Roman soldiers must have fallen off walls in their day. Except that . . .

I looked at George, who was sitting on the floor, smoking a smelly cigarette, waiting intensely for Rob to pause in his exposition. Odd, that George had talked about that meditation experience again just a few months before this class . . .

"Rob," George finally blurted out, "that's the same thing that happened to me! I have the exact memory as you do!"

It was funny, almost: George hastily telling the same soldier story; Rob reacting with bemused astonishment. I'd known both these men for about six years, but never had it been so obvious how . . . *connected* they were. Physically, they were of about the same age and general appearance. They had similar backgrounds:

Rob growing up in an ordinary Pennsylvania small town; George in a midwest family of middle-class means. Both are professional artists and excellent draftsmen; each had done lucrative commercial artwork in New York City before turning to his own painting; each made a living at one time doing anatomical drawings for medical books; each had worked in the comics. Both studied and used the techniques of the Renaissance Masters. Not an overwhelming set of coincidences, I acknowledged, for artists of their time: plenty of others had done the same stints. And after all, there were some pretty obvious *differences* between them. To start with, George had been married several times and had two children, and Rob wasn't actively pursuing a gallery-sales career, as George was.

But even these differences were . . . I groped for it—like complementary opposites. Was it any coincidence that George and Rob and Jane and I related to each other as we did? Both men were at least ten years older than the women, who were both writers. All four of us here, in Jane's class, like a Sumari quartet. And now, this falling-soldier thing. It all ached with something; the mind yearned to turn a corner and catch it there, elusive as it was . . .

I recalled Seth's recent remark about Warren's "counterpart" connections with Collin, the renegade priest—who had come to this class; *who had been here,* face to face with Warren. This wasn't some theory, then, about selves who in our terms were long gone and far away—this could mean *you* looking at *you,* living mirrors of identity; self seeing self and discovering something truly intimate, something quite unsayable. Were Rob and George counterparts; portions of the same self? Did this mean that they'd once "shared" this same Roman soldier? Or were they sharing memories (or perceptions) across a kind of spiritual synapse? But then, their entity names, as given by Seth, were different. Wouldn't that tell you something? Or was trying to define counterparts through entity names like trying to translate the Sumari songs on a literal basis? I felt dizzy, whirling with ideas I struggled to contain.

As George and Rob were exchanging details of this Roman-soldier scene, Seth removed Jane's glasses and listened, smiling, for a few moments. "I cannot tell you about the reality of your own psyche," he finally said. "You can only experience it for yourself . . . But in your terms, the population of the Earth is made up of counterparts, and so there is, indeed, a relationship; and when you kill an enemy, you are killing a version of yourself.

"There are deep spiritual and biological connections also, as I have hinted in one of our recent book sessions,"[4] Seth told Rob.

"For, as members of a physical race, so you are also members of a psychic kind of counterpart reality, and this straddles races or countries, or states, or politics.

"So, counterparts exist, in your terms, at any given time in history; and so are you indeed related; and there are no strangers, in deeper terms, upon the face of the Earth.

"You form your history. You form your reality, and no one is thrust into a position which first was not accepted as a challenge. And so you work out your problems and your challenges in whatever way you choose, historically, again in your terms; so that you and the Roman are connected; and the Arab and the American; and the African and the Chinese; and so are your identities intermixed with others that may seem to be strangers, but others that speak with your own voice—others who communicate with you in your dreams as you communicate with them. You have comrades, and you come, in your terms, to the Earth in a given time and place of your choice; and so do you reap and form the great challenges of your age.

"You are each individual. You are each yourselves."

So, we wondered after Seth withdrew, does this mean that you could literally have *hundreds* of counterparts? "What if you ended up being every solider in the whole Roman *army?*" Rob laughed. But in January of 1975, Seth named a series of counterpart relationships that existed among class members: including Rob and George, Rob and Jane, and Jane and me—a logic that certainly didn't surprise anybody. "Counterpart relationships appear when it suits your purpose," Seth says in Volume 2 of The *"Unknown" Reality*. "They mix and merge."

That January, Seth explained to class that "You have specific counterparts that are more related to you than others. It is not up to me to tell you who they are, only to let you know that the reality exists. Once you know that, it is up to you to discover your own counterparts . . . for you can all do so!" And so for class member Fred Lorton, this counterpart challenge from Seth became a creative exercise in perception, like his discovery of "reincarnational" selves.

"Counterparts—I sat stunned when I heard this!" Fred says. "About two weeks later, I tried self-hypnosis [*with the suggestion that he would see a counterpart*]. My first experience was quite interesting. [I saw] one of my counterparts, who is between sixty and sixty-five years old, lives in Turkey on a poor farm, knows all about raising and selling drugs and is responsible for some of my feelings

about people who sell drugs to people, especially young people. She
appeared to me, about twelve inches in front of my face, and stared
at me for at least two minutes, and then her face softened a little
when I realized who [this person] was.

"Counterpart number Two—about one week later. [I
saw] a cocktail party scene in Los Angeles, mixed crowd, well-
dressed, socially well-to-do. Suddenly, a girl about 5'11" turned to
me, drink in hand, and stared, long and hard. When I realized I
was staring back and that it was counterparts again, the scene faded
. . . again, self-hypnosis, six minutes."

In Session 732 for January 22, 1975, of *"Unknown"*'s
Volume 2, Seth had this to say about Fred's counterpart visualiza-
tions: "Many of the [class members] became deadly serious as they
tried to understand the [counterpart] concept. Some wanted me to
identify their counterparts for them . . . Instead, during the last
week, [Fred] let his own creative imagination go wherever it might
while he held the general idea in mind. He *played* with the concept,
then. In a way his experiences were like those of a child—open, curious, filled with enthusiasm. As a result he himself discovered a few
of his counterparts.[5]

"Most people, however, are so utterly serious that they
suspect their own creativity . . . "

On another level, Harold Wiles had felt a strong "recognition" when a young man from Boston walked into class in 1972.
The fellow gave Harold his name and address so he could receive
Seth class sessions, and the two struck up a correspondence. "We
come from completely different family backgrounds and don't share
the same interests or any of the things which one might think would
tend to bring two people together," Harold says. "But the fact is that
he was someone I 'knew.' We meet and communicate in the dream
state and out-of-body states and have had an amazing correlation in
our dream activity. We communicate telepathically, and none of
this activity is ever planned—it's completely spontaneous. It wasn't
until Seth brought up the counterpart information that I began to
wonder if that is what's going on.

"As an example: at noon one hot July Monday in 1977, I
was out walking on our farm. I wasn't going anywhere in particular.
I was just wandering—enjoying the sun and the heat and my apple
orchard and woods. Gradually, I became aware that I was not alone.
My counterpart was 'walking' with me, and we were conversing.

"The only way I can describe the situation is that I
seemed to move outside of myself, and there I was, walking along in

the sunshine, listening, as a third-party eavesdropper, to a conversation between myself and Greg. I was fully aware of what was going on. I heard me speaking with my physical voice, and I seemed to hear Greg's in my mind. I was aware of the 'alteration' and was able to lock onto it.

"Our conversation was quite personal and very specific. We talked about communication between people—communication in all of its forms. We talked about people whom we both knew and situations about which we are both familiar. The alteration lasted for about thirty minutes and then it faded. Again I was alone, walking through the fields."

Harold says that he wrote a letter to Greg that evening, describing the whole experience in detail. He later received a five-page letter from Greg that described his activities on the day before Harold's Monday walk. "He had been involved with many people about whom we had 'talked' on our walk, along with a multitude of other experiences," Harold says. "Our two letters—my report to him and his description of his Sunday afternoon—could have come from the same script. They meshed in detail after detail. It was uncanny. Greg's closing remark was, ' . . . so while working on Monday, and thinking about the events of the day before, I'm not surprised that I communicated them to you!'"

Harold rarely recalls his dreams, never had any alteration-of-consciousness experiences in class other than several door experiment "hits," never liked Sumari, and rarely had any type of paranormal experience. That he should have a communication of this sort with Greg, who lives in a distant city and doesn't share Harold's general interests (and is a poor letter writer besides, Harold adds), once again raises more questions than it answers. Do these two men "share" a common psychic ground? Yet of Les, his class-named counterpart, Harold can only shrug and say, "I don't know." Harold manages a shopping mall near Elmira and lives on the same farm that his great-grandparents worked a century ago; moreover, Harold's house is located a few miles from the third-generation farm where his wife grew up—a solid tradition of roots if there ever was one. In comparison, Les moved from New York to a small horse farm near Elmira in the early 70's and recently left the area to manage a horse ranch in Colorado. Harold and Les didn't communicate at all in class . . . outwardly.

In fact, it appears that you aren't even obliged to *like* your counterparts: none of the class-counterpart trio of Richie Kendall, Ben Fein, and Will Petrosky has any great affection for the others. Richie, a restless, aspiring songwriter "dreams of being spontaneous," as Seth puts it,[6] but hampered his own abilities with endless worries about creative responsibility and the sins of fame and fortune. Will was a compulsive talker with impulsive gestures (as witnessed in Chapter Eleven's wig incident) who is now writing articles on science-fiction for a West Coast newsletter. "He is very intellectual, proud to be one of the Boys," Seth acknowledges. Richie and Will grew up in the same New York City suburb; neither one could ever warm up to poor Ben, who attended class for a while in 1974.

"He trusts his intuitions fully and relies upon them; he is utterly spontaneous," was Seth's comment on Ben. "...but his spontaneity was embarrassing to adults; he was afraid of his intellect."[7]

"What does all that say about me?" Richie writes. "[Ben's] energy was strong but scattered, and he got on a lot of peoples' nerves...but I remember that 'Everybody's somebody's counterpart'...so I should be kind, at least in my mind."

In exploring the counterpart relationship between Jane and me, it's obvious enough that as writers, we're both exploring inner landscapes; both of us wrote prose and poetry from early childhood. At twenty-four, Jane's first published works of fiction were science-fantasies;[8] the first stories I ever wrote, at age eight, were science-fantasy-type ventures. Jane was born sixteen years before me, an only child in an upstate New York town, as I was. She grew up on the threshold of poverty; my childhood was comfortable and idyllic by contrast. Jane grew up a Catholic; my parents were agnostics, and I held a different religion: that anyone who went to church was guilty of perpetuating humanity's most blatant crimes against itself and the rest of the earth—this even though I was an avid reader of Bible stories as a child and was deeply moved by them.

Physically, Jane tends toward the lean, I toward the plump; yet our beliefs about food and nourishment are much the same (we both, for instance, have always felt a sense of furtiveness about eating). By choice, Jane has no children; neither of our childhood fantasies about our respective futures contained traditional homes and families ("I will *never* marry a nine-to-five man!" I pronounced fiercely, at age six, to my mother). Jane's quite specific career dreams were backed, however, with a great focused will, while my writing ambitions were much more ambivalent until my early thirties. We both went to college on the basis of our writing abilities, though: Jane winning a poetry scholarship to Skidmore; me honing my talents in journalism school.

Jane Roberts

In 1971, I started to write my first novel, a fantasy called *The Mediumship of Zachary LaRue* (unpublished), which initially was dictated to me in my dreams while characters acted out the appropriate scenes. I wrote down what I could remember and put the notes aside for two years. The book concerns a man who dies and then learns how to communicate with the living—and in the process discovers what I now recognize as counterparts of himself, alive in "his" time and in other times. I never mentioned to book to Jane before I finished it in late 1973; she never did read it. In 1972, Jane wrote *The Education of Oversoul 7*, about an entity and the problems of his Earth-bound personalities. Also in 1971, I had a series of vivid dreams involving a library that opened up from a corner of the woods behind my parents' house, and in which I could either do research on the nature of consciousness or travel out other doors into probable systems of reality.* In 1974, Jane began encountering her

* See Appendix 9.

own "library" in a corner of her living room, from which she wrote her brilliant *Psychic Politics*. Again, I hadn't mentioned my library dreams to her before her experience—in fact (as of 1981), I still haven't sent her transcripts of my library dreams. And then, in its way, my experience of letting Shirin "peek out through my eyes" reflects some version of mediumistic ability.

Susan M. Watkins

Jane and I have vivid dreams in which we often find ourselves aware of being in the dream state. To some extent, we can direct the focus and intent of our dreams. Frequently, we dream about each other, and recall coincidental details of dreams from the same night. In late 1969, one of my dreams beautifully foretold the counterpart exchange without my conscious knowledge of the concept: in the dream, I was trying to find a place to live in Jane's neighborhood, but the rents were all outrageously high. As I walked around the block near Jane and Rob's apartment, I looked up through their bay windows to see not one but *three* Janes standing there. One was a flighty, giggly version of Jane; the other was heavyset, aggressive, and mannish. Jane "herself" sat at her writing desk, which was piled high with her work. The three Janes gave me lectures on how to develop my writing abilities, then expressed their fears to each other about their contrasting characteristics, particularly between the flighty Jane and the "real" Jane. My dream self listened, but woke up without finding a place to live. "You see," Seth said, pointedly, after I'd related this dream in class, "Ruburt's way is too expensive—it is too expensive to follow another's way, and that is the message of the dream."

In the same fashion, both George and Rob have had double dreams[9] and inner experiences involving painting that correlate in surprising detail. Several times, for example, George would feel the urge to paint geometrical designs of intricate color and pattern, and then discover that Rob had taken a break from *his* usual style to paint geometric designs. Recently, Rob has been doing a series of small, evocative "dream" paintings in connection with notes he's been compiling on dream recall. At the same time (the two later discovered), George impulsively interrupted his sculpting to do some surrealistic paintings that are somewhat different from his usual methods in that these involve scenes from his own recorded dreams. Neither one knew what the other had been doing until several weeks passed by. Moreover, at one point in *The Seth Material*, Seth gave Rob some information on a probable self—a doctor who paints as a hobby.[10] As mentioned in the Volume I chapter on beliefs, George has recurring dreams involving a Scandinavian doctor who deals with conflicts concerning "the man in the marketplace"—conflicts, as noted in Chapter 5, that also affect George as an artist. George recorded some of these dreams, which he interpreted as having to do with probabilities, before he read *The Seth Material* or met Jane or Rob.

And then, remember *The Chestnut Beads*—in which Sue Watkins was the main "Jane"-character's *child*. If, as counterparts, Jane and I are dealing with the issues of creativity and womanhood, I can hardly think of a more appropriate way to pluck the concept out of the air and give it "life"!

Again in the context of class, Seth named Richard Bach (author of *Jonathan Livingston Seagull*) as another of Jane's counterparts. Richard attended class one August night in 1972 and exploded forever some of my worst fears. At the time, I was working in an Elmira printing company. I wanted to quit and write full-time, but was terrified of poverty—and failure. During break, Richard and I talked briefly about the risks of writing. "Don't hassle your job," he finally said. "When the time comes to quit and go out on your own, you'll know it—because you will have done it. And until then, it won't be the right time.

"But be true to what you love," Richard added, "because if you are, then it will take care of you—because that is the nature of love."

Thunderstruck fits my feelings at that moment about as adequately as "newsworthy" might fit the Second Coming. I gave notice at my job soon thereafter and began the real apprenticeship of writing, which led to my weekly newspaper work—and this book.

Jane's fourth class counterpart, Zelda Graydon, worked briefly for that newspaper and exhibited some reporting abilities. Later, she moved to the West Coast and entered a school for Unitarian Ministers—not your typical Jane or Sue choice of careers, but a parallel one, you might say. (Zelda was also determined by then, at age twenty-three, never to have children.) Outside of class, but related, I feel, to Jane, Zelda, and me in counterpart terms, is Sue Thomas, the woman who until 1979 co-edited (and owned) the weekly paper in our town. She never attended any of Jane's classes, met her only once, and didn't even finish reading *The Seth Material* when I tried to interest her in the book. Yet our lives and functions on the newspaper fit together in complementary fashion. Sue has an understanding of a newspaper's audience and a sense of what's newsworthy that largely escaped me, despite my formal journalism training. She, on the other hand, learned on the job, after buying the newspaper from a family who'd owned it for many years. As reporters, our considerations struck a balance: I was the one who wanted to know, "What is your philosophy of education?" and she was the one who'd rather ask, "Yeah, sure, but how much is that going to cost the taxpayer?" Our partnership served to round out one another's personalities, and the newspaper itself served a complementary purpose in the community, stirring local interest on both "philosophical" and "practical" levels.

Furthermore, Sue was born in Dundee, but many of her ancestors were from Elmira, forty-five miles away; I was born in Elmira but many of my ancestors were originally from this village (including my great-grandfather Baker, who co-edited the same weekly newspaper in 1878, the year it was founded). Sue's maternal grandmother bears an uncanny resemblance to my father's late mother; her *paternal* grandmother, on the other hand, resembles my *mother's* mother (also dead), not only in physical appearance but even in details of their backgrounds and beliefs. Sue quit the newspaper soon after I did to work as a psychiatric nurse's aide in a nearby veterans' hospital, where she had an offer to staff the in-house newspaper.

Oddly, Joel Hess, the third recipient of my "counterpart" dream's science-fiction trilogy, co-edited a weekly newspaper in Elmira during the same years that Sue and I were publishing ours. He's now living in Florida and has written a book about sailing; his writing background grew out of many years as a radio-announcer—and for a while, I was a news reporter for a local radio station. During his various careers, Joel was also an airplane pilot (as is Richard Bach), a minister, a teacher at Cornell University (where I once held an assistant teaching position), and studied at one point to be a nurse!

I'm omitting many personal details that fit throughout, of course; but by now, counterpart situations and their emotional interplay should be springing into the reader's conscious recognition. "Generally speaking," Seth says in Volume 2 of *The "Unknown" Reality*, "your counterparts are born in the same psychic 'family' [and are] your contemporaries." Since class ended shortly after the counterpart idea was introduced, however, we didn't have the opportunity to explore those relationships as a group. But I do believe that this awareness can make a profound impact on anyone's personal, day-to-day life, and on the world that he or she knows. For if your counterparts populate the world, then that sweet old adage of self-sacrifice, "Love thine enemy," becomes instead a simple acknowledgment *that the world is not filled with strangers.*

However, I am personally suspicious of slapping the counterpart explanation, Band-Aid style, onto every facet of human give-and-take, even when other connections might be involved. I'm fascinated and cautious in the same way that I'm fascinated and cautious about reincarnation (which I suspect is the accepted parable for what counterparts might be *hinting* at). Each person must discover the ingredients of his or her own subjective experience, and not limit that experience to a psychic score card of past lives, counterparts, or any other list of terms. I do think that the essence of the counterpart concept escapes the preliminary definition Seth gave us in class—as it was meant to do. If the reader can allow the counterpart ideas gathered here to blossom inside the scope of his or her own life, it can impart a kind of maturity all its own within human relationships, and within the personal identity sensed inside each individual.

"To me, it's obvious that counterparts work in areas we would like to have experiences in, and vice-versa," speculates Betty DiAngelo. "I suppose this is a desire for many experiences which aren't possible in one lifetime and cause communications on many levels. The counterpart thing was one of the ideas brought out in class that I understood when first confronted with it; and strangely, I can trace the idea back to my parochial school days.

"In a classroom, there was a picture of Christ's mystical body—it was an outline of Christ filled in with people of many nations. It gave me the feeling that we were all part of one another, and I had the secret idea that we shared souls. Also, it seems that by tuning into counterparts and becoming aware of them, we become closer to our multidimensional selves—or at least recognize different aspects of them. It is not an egotistical thing, but an exhilarating realm to delve into.

"I'm aware of many non-class members who are counterparts," Betty says. "I have—or had—a male counterpart I haven't seen in thirteen years; but over the years I've had numerous dreams concerning him and feel it's a way of keeping in touch. Our first meeting (I was nineteen) was a recognition on many levels for both of us—a Gates of Horn feel to it—unreal, yet super-real. From the first time we were together, I started seeing the world in a different light, and I had a curious occurrence along with it . . . I began seeing a small geometric symbol impressed on things—especially in nature, like in the sky, or on trees. I knew it symbolized the two of us together; it was a timeless sort of symbol . . . I encountered the same geometrical symbol on one other occasion, after the birth of my first daughter [who died shortly after birth]. And again, the feeling was that it symbolized our relationship together. On both occasions, [the symbol] was accompanied with a beautiful and exhilarating feeling of having recovered something precious that had been lost. I didn't think seeing this symbol an odd happening—it seemed a normal happening that heightened the experiences . . .

"Seth on one occasion pointed up a connection between Renée Levine and myself," Betty remembers. "I recognized its validity at once, and yet it is something very difficult to verbalize . . . She seemed like someone from my childhood, a more spontaneous and frivolous me.

"I've come to think of the counterpart experience as becoming aware of certain qualities [and bringing] them to fruition, [so] it affirms our own existence and keeps it growing. An analogy that comes to mind is a flower, just coming into bloom   . ."

NOTES FOR CHAPTER EIGHTEEN
    1. For more details of these other-life recollections of Rob's, see Volume 2 of *The "Unknown" Reality*, with exact page references noted in the book's index.
    2. From Session 721, p. 463, *ibid.*
    3. George has experienced other waking "memories" of death. One was a vision of a child trampled by cattle in a Middle-East country—"Absolutely real," George shuddered. Another scene was of a strange aircraft crashing into a mountainside. George said that he first tuned in on this particular vision while riding his bicycle as a young teenager. The details of the aircraft—its unfamiliar shape, its panels of indecipherable dials and controls, and its vivid destruction—were so immediate that he ran his bike into a streetlight. "This was not a memory of 'somebody dying,'" George said. "This was me, and I definitely felt it." In 1974 he asked Seth if this aircraft scene involved a future life. Seth's answer was that George had instead tuned in on a *probable* life, "but that essentially, you will learn that there is no difference." Once again, I connect this vision of George's with my own UFO sighting (described in Chapter 6) and Seth's explanation of this type of perception.
    4. In Appendix 22 for Session 724, pp. 768–76, Rob describes this Roman-on-the-wall perception in detail, and speculates on the various Roman seiges and military manouvers of that time.
    5. Page 556, Volume 2 of *The "Unknown" Reality*. Besides being a contractor, Fred also raises sheep on his farm. One spring day, he brought a new-born lamb to Jane and Rob's house, where the three of them watched it play on the living-room rug. Such is Fred's wonder and joy in his animals.
    6. For Volume 2.
    7. See *Ibid.*, Session 732, p. 556, plus Rob's notes on this session, for more details on class counterparts.
    8. In *The Magazine of Fantasy and Science-Fiction.*
    9. See pp. 153–56, plus Rob's notes, in Volume 1 of *The "Unknown" Reality* for more information on double-dreams and their meaning. According to Seth, such dreams can involve certain kinds of messages from the entity, or whole self, to the individual personality. I've had many double dreams (as discussed in Volume I of *Conversations*), and outside of Jane's class I've met several other people who tell me they've also had them. Interestingly, I had a series of double dreams involving Joel Hess during the time he attended class in 1971; Joel was the third recipient of my trilogy in my dream referred to in this chapter. I hope to do a book on dreams someday.
    10. See Chapter 15 of *The Seth Material* for Seth's discourse on Dr. Pietra, one of Rob's probable selves, who was attempting to communicate with other systems of reality—including Rob's.

CHAPTER NINETEEN

If It Isn't Fun, Stop Doing It!
(And Other Revelations)

RULE #1

dig your wings into the
roots of night and
fly madly scattering
buildings & sidewalks

—Barrie Gellis, 1973

*—The universe is a casual place,
not a suit and tie affair.*

—Barrie Gellis, 1974

"When my buddies ask me what you are
like, then I remember your dialogue, and I
say, 'Now, you will not ever, in a million
years, believe me, but there is a Sue, and
there is a Cannister Man, and there is a
Florence, and Steve, and Lauren, and
Fred . . . They are each at the center of
the universe! They are each creative! Now,
[my friends] want me to speak for *you*
sometime, because they find you all so
unbelievable. But they want the lights out,
so that the vibrations are good!"

*—Seth in Class,
December 17, 1974*

The discussion had somehow turned quite serious. The new spring air of 1974 wafted through Jane's apartment windows, hinting at apple blossoms, but nonetheless, we'd managed to turn ponderous and dour. It was Diane Best's turn to read from the yet-unpublished *Nature of Personal Reality*, and for some reason, all thirty-five of us seemed to feel a great weight falling upon us from the eloquence of Seth's words. The book was dealing at that point with the source of beliefs, and the assumptions that create our private and public world.

"Oh, god," Richie Kendall groaned as Diane paused for a sip of wine. "What really gets to me about this—what really, *really* gets to me—is how simple it all is. Your beliefs form reality, right? No bullshitting around—that's it! But if it's that simple, *what happened*? Why did we forget it all? Why aren't people aware of it? I mean, so much of the world is so *fucked up*! And Seth is saying that *all we have to do* is change our beliefs . . . "

"Yeah, right—*all*," Jane yukked. Her chuckles fell like a shower of rocks.

"Just think about it!" Richie hurried on, caught up in the throes of thinking about it. "Just think about it! *This* is what the whole world comes from *and we forgot it all!*" His voice rang out with real passion, and the rest of us were feeling it too. "How the *hell* could we have *allowed* ourselves to do that!" Richie wailed. "How could we have *allowed* ourselves to create a reality with all the pain and suffering, and wars and starvation, disease, cruelty, the whole bit? It's insane, that's what it is—*it's just insane!* I mean, how could we have *allowed* it to get this way? What justification can there possibly be?"

Silence, for once, reigned supreme. Jane shrugged; what could she say? "I don't know, Richie, who knows? But maybe it's that we wanted to—"

"What it means is that we all have a great responsibility now," Allan Demming suddenly pronounced. "It means that we have the responsibility of disseminating Seth's ideas to the world at large, so that people can understand the truth."

Jane screwed up her face in protest. "No, I don't know, Allan, I just figure we do the books, and if people want to read them and use the ideas, fine," she said. "I certainly don't feel 'responsible' about it in the way you mean—and I'm not about to start a crusade that I've got the truth and nobody else has."

"But you *do!!*" Allan wailed, ignoring the expression of dismay on Jane's face. "You say that we create our own reality, and I

think it's up to the people here to get others to read the Seth material—it's our responsibility to the world, before it's too late and we
destroy . . . "

Swiftly, Jane was yanking her glasses off, Seth's voice ringing out loudly in his familiar, "*Now*!!"

"Uh, oh," Richie grinned, "here it comes!" He leaned forward in anticipation of a Sethian scorch. What actually followed has
been labeled by those members who heard it as one of the most be-
lief-shattering "milestone" Seth session in the ten years of class.

"Listen to me!" Seth roared at us, "I thrust no responsibility upon you to carry my message to the world! I have, in those
terms, a responsibility that I give you—if you must start thinking in
terms of responsibility—the responsibility of being yourselves to the
best of your capacity; and if you fulfill that responsibility, the things
within your lives will be right, and your actions and your feelings in
the world will speak for themselves. For in being yourself, you bring
forth the message of freedom and creativity!

"The world will go its way. It may not be your way. It may
not be my way. But, it may! The world will take these ideas as it will.
I give them playfully, joyfully, and humbly, that they may fall as the
seeds fall from a gigantic oak tree. I do not say that every man must
pick up one of those seeds for himself and use it. I say merely, 'I am.'
And, to you, I say, 'You are.'

"*And whenever these classes are not fun, do not come to
them! And whenever you are doing something yourselves that is not
fun—stop it!!* "

"*STOP IT???*" Richie screamed, shutting Seth off in mid-
breath, "*Stop it???* You mean, just like that—just *stop* it? Anything—*anything* that's not fun?? Just like that??? Just—*stop it???*"

Seth nodded, smiling broadly at Richie. "Creativity and
the joy of the gods does not involve responsibility—in your terms,
now," Seth said. "Being knows its own actions, and when you are
yourself, you fulfill any responsibility that any god or man could lay
upon you from the outside.

"Now, back to the book, or your questions," Seth said,
and blithely withdrew.

"Anything that's not fun—*just quit doing it??*" Richie was
screaming as Jane emerged from trance. Everybody was talking and
yelling at once. "*Anything??* But the only thing that's fun for me is
playing paddleball!" Richie shouted. "So does that mean I should
just drop everything else, don't bother getting a job, and just play
paddleball for the rest of my life? That's *it?*"

"Hold it!!" Jane finally yelled above everyone. *"Hold! It! What was this?"*

"I don't believe it!" Richie yowled in exaggerated disbelief. *"Seth just said that we should stop doing anything that isn't fun!"*

"Well, I'll go that," Jane said lightly, reaching for her wine glass.

"Yeah, but—" Richie looked around at his friends and forced a loud, nervous laugh. "But—*anything??* What if nobody wanted to work any more? What if you just wanted to screw all the time? What if you decided it wasn't fun being a parent anymore and you threw your kid out the door? What if . . . "

"Yeah, or what if you had to take care of your old mother or something, and *that* wasn't fun anymore?" chimed in Rudy. "What if you thought it was fun to be a flasher in Central Park? What if *life* wasn't fun anymore and you decided to kill yourself?"

Richie Kendall

In a way, it was really funny—the group of people among us with the least number of responsibilities, conventionally speaking, were protesting this dictum of fun the loudest. Was it because they feared that fun was only a right of the chronologically young, which they couldn't hold onto? Or that the world really was out to get them in its jaws?

Jane lit a cigarette. "I don't know; it just seems to me that if we really were spontaneous enough to follow our impulses, that we'd just naturally do what was necessary—I mean, maybe if people were really spontaneous and understood the inner self, the person who'd thought all along that being a parent wasn't fun wouldn't have had kids in the first place. Or maybe when you got to it, some things you thought were so much fun wouldn't be. Maybe screwing would turn out to be a lot of work." Jane rolled her eyes and laughed. "Maybe, Richie, after you played 800 games of paddleball you wouldn't *want* to anymore; you'd find that you'd worked through all this pent-up desire from being too afraid of the impulse to let yourself go and *play* paddleball for three hours, or whatever."

"Well—" Richie began, doubtfully. But with that, Seth appeared again, with the advice that each of us explore our beliefs about fun versus responsibility by writing down our definitions of these terms during the coming week (see Chapters 5 and 9 in Vol. I).

"In some instances, you will find that you feel one way, it seems, and believe another," Seth said. "In those instances, privately follow your feelings, for they will lead you to your beliefs. I want you to deal with these questions on an intimate precept. You may find that they spill over into your ideas of good and bad [and] poverty—spiritual and non-spiritual—and, of course, bring those tender papers to class! It is your playful responsibility!"

During the readings of these papers in the next class, Ira Willis began things by stressing "the need for responsible action in a world capable of blowing itself up." Within seconds, Seth sprang to life with more remarks on fun and responsibility.

"My heartiest greetings to you all, and I knew I could count on you [*Ira*] to do it!" Seth began humorously. "[But] he is not alone in posing these beliefs. Now, I tell you that in basic terms, civilization is dependent upon the spontaneity and fulfillment of the individual. Your civilization is in sad straits—not because you have allowed spontaneity or fulfillment to individuals, but because you have denied it, and because your institutions are based upon that premise.

"You think that, left alone, the natural inclinations of man would destroy civilization. Then what, indeed, started civilization, if not the natural inclinations of man? What began the cooperation that allows people to unite even in tribes, if not the natural inclinations of man?

"If you learn to trust your being, then you will be able to trust your institutions and your civilizations. You equate spontaneity with irresponsibility; abandon with evil. If you abandon yourselves to yourselves, then what good would seem to spring out of the heavens of your being!

"Your world is not in dire straits because you trust yourselves, but precisely because you do not. Your social institutions are set up to fence in the individual, rather than to allow the natural development of the individual!

"I come here because it is fun. I have fun when I come here. I do not come here because I feel that I have any great responsibility for your beings or welfare. Who am I to set myself against the innate wisdom of your own individual being, or to take upon my invisible shoulders the great privilege or joyful responsibility for your behavior and destiny?"

A strange question, perhaps, if you were looking to Seth for definition of your being. But a very good point from someone who emphasized above all the authority of the individual self. And Seth's assertion that we should quit doing anything that isn't fun stopped class in its philosophical tracks for weeks—not surprisingly, of course. If everybody *really* stopped doing anything that wasn't fun, who would ever go to school again? Who would mine the coal, plow the fields, manufacture steel, wash the windows on the Empire State Building? Or would people who found these occupations fulfilling just naturally gravitate toward them?

According to Seth, that's exactly what would happen. And society can't be much more chaotic than it is right now. But Seth presented the fruitfulness of fun in an unforgettable way— since it's one thing to say, "Be spontaneous," and quite another to state flatly that "If it isn't fun—stop doing it!"

"Milestone" classes such as this one were sometimes placed in that category by members as a whole—and sometimes because one personal, pointed remark had profoundly affected an individual. Sometimes these sprang from Seth or Jane—and sometimes from the gestalt resources of the class itself.

Often, the sheer amount of material presented in the seven-to-eleven o'clock span was incredible, and of milestone nature in itself. Not only would members bring their week's doings to class and thoroughly dissect them, but there were many weeks when Seth's comments alone filled five to ten pages of single-spaced typed transcript. One class in 1974, for example, produced five pages of

Seth's comments on a wide range of subjects, leaping from a lengthy discussion of the "naked" class (of Volume I) to the nature of the animals' integrity to a comparison of honesty and true responsibility to information on why a friend of George's had died* to the introduction and explanation of True Dreams from the Gates of Horn.

Sometimes it felt as though the four hours had stretched somehow; yawned inside the spacious present and *enlarged* the moments. Many Tuesday nights, I would step out onto the dark and leafy streets of Elmira to go home, and feel as though I were "coming to"—as though my consciousness were snapping back from a lovely, warm, elastic state in which events had taken on a new fullness inside themselves. Perhaps everyone in class went into a trance right along with Jane—or at least re-focused their senses. Otherwise, it seemed impossible to understand how all that material could be delivered, discussed, argued about, clarified, and experimented with—and breaks taken in between.

It's a point that Rob has brought up in regards to the amount of information delivered by Seth during their private sessions. It could also help explain why it took such an effort of concentration to tell Jane what Seth had just said, no matter how unforgettable his comments—an effort very much like that required to bring a half-forgotten dream back into your conscious mind. Poor Jane would come out of trance, look around the room at twenty-five or thirty shining examples of intelligent *Homo sapiens*, ask, "What was this about?" and get nothing but mumbles, giggles, and blanks!

"The class is quickening," Seth said at the close of one Tuesday. "The time of quickening is here for many of you. So take advantage of it. . . . It is very important that you read the underside of class . . . and not skim along what you think of as the surface." I think that at least where these milestone classes were concerned, members were caught up in that "quickening" and on a very personal level were able to dip below the so-called surface of events—as the reader can do, too.

In July of 1975, class members met at Jane and Rob's new house for the first time since February of that year. Discussion, as usual, was vigorous and far-ranging; Sumari came through at one point and answered, in song form, George's momentary irritation over whether we were meeting as class or as "group therapy." The song was lovely, seeming to evoke a constant turnover of information among levels of the self.

*See Appendix 8.

"You know, watching Sumari again brings up a point that I wonder about a lot," Richie Kendall said as Jane came out of trance. "It's that I've been going out with this woman who's never read the Seth books, and she doesn't want to talk about it, and when I try to, she doesn't know what the hell I'm talking about; and so it makes me wonder, I mean, does having come to this class mean that in order to maintain any kind of meaningful relationship, I'll have to find somebody who's into Seth's ideas?" Richie paused for breath. "I mean, what do I have to do, send out a multiple-choice test before I—"

From his sitting position on the floor, Richie looked up at Jane and gulped. Seth was looking back, Jane's glasses in his hand.

"Now," Seth said, with emphatic softness, "there are people who are quite involved with my ideas who do not know my name! There are people, believe it or not, on the face of the Earth, who are very content with their lot, and they do not know my name! They know themselves. They are aware of the vitality of their being, and they do not need *me* to tell them that they are important. The flowers and the cats and the frogs and the trees do not need me to tell them that they are important, and there are people who do not need me either, for that reason.

"For they recognize the vitality of their own being, and they have ignored the belief systems of their times. They are ancient children. They may not read philosophy. They listen to the wind. They watch the behavior of the seasons, and they listen to their hearts. They do not need to read my books! They could have *written* my books, if they could write.

"They are the voices of nature and of the seasons, and they recognize their origin though they are not educated in your terms. And their heart speaks information that their intellect cannot possibly interpret, and in your terms would they seem indeed ignorant. They tend a tiny garden. They speak words that would make no sense to you, Rich, for they would not be intellectual. They would babble nonsense that in intellectual terms would make no sense!

"Yet would you recognize such a person, and the love within their being! They do not have to recognize Seth's ideas, but to recognize and enjoy the validity of their being. I speak to those who do *not* recognize the validity of their being. Those who recognize it have no need of me!"

"Well, yeah, I guess so," Richie said, "but don't you speak for more reasons than just for people who don't recognize the validity of their beings? I guess I find it hard to believe that we *all* don't—"

"There are those, my dear friend, who do not need me, for they are content," Seth interrupted. "They are content because they realize in the depths of their heart the joy of their own being. There are those who recognize the authority of their own psyche as it speaks to them in their private experience, and they do not necessarily even know the term 'psychic experience.'

"They, in your terms, may be ignorant. They may prattle — or sound confused. They are as wise and as crafty as a flower. They do not need intellectual concepts because they understand the nature of love and the nature of the soul. If *you* were satisfied with the nature of your existence, you would not be here! There are those who are satisfied, and they do not need my voice. They find sufficient reinforcement from the dawn and the twilight. They find sufficient reinforcement in their parents and in their children. They find sufficient reinforcement from their dreams and from their waking experience, and they may seem simple to you.

"They may build ditches, or throw sawdust hour after hour, as you did [*in reference to a job attempt that Richie had described*]. And yet they trust the simple authority of the twilight and the dawn. Speak to them of Seth, and the word is meaningless. They do not need me. They do not need *my* voice, because they heed the voices of the oak trees and of the birds, and of their own being; and, let me tell you, in certain terms, I am a poor imitation of the voices of your own psyches to which you do not listen!

"I speak to the world with it, and try to arouse within your beings the great exaltation that you realize is your own. If you had it, you would not be here! You sense it and you want it and I have it — but so do you! But the child does not need to listen to me. He is his own Seth and his own Sumari. And you have your own Seth and your own Sumari within you!

"I will be unneeded as all the ancient gods are unneeded, and gladly so, when you realize that the validity and the reinforcement and the joy is your own, and rises from the fountain of your own being; and when you realize that you do not need me for protection, for there is nothing that you need to protect yourselves against. You are as innocent as the dawn or as the twilight; as innocent as if you were created in this moment. *You are innocent!* There is nothing — no crime you are guilty of, no penance you need do [*to Lauren*], dear Pan!

"Do not insist, therefore, as you [*Richie*] have been, that a woman understand my words — only that she understand the messages that spring from her own soul."

Richie shook his head, "The question in my mind is—will that be enough for me?"

"If a woman understands the messages of her own soul, what is there that you could require?" Seth roared. "Understand the messages from *your* own soul, and then when you have so understood, put the question to me again!

"Now, we are about to close the un-class," Seth said to the rest of us. "But when you are afraid of your own authority, then you will accept almost anything rather than face the authority of your own psyche. A Mickey Mouse will do!

"The power of your own psyche, the authority of your own psyche, has brought you easily into the life that you know. When you were a fetus, you did not question, 'Where am I? Where am I going?' You exalted in the fantastic vitality of your own being.

"I tell you then, now, to listen to the authority of your psyche—of your being! To listen to the voices that you remember when you were children; the voices that spoke to you as you fell off to sleep.

"I ask you to recapture the courage and joy and expansion you felt as children—when each new day was a miracle to be explored, and there were no authorities to tell you how to explore it. Even your parents were but guides that had nothing to do with the reality of *you* in relationship to the day, or a flower, or a raindrop. I ask you only to rediscover your wonder. To look, even at the world that you know, from a different viewpoint, where there are no authorities but the joy and authority of your being; where time is not separated into moments; where you waken each moment as you did when you were a child—each moment a new birth, a new fantastic reality in which you had your place and your part to play; where the miracles were your own, and rose from the fantastic joy of your own being. That is what I ask you to do: recapture those moments that existed before you were educated.

"There were times, in your childhood, when you heard the voices of the Speakers[1]—when, as you fell asleep, the very miracle of your own being came upon you, and you felt it in the very depths and fibers of your being. Then feel it now!

"The most I can do is to acquaint you with the authority of your own psyche—to give you a trust in the nature of your being. For, if you trust what you are, you can never go wrong, in whatever terms you use. You can fly through belief systems as a butterfly flies through backyards.

"Some of you, more clearly than others, understand what I am saying, and so your dreams will multiply with glory, and comprehensions will come to you. You will begin anew the building of your City—the City* you began to build in your dreams as children. All of those childish, unintellectual, joyous dreams that were yours will be materialized in vitality.

"Not only that, but they will be beacons for others to use, if only—if only—if only! you trust the authority of your own psyche. And that psyche dwells in a world and a universe that is safe, in which you cannot be smothered or destroyed or ruined, in which you are always free."

Seth withdrew, leaving many of us considerably more humble.

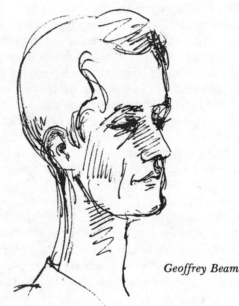

Geoffrey Beam

"One of the most beneficial and revealing classes of all, for me," recalls Geoffery Beam, "was in 1975, when Seth introduced us to the belief at the bottom of all our forts and defenses. [Seth said]: 'And each of you, to some degree or another here, believes that the universe is not safe, and therefore you must set up your defenses against it.'

"What a priceless statement! I have held it in my mind ever since, and have found it a source of great comfort," Geoffery says. "There are times when our worries overpower us, and we lose our equilibrium; but when things calm down, we can then recall this

*See Volume I for "The Birth of the City."

beautiful statement, and be comforted. If we can finally establish in ourselves a firm belief that the universe is safe, then nothing will be able to ruffle us." For Geoffery, whose defenses were rigidly policed, one simple statement began to make a real difference in his daily life. For one thing, he took the simple—though for him vastly difficult—step of calling people in his office by their first names. The familiarity implicit in this gesture had terrified Geoffery all his adult life.

Bobby Agan, another of the New York group (now studying acting on the West Coast), devoted his entire questionnaire response to "the greatest single 'win' I got from the classes. Seth said many things, the exercises we did were great . . . but the one single thing that produced the greatest change for me, in me, was a comment that Jane made.

Bobby Agan

"I'd brought up a point about different viewpoints. I forget the details of what we were discussing, but I said that 'When I have an opinion about something, okay, I feel strongly about it, but shouldn't you consider the other guy's point of view before making a decision?' You see, I was wishy-washy about confidence in my perceptions; wishy-washy in my knowingness. I can't remember exactly what I said, but I know Jane picked up on this two-sides-to-*everything* belief that I had, and then she looked me straight in the eye—and I swear her eyes were glowing—and I felt this surge of energy and she said something like, 'If you always think that way, you don't belong in this class, Bobby.'[2]

"She said this with a lot of affinity, tons of it—it wasn't a put-down. As soon as she said it, something went *click!*—no, more like, *BOOM!!* in me. From that moment on, I haven't been wishy-washy on anything! I mean, *wow*, I got it! The fog cleared, the sun shone.

"That is the one most intense moment . . . and it is a total validation for me on Jane's ability and knowingness. It changed my life," Bobby says.

"To single out one specific thing that Seth said in class," Derek muses, "would have to be something like this: 'The point of power is in the present, and it is a sad thing indeed that you need an old ghost like me telling you something that you already know—the point of power is in the present. Use it. Good night!'

"Seth would say that [kind of thing] with such energy of feeling and concern [that] I swore I could almost see him standing there shaking his finger at us, while smiling at the same time!" Derek says. "That statement—'the point of power is in the present'—had, and continues to have, an effect on me. I'm continually reminded of the way everything around me and within me seems to be constantly 'happening.' If I just mentally look up for a moment, I capture some inner force that seems to flow out of everything around me. Only my consciousness is biologically tuned into one aspect of a greater reality that everything has.

"However, with that expanded awareness, I can feel that greater reality that a blade of grass, a rock, or a bird has; not to mention my cells-self that is the one helping to make the event happen. So, in forming this moment and by turning the focus of our minds, we can see any aspect of 'reality' we want to.

"This knowledge has helped me to see the event of life in a kinder light, realizing the daring adventure we are all constantly participating in!" Derek concludes.

Matt Adams recalls the personal significance of a 1969 class that he didn't even attend—physically. "I was living in New York at the time, pouring over a mimeographed transcript of Seth sessions Rob and Jane had given to me," he says. "Suddenly, a very clear voice in my head told me to get a pencil and take down what it said. I obeyed.

"Ever since my rather traumatic meeting with Seth in 1968, I'd been mildly paranoid . . . [about psychic matters]. And now, with this Sethian voice inside me, I was even less equinanimous. 'It,' sounding just like Seth, then said, 'I have not been happy with your attempts to contact [a person at my place of business]. This damned voice kept playing Seth, giving me more information [about this person], and finally signed off. I was really bothered, and thought of calling [my girlfriend]. Instead, I called Jane, thoroughly forgetting this was a Tuesday night.

"Jane answered, and when she explained it was class night, I was ready to crawl under my East Side parquet studio apartment floor. But she—bless her heart—asked what the problem was. Rational to the last, I asked, 'Is Seth up there with you?' She said yes—does the Pope advise the rhythm method?—and she asked me what was going on. I explained.

"Whereupon, Seth took over and told me *over the telephone* that the voice was not himself, but a 'more dependable level' of my own consciousness. Naturally, Jane asked me what he'd said; naturally I tried to repeat it; naturally Seth broke in again to correct me. But the point of this whole story is that Jane brushed aside my apologies by saying that it gave class 'a good demonstration.' Jeez, maybe this was her Creative Writing Class, I don't know—but it was interesting to me that the class (whatever it was, and at that point) could have 'used' a demonstration of Seth in action."[3]

Another direct piece of personal advice from Seth was given to Bernice Zale in the first class she ever attended, in 1970. "Seth helped me to make a 180-degree turn in my life," she remembers. "During class . . . he suddenly excused himself from the rest of the people attending that evening and proceeded to address himself to me alone. Without anyone's knowledge [*including Jane's*] of my personal life, Seth talked to me on the subject of my stifled creativity and how I was the cause of that problem. He gave me suggestions . . . on how I might change my reality, open up my creativity, and alleviate my loneliness."

"You are not a guest, in those terms," Seth told Bernice that evening, "in that you are not a stranger.[4] I would like to take a moment here, and if you want to turn your face to the wall, then do it before I begin to speak. . . . You must learn to relate to outside physical reality. You need physical work to do. This will improve your painting, your creative life, and your psychic life. You are turning inward too much without knowing what you are doing, at this time. You need to compensate by direct and aggressive physical action, either in a job that will relate you with others, or in some aspect along those lines that will allow you to untangle the inner self and release your creative abilities.

"You badger your creative abilities too much," Seth told her. "You are at them all the time. You want them to produce. You need to do physical work outside of your home, and you need this now, in a very desperate way. This will take your conscious mind away from your subjective problems and allow your great vitality—for you have that vitality—to rush up from the unconscious and solve whatever problems you have.

"Now you are like a dog with a bone, at your problems, *at* them every moment; and you must get away from them. The sense of accomplishment involved in physical work will do wonders for you. It will take away the sense of unworthiness that you now have . . . this will automatically release your inner abilities. You are running down alleys of despair, and you need this doorway into physical reality. Now, how is that for a starter?"

Well, for starters, Bernice took Seth's advice at his literal word. "I went home, followed his suggestions, started meeting people, got involved in weaving, which somehow led to jewelry-making and a store of my own [*and many prestigious awards for her 'Sumari jewelry' designs, too*]. I ended up realizing that my marriage was detrimental to both my husband and myself, and . . . I moved to Albany, started a new life [*which included a writing job on an area newspaper*] and ended up meeting my present husband. Life is now totally different because of a few suggestions from Seth."

Very often, though, Seth's words of personal advice in class were not as overt as this and were instead couched in allusions understood only by the one it was meant for—displaying some neat psychological and telepathic footwork on Seth/Jane's part. One good example of this happened to me in 1970. I was writing a short story about a young married couple, based on Ned and me. At the same time, Ned and I were having serious marital problems. We didn't go into these in class, however, and I'd never told anyone, including Jane, about this particular short story. And so I was understandably surprised one Tuesday night when Seth turned to me and said, unrelated to his other remarks, "You are writing a story with a male in it. The character is too one-sided."

Not only did Seth reveal his knowledge of my writing project, but he'd given me a tip-of-the-iceberg piece of marriage counseling: for the male character in my story did indeed personify my angry projections on Ned's every mood. "The character"—my "creation"—was most assuredly too one-sided!

Large and small, class revelations wove through those Tuesdays in multitudinous form, neatly tailored to the needs and propensities of the individuals there. "[When] I came to class . . . I felt above it all, out of place, vaguely threatened," George Rhoads says of his first class in 1971. "I remained passive, observing, hardly letting the experience touch me. Jane wrote a poem inspired by my behavior that first session, and later I often read it over:

a man i don't know

he has a kind face
that looks sidewards, inwards.
he is passive,
sitting on his own spot
like a frog on a lily pad,
watching but slowly.
time eddies about him.
he never stirs it,
but listens.

people fall through him
into nothing
if they don't yell loudly.
he hates twitches and noises.
nothing matters.
he is so open to nothing that he gobbles
whole barrels-full of life
out of any body
and swallows it whole,
unblinking.

he stepped through himself
long ago
into nothing
and he's forgotten how he got
out of somewhere,
so now he's a cutout in flesh.
inside there's a hole
through which the universe could fall
if it didn't yell loudly.

"It was not until a year later that I came to class regularly," George says. "By then I had lost some of my other-worldly attitude . . . [and] a feeling of belonging grew. I began to feel more free about expressing emotions. I gave an impassioned speech in class about the evils of smoking, directed to the entire class, but really aimed at Jane, for whom I felt afraid. Seth assured me afterward that Jane's smoking would not hurt her. Later I took up smoking myself and was less disgusted by the truly thick atmosphere in class. I also relaxed my rigid attitude about nutrition . . . which I saw as my personal form of health insurance. I began to concern myself with my place in the world of 'reality.' Seth told me, on October 31, 1972:

"' . . . As you know, your person, *now*, is important. And one of the many un-messages I have for you is precisely that your identity is not swallowed up by a super-god or a super-self. The identity of one leaf *exists*. The word 'exists,' if properly understood, means there is no beginning and no end . . . and, if you fall through a hole into non-existence, you would create another existence at the other side, and greet yourself and slap yourself on the back— as indeed you have!'"

"When I remember class," Faith Briggs recalls, "several events stick out in my mind. The first was the evening I heard Seth 'come through' for the first time. It was electrifying. It was that, to some degree, each time I heard him. I felt very fortunate to be able to hear his words. Even if that were the 'only thing' that happened, it would have been more than enough, and that is a vast understatement.

"Nothing 'happened' at first in class or with class members that had a profound effect on me personally. It was what I was *reading*, at home (*The Seth Material*) and *hearing*, from Seth himself, that was so mind-bending. His remarks were so hopeful, so logical, so cheerful, and so challenging. Wow! Create your own reality?? Was it possible? Now I take this phrase as a matter of course, having subsequently encountered the idea in a few good books and in particular at the nontraditional church I attend. But in 1971, it was a completely new concept to me! As I said, provocative ideas were being pondered, and I had much to explore regarding past beliefs, ways of judging, looking at death, etc.

"The next event of special consequence was the night of October 12, 1971," Faith says. "I took my turn in the group and was relating my fifth dream of the week past [*involving a winter home in Europe*]. I had just gotten started when Jane said she was 'picking up' something on me, and started to talk very fast. At the same time, you [*meaning me*] said you were picking up things, too. The resulting reincarnational material was fascinating . . .

"Also, I remember Bette [Zahorian] . . . We met my first night there and became good friends. Man! She was the most out-spoken woman I have ever known! It took a while to get used to her casual swearing . . . [but] I'll always remember one Christmas Eve when my husband was working, our daughters were out, and I was alone. Bette, with a son and daughter, arrived unannounced at our lonely farmhouse. She brought a gift of carefully prepared fruit. But most of all, she brought herself and her friendship. Thank you, Bette."*

"Class constantly blew my mind away," Richie Kendall recalls, "with literally hundreds of little revelations, major and minor, going on all the time in what people said, or in their ex-periences they talked about, or in things Jane or Seth said, or—espe-cially, when I thought about it—in the things *I* did and said, once I got it through my head that it was *me* (and each one of us) that was the revelation . . .

"I had an experience involving 'invisible' Sumari songs that were all around us [in class] all the time," Richie says. "I felt like there were these holes in the air around us, several feet in di-ameter, and through these holes Sumari songs were constantly being sung. I got most of this poem right then and there; it was literally *given* to me through one of those 'holes' . . . I revised it a little and added a bit later on, but the experience automatically gave me parts of it . . . It's called, 'The Inbetweens of Time'·

In between the words we speak
where other meanings dance and leap
between the objects of our sights
others live, in other lights;

In the artist's aging hands
easels wait in other lands,
in composers' wrinkling skin
strange new sonatas twist and spin;

In the spaces of our fears
other faces dry our tears,
blue skies live within the rain
snowflakes carry yellow grain;

I search the Inbetweens of time,
looking for other kinds of rhyme;
I search the Inbetweens of time,
looking for, looking for . . .

* See Appendix 4, Volume 1, for a Seth session to Faith on her hearing difficulties.

"[In writing this song,] I felt like I was translating it from the Sumari but I was the only one 'hearing'—or more like 'feeling' this song," Richie says.

"Another thing, like the secrets session where I bared all [*described in Volume I*], was a little dream I had during class years," Richie says. "It was a very brief dream, but extremely powerful. I was in a room [*in the dream*] with only me and Jane. She was sitting in a chair directly across from me, and I was staring at her. All of a sudden, her image changed into this Mongolian warrior type. But he wasn't just a type—there he was, real as anything, sitting there with his sword and moustache, stocky body, and a face so strong and fierce it would scare even a tiger . . .

"I looked at him, transfixed, and said to Jane, 'One of your incarnations is showing.'

"The image very smoothly turned back to Jane and with a mixture of tender regard and a little sarcasm, she said, 'No, Rich—*it's one of yours!*'

"Needless to say, I awoke right then and there with my heart pounding and my instincts telling me the truth of her statement. [This showed me] how dreams can so easily give us reincarnational information, much more strongly and assuredly, than going to any psychic or reader!" Richie says.

But for Richie, the most revelatory experience of his class life sprang from an unexpected bit of "reincarnational" information Seth gave him one March Tuesday in 1972.

"I have been keeping my eye on you [*Rudy*] and you [*Richie*] and you [*Jed*], since you came to class," Seth said that night. Then, turning to stare directly at Richie, Seth added: "Now, the small but brilliant sardonic part of you was—and in other terms, still is—a very brilliant courtesan in sixteenth-century France, who sat with the philosophers and thought they did not know what they were talking about. Since you [*Richie*] were a woman with an excellent mind, you listened to these men who seemed to think they knew what they were talking about, and you thought, 'They have not the slightest idea in their heads, and yet they look at me and think I am beautiful and silly, when I can think rings around them!' And so you did, and in other terms, so you still do. This woman had much energy—and still possesses it!"

"I listened to all of this at the time, but it didn't affect me much—I let it sort of go by," Richie says. "It was interesting, but it just didn't mean a whole lot, other than the obviously ironic stuff about how this courtesan held her own in a court full of men . . .

"Not too long after Seth gave me this information, that June, I was having a real pits week," Richie says. "I had been feeling very depressed and worthless; I was scared about many things. On impulse, I went to the 42nd Street library to read. I got the urge to look in the encyclopedia about the painter Magritte.

"Now, I've never really had much of an interest in art or artists themselves, but I'd seen a few art books on Magritte and just decided to look him up. Anyway, listed below his name, I saw the name of Marguerite de Valois. *It literally jumped off the page at me!* Then I read that she was a beautiful woman in sixteenth-century France who lived at court, was queen for a short time, was known for her beautiful wardrobe of clothes and flagrant defiance of conventional attitudes in many areas.[5]

"The chase was on! I left the library that day a different person. I felt reassured. I felt that no matter what happened, even if I died on the street, *I was more than me.* I was no longer alone in my being.

"I started doing research on Marguerite," Richie says. "The idea of reincarnation came alive. There were many parallels between us. *She* came alive: I would read about her and my life would have incidents the same day that were parallel . . .

"I went to class the week after this, and as soon as I had a chance, I asked Seth if he had anything to say about a Marguerite de Valois, Richie remembers gleefully. "I remember Seth's expression when I asked. It really seemed that Seth was *surprised* by my question—surprise being a rare reaction for Seth—and this always stuck with me. I could have projected the surprise, but there was a strangely reserved look he gave me. He said, 'Not now, I don't,' and left it at that. Later that class, he came through and corrected me on the pronunciation of the name, and said no more!

"I continued the search, though, and at the library I discovered that there was a very rare book called *The Secret Letters of Court*—by Marguerite de Valois!" Richie says. "I wasn't allowed to take the book out, so I read a lot of it right there, and I nervously went through the pages—I mean, think about it: reading your own autobiography! Marguerite composed songs on the lute—I do on guitar. She was obsessed by her beauty—I've always been over-concerned about my looks. She was 'rich' and lived at court—I always felt strong feelings of wealth as a child and strong feelings toward France then. I've also always felt that I'd be more comfortable as a woman, and felt it hard adjusting as a man; I felt women had more power than men, and was jealous of beautiful women.

"The other aspect of this was Seth's comment about her sardonic side," Richie says. "I began to really think about that and made changes in that aspect of myself that I'm convinced would have taken far longer had it not been for Seth's comment, and my life is much 'en*rich*ed' for having worked out that aspect. Of course, the real 'chase' is within my selves, and as Seth said, this woman *possesses*— not possessed— much energy, so there is far more to be seen from this information to me . . .

"The strongest effect the information has had on me is not specific psychological insights, but the feeling of vastness and some kind of interrelatedness with the universe that's hard to explain," Richie concludes. "It's funny, too, that while I was looking up stuff on Marguerite, I found a picture of Henri de Lorraine, Duke of Guise,[6] who lived in that same time. He looked *exactly*, and I mean exactly, like Rudy Storch . . . and there were many parallels between them, too. Not that you always look like your reincarnational selves or that physical likeness has anything to do with it, but about a year before I got this from Seth, Rudy asked for a reincarnational dream and went back in time in the dream, where he met an aristocratic person, a duke of something, in Old England or Old France, he wasn't sure where . . . "

Marguerite de Valois and Henri de Lorraine, Duc de Guise (courtesy of Richie Kendall)

His fascination undaunted through the years, Richie continued to do research on Marguerite de Valois. In an informal class get-together in 1979, he passed around Xerox pictures of both Marguerite and Henri de Guise. "I keep wondering and wondering, though: *was I this woman?*" Richie repeated several times in Jane's direction during his explanation of Marguerite's life. "I mean, was I actually this person, or *am* I actually this person, who ended up in history books—I mean, think about it: am I reading about *myself*, a part of me that took my basic purposes and characteristics and went with them in another way??"

"Now," Seth answered smoothly, removing Jane's glasses with thumb and forefinger, "you create your own reality." He stared pointedly at Richie.

"Are you going to be crafty and keep me wondering?" Richie said in mock exasperation.

Seth placed Jane's glasses on her round work table, smiled briefly across its expanse of pens and papers at Rob, and turned back to Richie. "If you really understood, you would realize that the statement answers your question, but since you do not, I will elaborate," Seth replied. "You hit upon it yourself—regardless of the sneaky ideas you get now and then that make you believe that time is a series of moments and years and centuries.

"All time is now. When you told your story [*of Marguerite's life and Richie's research*], you wondered whether you had been that woman. And the syntax of that sentence sounds quite correct. It is quite as proper, of course, to say that woman was you. It is much more basically truthful to say that a *correspondence* exists between you and that woman *now*. And that that correspondence creates a *relationship*. And that that relationship then, in your terms, seems to bleed backwards into the past. In whatever terms you think of, there is a correspondence between yourself and the woman, *but you are yourself now,* and not the woman."

"At this point," Richie relates, "I couldn't stand it another minute. I asked Seth if Marguerite was indeed the woman he meant when he gave me the original information—and he said that it was. Then I asked if Rudy and the Duke of Lorraine, Henri de Guise, were the same. 'And the same applies to our spooky Duke over there,' Seth said, meaning Rudy.[7] Then he had another bit to say about mass beliefs that was really outrageous:

"'And again, these events seem strange and nearly unbelievable, only because you have all taken the structure of reality, as you have been taught it was, for granted. Whatever I tell you, you have previously appended onto it the beliefs that you had. Or you might whittle away a little bit at a past belief.

Rudy Storch

" 'What I want you to realize is that you have not only your personal beliefs about your individual families and sexes and problems and countries and so forth, but that you have been drifting on a mass raft of beliefs about the nature of reality in general. About the nature and origin of the world and of yourselves. If *I* believed that I—and my reality—existed because some chemicals and atoms and elements happened to come together, without purpose, and accidentally through the eons managed to form my identity; or if I believed that I was created by some god out in objective heavens who then made me and my kind in a perfect world, but did not have the creative abilities to keep it perfect, and in it I instantly began to decay—then I would have a very poor conception of my self-worth, and I would not think very much about my colleagues, either. *But that is what you have believed!*' "

"There is one statement by Seth that overall has had a profound effect upon my life," says Betty DiAngelo. "It was from

1973: 'There is no question that you can ask to which you do not have the answer.' It is like possessing a security system and has gotten me through many problems, large and small . . . To a certain extent, it hearkened back to my childhood when I had the belief that anything was possible, and when I heard this statement in class, I know that my entire self heaved a huge sigh of relief . . .

" 'You create your own reality' of course opened a whole new universe and has had an inestimable impact," Betty adds, "but it does take much thinking and is a long process at times, getting at those source beliefs that create each moment of our lives.

"Warren's interpretation of [the Sumari song] 'Creation' on the cello was one of those [revelationary] events—a gift to the entire class, that made class almost painfully special at times. Then . . . Seth said, 'Ruburt goes ahead for you as well as for himself.' I think about this often, especially since classes have ended. This didn't register fully until I read *Psychic Politics*. I had to keep leafing through my dream notebooks and journals, as so many of Jane's experiences in the book correlated with my own in this time period. And the concepts she was working on were things that I'd been thinking about at the same time—really blew my mind. In fact, I've decided to make a list of all the correlations next time I read the book.

"Most notably, though, was her healing dream concerning the pyramid of light that turned into the 'silver guide,'"[8] Betty says. "I had the identical dream experience the same day, and I too was ill at the time—though my dream had a different type of conclusion.

"I am thinking that [the question of revelation] is quite difficult because at different times it was one statement more than others that had impact, and in re-reading [class] transcripts, I am having new experiences from statements—sort of a delayed reaction," Betty says. "A July 1973 [class] session says a lot about this sort of thing, and for me it was like Seth was talking to my future self; he said: 'Now, I am making you grapple with yourself, and you are making yourselves grapple. But in certain terms, now, there is a kind of acceleration of consciousness in which you are indeed involved, and that acceleration requires that you work with the contents of your own psyche . . . You are given to terms of higher and lower, so to help you understand—and *only* to help you understand, from the point at which you think you are—we will say that certain questions accelerate within you the functions of a higher intellect and open up channels within yourselves which are indeed inherent in your creaturehood; that bring you *through* your creaturehood into other dimensions that must, however, intersect with it.

" 'These accelerations then change the nature of your creaturehood, and alter the consciousness of your species in physical terms . . . There, you achieve, in those terms, potentials, and open up channels of creativity and activations that you can sense as I speak, and that are a part of your own being, and that can be activated in your space and time . . . what I am saying has an importance that is not verbal; that each of you will intuitively comprehend . . . think—I am borrowing from Ruburt—think of dogs trying to learn math, and more, trying to communicate a complicated problem to their peers. What eerie barking!'

"Well," Betty concludes, "we eventually try to verbalize these things anyway. But that is how I see class—'some things have an importance that is not verbal'—and how I deeply feel about it, and all of us who were involved."

NOTES FOR CHAPTER NINETEEN

1. According to passages in *Seth Speaks* (and within the story of *Oversoul 7*), the Speakers are teachers, both physical and nonphysical, who have helped humankind throughout the centuries, especially in remembering the "inner realizations that would take [Mankind] both within and without the physical world that he knew." Speakers also communicate on other than physical levels, according to Seth, with "much of the most pertinent information . . . memorized by trainees during the dream condition, and passed on in the same manner . . . Some Speakers confine their abilities to the dream state; and, waking, are largely unconscious of their own abilities or experience." (From *Seth Speaks*, pp. 287-90.)

2. Of Bobby's description of her remark, Jane says, "I know there must have been more to what Bobby said to me that night—I just wouldn't have been that emphatic with the little bit leading up to it that he recalled. But the *way* he recalled it is what has meaning for him, and that's what's important."

3. In fact, this was a hilarious one-time "demonstration" of Seth's "telephone manners"—suddenly, Seth was roaring with his usual gusto into the receiver, waving Jane's glasses in the air in time to the rhythm of his words, and pacing back and forth between the living room and kitchen on the very end of the stretched-out phone cord. ("Does Seth speak for Bell?" someone quipped during this *double*-long-distance call.)

4. Seth mentioned several times in class that Bernice had been involved in class dream activity before her first visit there, even though she wasn't a "regular" member. (Bernice was one of the few people I knew, before Jane's class, who habitually recorded her dreams.) Once in March of

1972, Seth mentioned in class that Esther, an occasional visitor from Rochester, New York, was particularly connected in the dream state with Bernice and me—in healing endeavors. On impulse, I asked Esther after this class for some details on where she lived in Rochester and discovered that she knew Louise H., another Rochester native, who'd lived in the same Syracuse University dormitory with Bernice and me. Louise also remembered (and occasionally wrote down) her dreams, and we'd all spent many hours discussing "psychic" experiences.

On top of this, a few nights *before* this class, I'd had an extremely vivid dream about Louise, in which I was "told" to write her a letter at her old Rochester address (which I'd once known but had consciously forgotten)—an address, I discovered in class, that was but doors away from Esther's house! Although we hadn't corresponded since college days, I wrote a letter to Louise the next day, using the address suggested in my dream (which omitted only the zip code)—and was *doubly* surprised when I received an answer from her a week or so later, since in her letter, Louise told me that she'd recently read *The Seth Material* and had seen my name there, much to *her* complete surprise . . . (Her father had forwarded my letter to her residence in Maine.) It's also interesting to note Seth's remark about Bernice's involvement in *healing* dreams in connection with this coincidence between Louise and Esther: Louise had been diabetic since childhood, and throughout our college days, much to our concern, she struggled with numerous physical difficulties related to the disease . . .

For another class-related incident involving Bernice and me, see Appendix 7 in this volume.

5. Marguerite, or Margaret, de Valois, also known as Queen Margot, was born in 1553, the daughter of Henry II of France and his queen, Catherine de Médicis. In 1572, she married Henry of Navarre, who in 1589 became King Henry IV of France. The 1958 edition of *Collier's Encyclopedia* states that Marguerite was "noted for her beauty, wit, learning, and her elegance of wardrobe," and that she was involved in "many amorous liaisons" throughout her childless marriage. In 1587, Marguerite was banished from court as a result of her entanglement in political intrigues, and she lived in Auvergne until 1605. Her marriage to Henry of Navarre had been one of policy, however, and after he became King of France, the union was dissolved by Papal edict in 1599. Marguerite lived the rest of her life in luxury in Paris, where her house became a rendezvous for the learned and fashionable of her time. On good terms with her former husband, Marguerite was unofficially recognized as Queen of the French court until her death in 1615. The best edition of her poems, letters, and memoirs was published in 1842 by F. Guessard.

Interestingly, *Collier's* notes, Marguerite was the mistress of Henri de Guise until her marriage to Henry of Navarre—this marriage taking place five days before the infamous St. Bartholomew's Day massacres, a Huguenot slaughter personally supervised by Henri de Guise.

6. Henri de Guise, Duke of Lorraine, was the third Duke of the

House of Guise, which rose to great prominence in sixteenth-century French politics. Born in 1550, Henri is described by the 1958 *Collier's Encyclopedia* as "popular and personable" in his day, champion as he was of the Catholic interests in France. Early in his life, Henri vowed to avenge the murder of his father, François de Guise, who had been assassinated by a Huguenot fanatic in 1563. Out of this vow came the St. Bartholomew's massacres and the assassination of Huguenot leader Gaspard de Caligny. Henri also took the lead in organizing the Holy League in his country, which was meant to prevent the spread of Protestantism. A wound received during this time earned Henri the nickname of *le Balafre,* or "scarface."

      History sees Henri de Guise as one of the many politically powerful aristocrats who attempted to place themselves in position to become king of France upon the death of childless Henry III. For this and other reasons (one can speculate on his relationship with Queen Marguerite as being included here), Henri de Guise was assassinated by order of the King in 1588.

      7. If one assumes that Seth's information to Richie and Rudy is correct—or, perhaps, that it *became* correct with Richie's "corresponding" enthusiasm for the life of Marguerite de Valois—then the speculations, questions, and parallels across time become literally endless. For one thing, to my knowledge, only two other people in the context of class were connected by Seth to historically known figures—one Elmira college girl, as mentioned in the *The Seth Material,* described by Seth as a distant cousin of Joan of Arc; and Bette Zahorian, described by Seth many times in class as having been (or as being) "a cousin of [Cardinal] Richelieu."

      Understandably, Rudy's reaction to the historical data on Henri de Guise was of considerable revulsion. "He was a pretty disgusting dude," Rudy remarked mournfully in that 1979 un-class. Nevertheless, of all the Boys from New York, it was Richie and Rudy who hounded, badgered, worried, and fumed over the most casual innuendo of Seth's comments; who argued the most passionately—and usually with each other—over applications and possible *mis-*applications of Seth's ideas in the world. (Once, in fact, Seth interrupted one of their more heated wrangles in class with the observation that the two of them were perpetuating "a religious war" of ideas.) And then, it was Rudy (in Volume I) whose beliefs about manhood, power, and "*safety*" of personal energy led him to walk through a plate-glass window!

      However, the real vastness of this kind of "historical" revelation lies—for me, at least, as I know it does for Richie and Rudy—less in "factual" parallels of personality or circumstance than in wondering: how much of Richie's "correspondence" with a so-called "past" self sprang full-blown (and with complete validity) into being with the growth of certain characteristics of his own—stimulated, perhaps, by Seth's class comments in 1972? For that matter, how much of *Marguerite's*—and Richie's—own history sprang anew into being at that point?

And then there are the implications of counterparts, and their "historical" interrelationships. Is there more than one person who "was" Marguerite or Henri? Like your counterparts, then, are your "reincarnational" selves constantly rising and falling into being in answer to the needs and beliefs of your personality at any particular stage of your life? In other words, was Richie, for example, a twentieth-century version of Marguerite from the moment of his birth as he understands it—or was Marguerite (and in some fashion, Richie) "born" within the moment of his awareness of her existence?

8. See Chapter 9, "The Ape and the Silver Guide," in *Psychic Politics*. Apes appear in numerous class members' dreams too; I recall a vivid one in which a gorilla was squeezing me, vice-like, between its legs, until I nearly suffocated. Suddenly, a friend appeared in the room and said, "That's just your limiting beliefs you're seeing!" Immediately, the gorilla and I were sitting in a restaurant together, eating lunch and talking like old friends . . .

Similarly, Richie recorded this dream during class years: "Good and evil was a topic Seth often explored, trying to get us out of that framework, and trying to get us to realize our beliefs about these concepts and how they affected our everyday lives and actions," Richie says. "This particular dream played out my beliefs along these lines simply and dramatically.

"I was in some kind of arena, like where gladiators fought, but there was no crowd or stands, and the whole arena was dark and foreboding. I was alone.

"All of a sudden, this huge and very strong caveman type (like a gorilla) came at me with a club, and the struggle was on. I was fighting for my life in more ways than one, and the battle seemed literally endless, with my opponent far from weakening. Then all at once I heard this voice in my head and it seemed at the same time I spoke these words—feeling their full emotional impact. The words were: I AM NOT EVIL—and I repeated them out loud in the dream over and over.

"Then what happened was fantastic. My opponent just put down his club, stepped aside, and these big black iron gates that had enclosed us just opened up, and I calmly walked outside. As I did, the sun rose as brilliant and beautiful as you could ever imagine, and I just took off—and flew—and the feeling of freedom and power and grace was wonderful."

CHAPTER TWENTY

The Girl on the Old Purple Mountain —
(Does All This Stuff Really *Work*??)

JOYFUL RAIN

Together we dream and spin life's song
Been singin' the blues for far too long;
So afraid to touch, afraid to smile
As if being human was out of style;

> I'd rather sing of joyful rain
> That peaceful falls on purple plain
> But I've been singin' blues so long
> Help me find a happy song.

Some people say you must pay your dues
Before you win you must learn to lose.
Was life really meant a vale of tears
Where laughter dies in empty fears?

> I'd rather sing of joyful rain
> That peaceful falls on purple plain
> But I've been singin' blues so long
> Help me find a happy song.

The sun shines proudly every day
Beneath its wings the eagles play,
Be you a beggar or a king
Let the life inside you ring;

> This earth was not conceived in pain
> Joyful falls the morning rain
> But I've been singin' blues so long
> Help me find a happy song.

— Song by Richie Kendall, 1979

"For once, in your terms, in the history of your planet, in your
terms again, you must learn to trust the integrity of your own
individual being, and stake your life upon your own integrity and
creativity. *For only then, in those terms, can you save your lives
and your planet.*"

*— Seth in Class,
June 18, 1974*

Okay—we heard it a thousand times: You Create Your Own Reality. Beliefs make the private and public world that we know. Change your beliefs, and you change your reality, on all levels.

Yeah, but . . .

Admittedly, most anybody running into the idea that his circumstances are entirely of his own making has a collection of objections—and understandably so, since "You create your own reality" flies in the face of nearly every "rational" and "logical" law of cause and effect accepted by civilization. If your situation is really dire, it might seem insultingly glib to suggest that *you* are its source. (On the other hand, if your life is fulfilling and happy, the thought that *you* created that condition seems much more palatable.)

My particular "Yeah, but . . . " ran something like this: "Yeah, but . . . what difference do the ideas of twenty-five people in Elmira, New York, make to the starving millions of the world? How could you look them in the eye and say that 'all' they have to do is change their beliefs to change their condition? What kind of megalomania is that?"

Or: "Yeah, but . . . the history of mankind is soaked in wars, cruelty, and stupidity. How is a species with a background like that supposed to trust spontaneous action? Aren't we wrecking the planet right now in the name of spontaneous consumerism?"

Well, Seth is not, of course, advocating that people stop trying to solve problems in external, practical ways—as mired in international bureaucracy as that route can get. And he's certainly not saying that we should just ignore, say, the obvious benefits of medical science, even while maintaining that the *necessity* for these is a result of beliefs on a mass scale, and of a certain kind of direction taken by consciousness—a direction that's gone as far as it can go. The point of "you create your own reality" is most assuredly *not* a sop thrown to people in trouble, in a sneaky variation of the old idea that the poor obviously deserved to be that way because God doesn't like them (or that the poor were the "spiritual" ones that God *did* like).

What Seth *is* saying—and it's tricky indeed—is simply(*!*): Our beliefs create whatever we've got, period. The framework of our birth represents the framework of our intent in physical life, period. And the complicated exterior manipulations of history and circumstance—all the methods ever used to sustain, change, or modify our physical situations—are the output of individual and mass beliefs, and affect that exterior framework only. And if we don't like things, we have to change the inner precepts, or nothing else will change. We have to evolve a new consciousness.

In other words, for instance, the typical anti-pacifist arguments of "Yeah, but . . . you had to fight to save the world from Hitler," forgets the private and mass beliefs that enabled Hitler to come to power in the first place. Hitler (or whatever figure or group of people you can name) precipitated war upon a world in which the beliefs of humankind had *already* justified war as a means to an end. The stage was set — again.

"I have told you time and time again in class, and I tell you all again . . . and Ruburt has told you: *You form your own reality*," Seth said in a fall class in 1969. "You form the world that you know — and you form your own images. And there is no justification for violence. Now the words sound simple. *None of you has fully accepted them except as they apply to others.*

"You must apply them to yourself. You must look within yourself and apply these truths, and learn from them. They are not theoretical ideas. They are realities.

"You operate in accordance with these truths whether you realize it or not. It is not enough to listen [to me] — you must look within yourself. It is not enough to play games. It is not enough to squint at yourself . . . to look at one motivation . . . to accept partiality.

"Do you want to know what freedom is? Then I will tell you. Freedom is the inner realization that you are an individual — that you *do* create your reality; that you *do* have the freedom — and the joy, and the responsibility — of forming the physical reality in which you live. *Then* you can change the reality. *Then* you are free to move . . .

"You are not free when you say, 'The idea works for everyone but me — *my* symptoms are caused by something else — and when *I* am violent, different rules apply. Everyone else forms their physical reality, but not *me* — *my* reality is caused by heredity or environment. Every other nation, every other people form their own violence and [are] responsible for their own miserable condition, but *my* people — *they* are right! Any problems that they have had are caused by other agencies beyond them!'

"Then, you are not facing yourselves individually or as a people. You are meant to look at your physical condition, to compare it against what you want, and what is good — and change the inner self accordingly. Any evils in the world are symptoms of your own inner disorders and are meant to lead you to cure them.

"There is a beauty and a strength and a joy in looking within yourselves—and a freedom from bondage. And I hope that when I am finished with you all, you will taste some of that joy and freedom! You will not get it from a book. You will not get it like your chocolates [*indicating some candy on the table*], wrapped up in a merry box. You will not get it by making exceptions. You will not get it by saying, 'I am the exception to the rule!' You will not get it by running away from yourself. You will find this freedom by learning to look inward, and by realizing that you create the reality that you know.

"There are no exceptions to this rule. Your successes and your failures alike, you have yourselves created. If you would but understand, *this is the truth that would make you free.*"

But class still questioned and debated and challenged—with its usual irreverent vigor. If you changed your beliefs, could you regenerate a missing arm? "When you decide to enter into physical experience, in your mind and in your consciousness you form the frame within which you will operate," Seth replied to that one. "When anyone comes to this class, however, with three arms instead of two, who had only two yesterday, then I will give you a gold star!" What difference *does* it make for a handful of people to realize, however hazily, that beliefs create experience? "You forget those you communicate with in the dream state," Seth said, indicating a wider kind of communication among the species. If the past is really as plastic as the future, then why do millions of people remember the same events? (If you could interview each of them, you'd find out that they don't "remember" the same events at all.) But why have we as a species allowed ourselves to develop a technology that could destroy us? It is safe to eat chemically-laden food if I really believe it won't hurt me? Why would I *want* to get sick? Why would a *child* want to come down with a horrible disease? Why did all the elm trees die? How come my cat lost all her hair/ran away/chose to be a certain color???

One June Tuesday in 1974, class had been mulling over such philosophical worries for most of the night. The latest conflict between Israel and the Arab states was again ripping the Mid-East apart, while drought and famine were sweeping through large portions of Asia and Africa. Some members talked about how ideal it would be to set up a school based on Seth's ideas and shut out the rest of the nasty old world; others (Jane and me included) objected to this vigorously. By 10:30, the issues of war and peace, wealth and poverty, good and evil, beliefs and reality had all been hashed over again for the nth time, when George Rhoads cut through the babble of conversation with his explanation of how the victims of starvation in India withstood their plight: by intuitively knowing, he said, that life was an illusion.

"That's why the Oriental seems mysterious and stoic to the Western observer," George went on. "They know what's going on—the Western man doesn't."

"Bull—*shit!*" screamed Mary Strand, half-leaping off the sofa in fury. I could see that George's remarks were really going to start a good one this time—but at that moment, Jane pulled off her glasses and there was Seth, carefully placing them on the cluttered coffee table.

Mary Strand

"My dear friend," Seth began, nodding at George, "forgive me for interrupting. But I have been physical many times, and that physical nature, *while* I was physical, made several 'facts' apparent. One such 'fact' is this—and granting the basis of which you [*George*] spoke, and I understand your intent; I am simply using your remarks as a springboard—it is easier to go along with the nature of reality as an illusion when it is a happy one, and the empty belly still hurts, in your terms, more than the full one!

"Those of you who are affluent may think that it is spiritual, even sophisticated, to diet, to deprive yourselves, or to go upon a fast so that you can become spiritually oriented. The starving man can afford no such spiritual luxury—his guts ache until his brain spins!"

Seth looked around at each of us in turn, his eyes wide, dark, and penetrating. "Again, individually and *en masse,* you choose your reality," he continued, his voice now rasping out in a throaty whisper. "So the starving in India represent something—the part of the planet that is in pain; the place where beliefs do not mesh; where the spiritual and the physical are so divorced in practical terms. The gurus may go on fasting retreats, but in the meantime, they eat well! They do not lie in gutters in their own vomit!

"Those of you have enough money to live may adapt the garb of the poor. You may disdain what you think of as wealth, yet by those [starving men's] standards, you are indeed each a king!

"What use have those rituals been? And I use the word 'ritual' because you understand, in your terms, what you mean by it. There is a ritual in starvation; a ceremony. It is the opposite of the ceremony that takes place with chandeliers and shining silver and china plates. It is the opposite of the ceremony offered by the gurus."

Seth bent forward in Jane's rocker, looking quite stern. "There is a ceremony of the seasons; a ritual of the seasons that is blessed and exuberant and knows its own order. The guru can well afford to luxuriate in it!

"Here [in class], comfort blankets are taken away from you. Or, rather, you take them away from yourselves, though now and then you tug for them, and think how lovely one would be, for just a moment!"

Then Seth's voice really rang out:

"You are your own great ceremonies, as the seasons are their own great ceremonies. If ever there was a time when natural ceremonies should be recognized, the ceremony—indeed, the loving ceremony—of the seasons and of spontaneous song and of spontaneous joy, then this is, in your terms, the time!

"It is not the time to set up new rules or regulations or even loving dogmas. In your terms, you have been through that before. Each of you, in your own way, will creatively do your thing, with the material or the Sumari, or your interpretation of it; and that is good. That is what it is for. We give it to you to use as you will. But there will be no new organization, no new church, no new cult. *There will be a brotherhood of men and women who know themselves, and who explore the nature of their own reality, subjectively and objectively!"*

Seth paused in his delivery, and Allan Demming, who had been arguing in favor of a "Seth school," spoke up. "Are you really telling us that reality is *entirely* isolated within the individual?" he said. "If so, then that seems to mean that there's no joyous coming together possible, because—"

"Now, raindrops fall," Seth interrupted. "They are all individual. They do not stop and together think, 'We must all fall together upon Elmira, New York, at four o'clock this afternoon!' Yet, by being themselves, they bring freshness and vitality to the grass and flowers by thus falling.

"You cannot separate yourselves from others or from your world," Seth said to the class in general. "Indeed, neither can you immerse your individuality, as you know, in others. But by being yourself completely, you are automatically doing what you yourself want to do—fulfilling the purpose that is your own, and joining with others of like purpose. And you become, therefore, a force of nature, and in trusting that force that is yourself, you flow naturally into those areas of your own interest and the interests of others.

"You *are* a brotherhood—you do not need to form one! You meet with other [Sumari] in your sleep. You do not need credentials—none of you!

"Now, I understand your need, because of your historical existence, for exterior organization," Seth went on, his voice now soft and affectionate. "But I say to you that the real organizations are inside. And when you thoroughly understand this, there will be no need for exterior ones, for they will naturally appear, as the raindrops naturally appear—and you will change yourselves and the world; as raindrops change the world each time they fall."

Seth ended this exposition while staring directly at Richie Kendall, who was sitting next to Mary on the edge of the blue sofa, obviously waiting anxiously for a chance to ask a question. Now he and Seth grinned at one another, and Richie launched into it with his familiar playful intensity.

"So," Richie said, punctuating each word with exuberant gestures, "practically speaking—if I have a desire for a beautiful house, pretty clothes, a beautiful car, et cetera, et cetera, and I fulfill that desire—then, practically speaking, I am in some way acting to actually alleviate a future situation such as exists in India with starving people. Right?"

Class roared with laughter. Richie worried endlessly about possible material possessions that he didn't have. ("Which was probably why he didn't have any," Jane observed years later.)

"Even I have trouble following that reasoning!" Seth bellowed humorously.

George's "Cosmic Comics," signed with his entity name, poked fun at Seth and Richie Kendall

"Well, by being spontaneous," Richie shouted over the laughter and guffaws, "wherever my spontaneity takes me — Come on, you guys, shut up! — If I'm being spontaneous, then naturally I'm helping the world of which I'm automatically a part of, right?"

"You are indeed!" Seth answered.

"All right, so even though there are people starving in India and money could be sent there to feed them — if my spontaneity leads me toward buying a beautiful house, a beautiful car, a beautiful —"

"If you allow your spontaneity its own freedom, then you can quite happily have whatever you want!" Seth roared back. "But spontaneity will *also* lead you to thoughts of love for others; it will lead you to realize that you cannot plunder your planet; and it will lead you to realize that as long as one person is starving, then you are starving in ways that you are too ignorant to realize!"

Richie's grin hadn't left his face. "Ah-huh!" he responded. "Sure! That clears it *right* up!"

"Now Richie's gonna run out and spend all his money on new clothes!" someone laughed.

"Seth," Warren Atkinson said at this point, the seriousness of his voice cutting through all the noise, "Could you give us a comment on this thing going on in the Middle East—where much of our energy seems to be focused, when a few thousand miles to the east, there is this fantastic drought and all these people are dying?"

"To some extent, and, I admit, opaquely, I am discussing that in our present book,"[1] Seth replied. "But each portion of the world, in your terms, has certain meaning, and the people of course accept their own reality, and form it.

"Each area—the area of which you are speaking, and this area in your country, for example—these areas are important focal points; each working out certain beliefs in exaggerated form. If you think, those beliefs will come to you, and you will see why the conditions exist in each area."

Seth withdrew, and class tried, clumsily, to tell Jane what had been going on. "It just really flips me *out*," Richie said, still perched on the sofa's edge. "If what Seth is saying really works, then does that mean it's really *okay* to go out and just buy and buy, and throw away, and buy some more, and have twelve kids, even if that means cutting down all the trees to build beautiful houses for everybody to live in—" He stopped in mid-sentence: Jane was removing her glasses again."—All totally spontaneously, of course!" Richie added hastily.

"There *is* abundance," Seth said, blinking Jane's darkened eyes at Richie. "There is also the fact that you dwell on a physical planet. With a sense of love and identification, your idea of survival would not include annihilating other species so that you could live. You would understand that all of you share this reality, and that all of you are bound together in a gestalt of creativity . . .

"The animals, knowing their own grace, breed with a joy and spontaneity that know their own order. The cow, giving birth, knows how many caterpillars are within a meadow, or a field, or on a continent; and in your terms—but in your terms only—the other species gracefully acclimate themselves.

"They give and they take with a graciousness that you are only now beginning to recognize. They are not gluttons!

"You have chosen a different kind of consciousness. That kind of consciousness necessitated a different kind of challenge, so that with your new kind of mind, you would come to different crossroads. You would forget what the animals knew. But with a different kind of consciousness, you would triumphantly then become *aware*, but in a different way, of the animals' blessed knowledge, and use it again in *new* terms as conscious co-creators. You have not as yet reached that level, but you are working toward it.

"That is a partial answer to your questions," Seth said, turning to Richie again. "There is a great conscious revelation that in all probability can come to each of you, and to those of your species, in which you understand the nature of your own grace, and your relationship with All-That-Is within the reality that you know; and then you will realize many things.

"When you do not define your existence as physical only, then you will not feel that you must breed indiscriminately because you have been told that you should breed; or because you feel that your immortality is dependent upon the seed that falls from you into the earth. You will recognize your own *immortality* and therefore be free and joyous with your *mortality*; and you will gracefully take your part as co-creators on a conscious level, with all the conscious and unconscious beings that dwell within your physical reality . . .

" . . . Here [in class], you are returned to the integrity and joy and creativity of yourself, and there is where the hope of the world rests—in *your* being, and not in mine; in *your* reality, and not in mine; and in your beliefs in yourself, and not your beliefs in me. Only as I serve to remind you of your own greater reality do I serve you, and do you learn from me. And only, as through this performance with Ruburt, as you recognize the abilities of your own individualities, do you learn when you come here. You do not have to speak for others, or work fine psychic feats to know yourselves, to follow your consciousness in the waking and dream states, to walk joyfully and triumphantly through the corridors in times and spaces of your own being."

In April 1977, during one of the infrequent post-1975 "un-class" meetings held in Jane and Rob's new house, Seth continued this theme in a message of springtime: "You cannot help yourself and you cannot help your species by identifying with your own weakness, or with the weakness of your species," he told us. "When you are safe, you are safe, and you are in a position of strength and you *can* be in a position of tranquility. Then you have the energy and the exuberance to think and feel clearly, and to help others.

"When you are in a position of safety, you do not help by pretending that you are not safe, or by taking upon yourself the agony of others. Your reality, when you are safe, is a reality of security. From that framework you have strength, validity, grace, exuberance—additional energy that you can send out to touch the hearts and the realities of other people.[2]

"If you become so frightened of realities that are not your own; if you take upon yourselves tragedies that do not exist in your reality, in your moment; then you weaken your position and you weaken the position of those you *think* you are helping. You look about you and you see only hopelessness and helplessness. *You organize your reality according to the tragedies of the newspapers!*"

My own journalistic ears perked up. This was a question that I'd often agonized over, even as the co-editor of a small weekly newspaper: what was the effect on the reading populace of reporting tragedy after tragedy, myriad bunglings of local government, disastrous environmental mishaps, and all the other endless mires of bad news? What were my responsibilities as a reporter who was at least aware of the nature of suggestion and beliefs? Should I try to root out injustice, expose it, give people grounds to protest? Or should I somehow "make" all the news optimistic, even when (on the small weekly scale) it wasn't?

"The tragedies of the newspapers are symbols," Seth continued, as if in answer. "Those symbols *represent* 'real' tragedies, but those tragedies do not exist in *your* moment unless you are participating in them. Those who are involved in such tragedies feel a sense of hopelessness and the loss of power in the present — *and you do not help them by taking on the guise of hopelessness!*

"What I am saying this evening is indeed simplified . . . but you must operate from strength, not from weakness. When you stand upon a firm shore, you can extend your arm to the man who is in quicksand. You cannot help him by leaping into the quicksand with him, for surely both of you will go down — and he will not thank you!"

"Then we're doing that as a nation?" Warren asked.

"Individually — as you read your paper, as you watch your television," Seth replied, "whenever you look around you and say, 'Other men are fools'; whenever you look around you and say 'The race is ruining itself — it is insane'; you are doing the same thing — you are jumping into the quicksand, and you cannot help.

"Organize your reality according to your strength; organize your reality according to your playfulness; according to your dreams; according to your joy; according to your hopes — and *then* you can help those who organize their reality according to their fears."

Seth turned to look at Lauren DelMarie, who had just returned from a trip to California. "There are those who prophesize a great holocaust that will destroy the species," Seth said. "There are those most certain, my dear Pan, that California, as the new state of sin and iniquity, will be banished from the face of the earth. There are those who prophesize, and have prophesized since the beginning of time, that tomorrow would never come because you are so sinful—because you are such idiots! There is no difference! You can condemn yourself because you are sinful and the daughters and sons of Satan. Or you can say, 'That is nonsense. We are not sinful nor the daughters nor the sons of Satan. Instead, we are the idiot offcasts of nature. We are going to destroy our planet. We are rotten, not because we are the sons of Satan, but because we are insane atoms and molecules gone astray!' Only the vocabulary is different!

"Do any of you actually believe that your existence is a cosmic accident? Do any of you really believe that the integrity of this moment is an accident? Do you really believe that all nature is sane but you—that nature in its great holy being had good sense except when it created men and women, and only then did it go astray?

"If you organize your reality in that fashion, then you are in the quicksand! If you want to help, *stand on the firm ground of your creativity and being!* You are only fools if you cast off your clothing and jump into the shifting ground. Who needs a hand that is going to sink beneath the mire? Some help *that* is!!

"Therefore, again, I return you to the common sense, the common joy, the common integrity that each of you know to be your own. And if that is Satanic, then what sense there is in Satanism, and some of our good spiritual people could learn from it! However, poor Satan stands also in the middle of the shifting dirt! And it is a pity, for the concept is an important one . . . *and that [concept] is the right to object*—the simple right to say, 'I do not believe whatever it is anyone else is saying!'

"You can refuse to believe out of ignorance, stupidity, pride—it matters not. You have the right to say NO! And, in all Christian terms, Satan said 'No!' He looked at the grandeur of God—as it is understood, now, according to your Bible—and I am speaking in your terms, and not in my own—as the Bible is understood, and as the Bible was interpreted, and not as reality was at all. But in the terms of the story, God said, 'I am just. I control the universe. I am truth. I am reality.'

"And Lucifer stood there, and he said, 'No, you're not!' And God said, 'Out!' And out Lucifer went. And in those terms—and I am quite aware that this can be delightfully misinterpreted—but in those terms, Lucifer was saying, "No one can create my reality for me!'

"Now, Lucifer was not evil, but in the terms of the story, Jehovah was not good! Lucifer did not send floods to destroy whole populations! Lucifer did not turn people into salt. Lucifer said, 'Listen to nature and maybe you will learn something.'

"But those are old legends. They are old, ancient legends, and both God and Lucifer—Jehovah and Lucifer, in those terms—are done poorly. The characterization is weak!

"That is my Easter message! I bid you all a fond good evening . . . "

For many, the basic message of Seth's words might be a little hard to swallow, except as interesting philosophy. Accepting as fact the idea that only by changing one's private reality can anybody really change the world may seem just too far-fetched, or hopelessly narcissistic. Yet how else did the world get to its present collective state, except through the intense concentration on the part of its inhabitants?

This book is full of class members' testimonials demonstrating how Jane, Seth, and class itself made a real difference in their lives, and how the ideas embodied in Seth's words opened up realms of selfhood and personal power. Jane and Rob's mail is also filled with examples of everyday people taking charge of their private lives and getting results—often dramatic results—by examining beliefs, the contents of the conscious mind, and using the exercises suggested in *The Nature of Personal Reality* and in this book. Nonetheless, Jane's class was not a group set up to prepare initiates to go out and proclaim the new Messiah, or to tell people that *their* private realities were wrong if they didn't "believe" in the Seth material. It *was* a group that came together to explore private reality—and its worldly results—in a way that had, quite simply, not been done before, at least in recent times.

"Now, within the psyche that is your own, there is your own personal model," Seth said as he led us through an altered-state-of-consciousness exercise in late 1974.[3] "I want you to sense the models that exist within your own psyche . . . Within the psyche that is your own, there is your own personal model. It is the personal self that you have chosen, and you will follow it through all realities and in all worlds that you will ever know . . . Each of you will have your own images, and your own feelings, and your own symbols. These are highly important, for they are, at least symbolically, your personal paths to what may seem to be to *you* the impersonal nature of the universe.

"If you remember some of the exercises in *Personal Reality*, then you will see how this correlates with *your own true tone.*[4] You can follow that tone. You can get the feeling of your own model, or suggest that it appear to you in the dream state, and then follow it. It is your personal line to all the realities with which you will be involved . . .

"Now, I have told you that you live in many worlds. I invite you to become aware of your own other realities, or at least a tiny corner of some other reality. I invite you, then, to become even more aware, in practical terms, and not to be afraid of your own consciousness, or your own reality . . .

"You form your own model, so you need not fear it! On the other hand, as you are inviolate, so within you have you kept inviolate the knowledge of the model that you yourself have created.

"Ruburt is quite correct [in saying earlier that] some of you are beginning to sense for yourself your own tone, in whatever way you choose to put it. You will become more effective in all worlds, and this world will become more *rich* for your realization."

Turning to me, Seth added: "The ghost of the old Nebene did you a service this evening by showing you the model for your book.[5] And the model for your book, Lauren,[6] is there and you have seen it; and the model for each of your lives is within you for you to see and interpret in whichever way you choose. And do not discard it, but use it joyfully. Do not judge it according to what you have read or heard, lest you find it wanting . . .

"If you really want to increase your experience here, then try to sense within the [other class members] the models that are within them, and feel the eccentricities, and learn to relate with the realities within yourself, and with the realities that exist between yourselves and others . . .

"You must make this information your own. Then, for you, it becomes psychologically valid and real. And, using it, you can indeed alter the nature of your reality. But you must be willing to be kindly to yourself. You must believe that when you send out pleas, they are indeed answered, no matter how impersonal the universe may seem at times.

"You must realize that your personal self grows as naturally out of that universe as, in other terms, any star does, or any flower, or any oak leaf. You are a part of that system. *And when you send out a plea, you do indeed set the universe in motion, so that the plea is answered!* And so do you also send help to others, often even when you are not aware of it, as a flower sends out help to someone simply because it is beautiful . . .

"You can stand up and say, '*I am myself, and I am good, and I refuse to accept the beliefs of others with which I do not agree!*'" Seth continued later on the same theme. "Then, you . . . make your own direction. *You must make that choice!* The choice is always yours.

"Cow before beliefs that you no longer accept, cow before the past — or assert your individuality and being in the present, the full divinity of your being, which includes a conscious mind — and refuse to be cowed by any elements in the so-called past — *and you begin anew!* That is of greatest importance to each of you.

"As long as you believe in the basic evil of man, then you must project upon yourself great punishment. You must see your world destroyed, and so will you have prophets to tell you so, and so will they speak the truth, for they will speak from your own beliefs in the idea of your own evil.

"Now, there is no holocaust unless you believe that you are so evil that you must punish yourselves. But there will always be benign old spirits like me that tell you that though you are bad, you are *perfectly* bad, and utterly beautiful, and nothing will destroy you unless you are convinced that you are so evil that you must be destroyed! *And even then, only those who so believe will partake in that probability, and those of you who refuse to accept that belief will learn instead, as I have said, a loving technology, and will learn to deal with your universe and your earth with technology, but with love.* You will breathe love into your machines, and that love will bring truth.

"The prophets speak truly, that speak of doom. They speak truly when they speak from a framework that believes in doom. But that framework is a mere probability that gains its strength only from a belief in evil. So the prophets feel that belief, and emotionally understand that while that belief is held, it will express itself—and so they are themselves terribly driven by those beliefs; and they paint dire pictures that reside individually in the psyche of each person who feels damned.

"I tell you, you are full of grace. Your planet is full of grace. When you understand that, you will not need to pretend to destroy yourself, or your planet. You can live lovingly with yourself, and with your planet!

"There are directions that your consciousness can take, and I am trying to tell you what those directions are. And if you take those directions, then indeed, in your terms—in your terms—there is a birth of a new kind of species—a species that understands its blessed creaturehood, and a species that understands its biological spirituality; a species that consciously creates a reality of which it can indeed be proud; a species that does not despoil its planet, but considers that planet sacred; a species that consciously and purposefully creates the kind of world that a sane god would create; a species that creates a god that is themselves; a god who has no need for a heaven or a hell!

"Forget your ideas of present and past. Forget the occult nonsense that you have learned, and look at your present with the wondering eyes of a new self."

NOTES FOR CHAPTER TWENTY

1. This is a reference to *The "Unknown" Reality,* but the subject is also explored in Seth's two later books, *The Nature of the Psyche: Its Human Expression,* Chapter 11; and in *The Individual and the Nature of Mass Events,* published in 1981.

2. For more on the "safe" universe and suggestions on how to sense yourself within it, see both volumes of *The "Unknown" Reality,* especially page 310 of Volume 2, Introduction notes.

3. See *Psychic Politics* for more on personal models and eccentricities.

4. This remark reminds me of the individual Sumari "songs" that were given to some class members, as described in Chapter 7 of *Conversations*.

5. That night, Rob had suggested to me that I write a book on my own dreams and psychic experiences; he even gave me some examples for chapters that I could include in such a book. I was immediately fascinated with the suggestion and later wrote some sample chapters, titled *Sideways Lives*, and sent them to my present editor. Although other events diverted my interest and I never completed that particular project, the manuscript was one of the factors that eventually led to this book, and much of the material about my life that I collected for *Sideways Lives* appears in *Conversations*.

6. A reference to a science-fiction novel that Lauren later wrote; at this date it's unpublished. Lauren has also put together a manuscript of interviews with science-fiction writers.

CHAPTER
TWENTY-ONE

Nobody Does It Better:
Class and Un-Class Ever Since

CHILDREN OF ALWAYS

I. The night

We sat,
Minds splashed by the hours
Breaking over the shores of tilting rooftops,
Drifting downward, lost projectiles,
In the worm and flower-laden air.

       hallelujah
       mouthed the stones, waking.
       hallelujah
       mouthed the stones, standing up inside
       their round and whirling cathedrals.

Wading in the winey hours,
hip-deep in night and dawn,
tumbling down the music's stairs like autumn flowers,
mustily the breezes of time's great flight transfixed us.
wine like liquid always spilled upon the floor.

       stand up children of always
       mouthed the stones
       from their trances.

Greek children danced as we dance,
dangling downward over aprils,
staring into the spooky eyes of flowers.
forever sprinkles holy water on their answers,
and february plunges clouds through the wintry tangle of their hair.

Gather up our fruit
mouth the stones.
they fly to the ceiling of the sky,
thrust like cosmic thumbs in the holes
through which always once forever after poured.

       hallelujah shout the worms
       genuflecting inside the apple.
       our infinite thoughts surround you.

Ah you Sethites, scramble up
the hills on the underside of truth

hallelujah says the worm,
timidly holding out his hand
from the rosy apple.
take my hand friend, take my hand, take.
who will befriend the worm
and who dares not?

II. The people

see us here so assembled.
our shadows burn like lighted torches.
nodding, smiling, half unknowing
we dance inside time's giant whale belly.

mr. stephens stand up and be counted please.
      gentle Darren lost in cloudy jelly cubes of air,
      wandering gelatin roads that solidify and melt.
      he flows out, mixing with eternity's ingredients.

mrs. granger stand up and be counted
      sister maggie, secure and elemental
      digests reality without a qualm,
      sees forever in today's face
      and holds her ground
      but resents sharing it with the animals
      who hunt her down.

mr. butts stand up and be
      aloof rob a sometimes wizard
      flies inside his soul
      through skies unending smooth and wrinkled.
      now he smiles at the door of himself
      and guards the partially opened door.

miss mullin stand up
      and sue, squirreled in tangled treetops
      dangles like a sliding summer moon,
      cool, climbing higher
      but looking scared. above
      the constellations prowl like animals.

mr. granger stand up and be counted please
      brother bill, several people grouped

together in one skull,
tonight violently drawn out,
one to watch a firing squad,
one to aim, one to stand blind-folded
but without alarm.

mrs. butts stand up and be counted
unblinking jane, priestess powerful and frightened
wages wars on battlefields impossible to find,
munches tidbits of peace flown in by ghosts
and warns demons off with noise

mr. watkins stand up and be
laughing ned winks at the gods
who wink through the grass.
he steadies the air about him
and stretches out full length upon the floor,
pulling the universe up to his chin like a cover.

stand up children of always
mouth the stones from their trances.
gather up our fruit sing the stones.
hallelujah shouts the worm,
genuflecting within the apple.
now take your names off.
take your names off
in this night of fire
and reach out
for my hand.

hallelujah mouth the stones, waking.
hallelujah mouth the stones
standing up inside their round and whirling cathedrals.

III.

brother bill smiles inside mr. granger.
gentle darren feels his gaze escape his skin.

take
take my

sue climbs in panic higher and finds one moonshaken branch,
ned crumbles greek-like, dreams cracked beneath the star's weight

take
take
take my

maggie with eyes wide open turns her back away
rob cautiously steps out onto his soul's porch
jane stares fascinated into the worm's head.

take take my hand.
who dares befriend the worm
and who dares not?
children of always stand up and be counted.
take my hand timidly says the worm, ascending
to the top of the apple.
twirling above its rosiness, he addresses us,
still smiling.

IV. The worm's song

children of always it is time now.
step blindfolded into my ever-expanding eye,
nameless into my vision.
greek children come home now.
in my eye find your focus.
let your many images spin into one
self you have forgotten.

you have walked before
through the circle of my great dimensions,
swirled in the retina of my devotion
were discombined and reawakened.

hallelujah mouth the stones, waking.
hallelujah mouth the stones, standing up inside
their round and whirling cathedrals.
hallelujah shout the children of always,
waking inside the worm's infinite eye.
they peer over the rim of the world
and smile down upon us in this room.

welcome children of always, sister and brother,
we greet you, those still entranced and those awaking

take my
take my
take my hand says the worm.
who dares befriend the worm and who dares not?
all walk
into my eye hand in hand
dear greek children of always sing. . . .

hallelujah
mouth
the
stones.

—*Jane Roberts, 1968*

"When we moved to our new house, it just didn't fit in somehow," Jane says of her decision to end the class in 1975. "At the old place, we had the two apartments, and there was a way to divide things up, along our ideas of privacy—class had its "own" living room and we had ours across the hall and I could leave my papers out on my desk over there, or go over and shut the door during break . . .

"I'm not sure what part of me it was that I left in that other apartment during class, but whatever it was, our new house just wasn't set up the same way, not for the same kind of regular mob. If we'd taken the big old house on Foster Avenue[1] that we looked at, I would have had class going in two weeks . . . that place had two living rooms and two bathrooms, see . . . I always had the feeling that if I stopped having class once, that would be it; that I had to keep the 'habit' up . . . but I do miss it: the people and the exuberance and the, I don't know, the *immediacy* of it . . . "

But even without the difference in physical set-ups, by the time Jane and Rob had settled into their new house and started thinking about class again, members had scattered far and wide, toward new careers, new turns in their lives—even holding "Seth" classes of their own. Caught up in the preparation of manuscripts like the massive *"Unknown" Reality,* and deluged by ever-increasing amounts of fan mail, Jane and Rob began putting more and more of their own time into their private work. And so, with the exception of occasional small get-togethers with some former class members, Jane's ESP class ended.

But in all likelihood, 'the Experiment' continues; a new *framework* begun.

"Because of class I feel a kinship with more people than I ever hoped to," says Betty DiAngelo. "And lately I'm aware of things going on under the surface that are adding interesting aspects to my experiences. Seth once said that we are always searching for ourselves, which in turn leads us to ask more and more questions of ourselves . . . Class gave me a context for certain experiences and the confidence that I could search for answers and find them within myself.

"I could not but help have Seth/Jane concepts affect the way in which I interact with my children," Betty notes. "I feel that these are my concepts too, for one thing. I have passed on Seth's 'safe universe' concept to my daughter, as I know the world can often be overwhelming for small children. My daughter has never forgotten it and uses the phrase, particularly when she is feeling sad or frightened for no apparent reason . . . it is something I am working on also and feel it can only add to her own independence as time goes on . . . I think I encourage her to look behind the surface of things and I think most children do anyway, but don't voice their impressions from fear of disapproval. I want her to feel her impressions are valid, even if different from others.

"Now and then my daughter and I do relaxation and Alpha state experiments, and she is quite delighted with them. I also encourage her to remember her dreams and talk about them—and not surprisingly, we have similar dreams. In March of 1979, I had been thinking about Sumari a lot, probably because of working on your questionnaire and also I've had many experiences of hearing Sumari singing in the past two years. One morning in March, my daughter came into our bedroom very excited; she said that she was hearing singing and didn't know where it was coming from, and also that it was a whole group of voices. She even remembered one of the refrains. I am certain that it was Sumari, because our experiences and feelings are often along the same lines. I've taught her to see her own aura at night and she has a lot of fun with that and thinks it's great . . .

"I can give her suggestions about her nightmares, which often frighten her, by telling her that maybe they are hidden *ideas* she has, and so she dreams about them. I found that she does something quite interesting, and I have a feeling that most children probably do this: she plays out her dreams, particularly her nightmares, and it's interesting that in most 'primitive' cultures people are reported to do this—as a case in point, most American Indian tribes did this; they felt that it was vital to a person's emotional and physical health to act out his or her dreams . . .

"I hope I've 'graduated from kindergarten,' as Seth puts it; there were times at class that I felt like the class dunce, and doing this questionnaire has been like a final exam," Betty concludes. "I no longer go around espousing Seth or punctuating conversations with 'Seth says' this-or-that. And maybe we all feel now that it is time to try our own wings and that we are capable of determining reality for ourselves . . . I could go on and on I suppose in detailing how much my life has changed since working with beliefs. I myself wasn't aware of the complete impact until now. It's very freeing—it's not like a religion where one's given an outline on how to live one's life, but quite the opposite, in that we discovered, through class, tools that were always there for the taking, and the best part is that it's an ongoing thing. I don't feel there is a dead end to this or a stop sign in sight."

As for developing a different kind of reference framework with your children, it's my feeling—as Betty expressed—that understanding the inner orders of logic from an early age can literally begin to birth a new kind of awareness in the world. Parents who responded to my questionnaire all stated that they encouraged their children to remember and interpret dreams and gave respect to their children's subjective lives. Not only is this aspect of parent-child relationship vital—it's wonderful, fascinating fun.

Recently, I had a strange and largely untranslatable dream involving geometrical patterns. In it, Sean and I were progressing up through a series of vertical rooms that towered above a flat, lined plain. Each group of rooms fit like boxes inside one another, from small to large, and as we traveled upwards, the whole group would start moving in the direction of our climb. Then the rooms would change into another series for us to navigate in another direction—sideways, or on a diagonal. I'd never dreamed anything like this before—and throughout, Sean seemed to know exactly what we were supposed to be doing.

I wrote down the dream before waking Sean up for breakfast. Casually, I asked him if he remembered any dreams. Incredibly, he proceeded to describe what he called "a bunch of things hard to say in words": that he'd been watching a series of concentric submarines, each fitting inside the other, floating on top of the ocean. One by one, the submarines emerged: the smallest from inside the next largest, then that one from the next size, on up until the largest one was empty. As each submarine appeared, he said, they reversed direction and sank, horizontally, beneath the sea. As the largest submarine sank, the scene flashed to a picture of three identical stones sitting in a line on a *flat plain*—"You know, that kind with the lines that all go to a point at the back," Sean said, describing the same "plain of perspective" that I'd seen in *my* dream. "And there was something special about the way those stones were arranged, some lesson but I don't know what," he finished.

I wrote down his words and then read my dream account to him. "Well?" I said expectantly, looking up from the paper. "What do you suppose that means?"

Sean groaned and clutched his forehead. "Oh, god!" he wailed, "I suppose that means that I'm gonna end up being a *writer!*"

One morning, during a bout with the flu at age three, Sean eagerly told me all about "the doctor man who comes and talks to me while I dream and tells me how I can get myself better." Sean said that this man "wore a tall black hat and a long coat with two tails and sometimes was the Easter Bunny but sometimes didn't talk, he just threw thoughts at me." At that time I hadn't made any dream suggestions to him along those lines. A few months later, we were riding in the car listening to a popular rendition of "The Boogie-Woogie Bugle Boy of Company B" on the radio, when Sean suddenly launched into a detailed and lengthy description of what he called "the other time I was alive, in the twenties." (Again, I did not give Sean "Seth material lectures," and still don't dwell on it much, as such, in our conversations.) For at least a half an hour, Sean spun a lovely tale of "my own self John Keelish, when I danced an' had a wide horn. Five people danced with me. So did a lady, but she didn't have a horn, she jus' had a singin' mouth. . . . I was born in the Cabbage Song City an' I died 'cause I drank that stuff too much." In spite of my many questions, he never mixed up any of the details of this tale, or contradicted himself. Complete fantasy or not, Sean was at the very least displaying a delightfully provocative story-telling ability and my encouragement was for him to "keep seeing those pictures and tell me all about them." How many people, however, are cut off from spontaneous acquaintance with aspects of their own identity? How many children are kept from expressing these kinds of images by the admonition that such stories aren't "true" and are therefore "bad"?

Again, I'm not about to start rushing around on Sean's behalf in a mad search for encyclopedic references to a horn player from the 20's. Besides my personal suspicions that nothing stays that literal, I'm also not about to cram Sean's inner perceptions inside another set of definitions that, like the ones I looked through as a child, don't even begin to live up to personal experience. For me, the encouragement of creative play, intellectual integrity, and trust in the spontaneous self is what's important — and in immediate earthly terms, I think our survival depends upon it.

"Everyone thinks I'm crazy — precognition? Bah, humbug!" Bernice Zale wrote to me in June 1979. "But in a baby, no less . . . !

"On Thursday, my mother was visiting for the day [*from a town thirty miles away*]," Bernice said in her letter. "We put Ben [*Bernice's son, then aged eleven months*] down for his morning nap at 10:45 A.M. and at 11:15 he was suddenly awake, screaming and crying like I've never heard him do. It took me only a few seconds of holding him to see it wasn't physical pain. Rather, it was stark terror. It took a lot of walking and patience, with lunch and then an hour's carriage ride, to bring him back to normal! Ben, as you know, is just the opposite of this. I felt that he'd had a bad dream.

"Late that night after I was in bed, I heard my husband answer the phone. My mother had called . . . to tell me that my father was in the hospital. At just the time Ben was napping that day, my father wasn't feeling so well. He was downstreet [*from his home*] and practically dragged himself home to lie down on the living-room couch. . . . At 1 P.M., he began to bleed . . . the blood poured from his mouth and rectum. He crawled out into the hall but found he was unable to make it to the telephone and only managed to get into the bathtub where he felt he could die without making any more mess than he already had. My mother arrived home sometime after 5 P.M., to find an incredible trail of blood leading to the bathroom and my father entering shock from loss of blood. . . . An ambulance got him to the hospital. It seems that his ulcer has been bleeding for a few weeks and he's been taking *aspirin*,[2] without telling anyone, to alleviate what he thought was back pain! He's fine now . . .

"In the meantime, I believe Ben's nap was disrupted by a nightmare. He's very fond of my father, following him wherever and whenever he can. I think Ben dreamed of what was soon to occur to his grandfather. I don't know if any of this will be of use to your book, but . . . it seems that Ben's experience may be pertinent."

"How did class change my life?" Harold Wiles muses. "Probably by developing tolerance for my fellow man. I know that as I create my reality, so does every other person create theirs. Who is to say that these realities should coincide? If they don't, why hassle it? I guess that's the most important change. I know (and believe) that I create my reality. I may not like it at times, but I know that there's no one else to blame. I think that's kinda neat!"

Other class members grouped and regrouped in their own ways, went it alone, found other philosophies through which to explore their ideas. Charlene Pine and Rudy Storch hold their own classes in New York based on transcripts of Jane's class; Charlene is piecing together a book on her personal healing experience. Lauren DelMarie and Will Petrosky are writing for a Berkeley radio station; Lauren is also getting his science-fiction book ready for publication. Camille and Warren Atkinson are busy with their six teen-aged children; all of them are musically gifted and they've enjoyed transcribing some of the Sumari songs from Warren's tapes. Richie Kendall is writing songs; his "Joyful Rain" was recorded by a professional studio group.

In short, for all its impact upon the individuals who attended, class as a group disengaged easily—and perhaps appropriately—when the time came. "Class ended because Jane and Rob did not need class any more," Warren Atkinson says. "Also many class members didn't need it, as a group, anyway. But the experience developed and changed me. I was the observer, the internalizer—the Cardinal—a conservative being stimulated by a discarnate visitor." Class transcripts and tapes (though protected by copyright law) circulated around the country for several years; and Seth-oriented groups have sprung up in dozens of places, from New York to Florida and California.

"Some of them are great," says Richie Kendall, who's attended several of these "maverick" classes. "Some are really poor excuses for one person to lay a lot of his own power needs on others. Well, I guess people who go to those have their own reasons, too.

"But one thing I run across sometimes in people who've read Seth is a kind of weird process by which they use Seth's words to justify any old bullshit they're into, without examining their *beliefs*," Richie adds. "In a strange way, you can end up using the 'you create your own reality' bit to *not* look at how or why you're creating the reality you have. It's a superficial use of the idea at best; or the same old nonsense with a new justification at its worst. Because when you really start examining your beliefs—I mean *really listening* to yourself and really accepting that *you* create all of your experience—when you strip away all the bullshit and start honestly looking at your beliefs, *you take a step,* a sideways step, into a literally new world of action. And strangely enough, you become *less* divorced from the world at the same time. The world becomes an intimate thing. Because of course it *is* an intimate thing. But you don't really understand that until you take that step.

"You can't just spout Seth's appropriate words from page so-and-so for every situation you run into. The words are meant to lead you toward your *own* experience—toward that step back to your own self."

"You know what I think?" Joel Hess concludes about class. "I think that one of the major contributions of the class was the way it built a link between us sophisticated twentieth-century technocrats and our ancestors, even back into the proverbial mists of time. It gave us a place to discover that dreams and so-called 'psychic' experiences aren't imposed upon us but are a part of us, meant to be used as part of us. It showed us how plausible it is for sensitive and intelligent people to come to believe in spirits, ghosts, gods, angels, contact with other beings in other times, and to believe in open-ended dreams. It provided us with a glimpse of ourselves; our parents, as it were, sitting about a fire dark eons ago, curing cuts and bruises by prayer, incantations, hexes, Alpha . . . *willing* a sick child back to health . . . and talking *with* the gods about where the hunting will be best tomorrow.

"We no longer think of those ancestors as silly, superstitious people who saw a god or demon behind every bush. If there is nothing to all this other than a psychological human need to have a supernatural explanation for otherwise mysterious events in the natural world, then we have possibly manifested those same drives in our own time, and didn't feel silly or superstitious, certainly not weird, crazy, or off the wall . . . In that case, we can appreciate the human drives that prompted the birth of so many of our legends, religions, gods, powers, omens, and practices. Or perhaps, just perhaps, our forebears knew and used secrets and called upon powers in themselves and the world around them that we are only beginning to rediscover."

EXCERPTS FROM AN "INFORMAL" CLASS
HELD DECEMBER 2, 1978

Several people from ESP class days got together at Jane and Rob's house on this wintery Saturday night. Most had driven the 250 miles up from New York City. We sat around on the cozy living room's thick shag rug among the jungle of plants and bookshelves, Robbie's paintings peeking down from the cream-colored walls—paintings in deep, echoing hues of light and shade. We talked about our current projects. Jane and Rob sat across from each other at Jane's round worktable, listening attentively, affectionately. My proposed book on class had received an enthusiastic response from my editor; I was uneasily on the edge of my first contract. Vic—a concert pianist and composer—Charlene, and Rudy all described their "Seth" classes. "What do you do in them, exactly?" Jane quizzed, grinning. "Do you get into sexuality? The man-woman divisions? Do you work with beliefs, tell secrets, take your clothes off?" We all laughed. "In short, loves," Jane said, "do you get down to the nitty-gritty?" Vic said that his class dealt mostly with getting reincarnational material; Charlene spoke of her experiments with healing; Rudy talked about the belief papers he assigns to his students. Richie Kendall then read a lengthy essay on the nature of Art and Life. As he finished, Jane pulled off her glasses and Seth's familiar dark eyes and somewhat amused expression regarded us once again from that incredible, invisible window in time and space.

Now. The sun shines, the writer writes, the artist paints, the thinker thinks, the dreamer dreams, and each of you, whether you know it or not, naturally follows your own natures. You bloom whether or not you recognize the pattern of your petals. You sing. You are like a trans-species, as Ruburt would say. Something happens when you meet the world, something happens when you meet each other, something happens when you have a child, when you think, when you look at each other. Something happens the moment you are born and the world is different. Because you are, the world is different. It is a world of individuals, and distorting an old historic statement: God must love individuals, because he never made anything else.

You are not born as members of a nation tied tail to tail. You each are aware of the difference of your thoughts. And when your thoughts meet the world, you change the world.

Now, you are also changed by the world, since you are not made of concrete. But if I have taught you anything, I hope I have given you the grace to know yourselves to some extent. To recognize that you are, indeed, in your way, world-changers. For as you change yourselves, as your grow, you change the world. The world changes because you are.

Now if you listen without listening too hard, in any intimate moment you can hear your molecules shout, if you will forgive me, with their own optimism. Each molecule is its own world. *Each molecule is its own world.* Your thoughts form worlds. I say what I say and I say more than you hear, and yet you hear me silently. When I speak of responsibility, I speak of the cat's responsibility to lift its tail or twirl its ear. *Billy II, the gray tiger cat, was sitting in a corner, swishing his tail, watching every move this strange gang of people was making.* No cat says, "I must hold my backside in such and such a fashion," or "I must play with the catnip." And yet a cat is a cat, whether it is flawed or has a broken foot, or whether it can hear or not hear, whether it is ancient or young. A cat is a perfect cat. Now you can understand that. But in the same way you have a responsibility to be yourselves as a cat has to be itself. To express the joyful creative nature that is your own. And through that expression, your spirituality will flower. For it will not flower if you pretend that the spirit is elsewhere and you are here.

So, those of you [*holding classes*] who speak on my behalf, let there be times of boisterous activity. Let there be play. Let there even be time for discord if that is what is needed; but never—and I know you would not—never impose an artificial ceiling of peace. For peace is active. And so if there is any message that I have for your students [*to Vic, Charlene, and Rudy*], as usual, it is not a quiet one. When you feel your own vitalities fully, then that will be understood by your students. And when each person feels and releases their own creativity [*to me*], there will be no need for books about Seth classes. But now there is such a need.

So you have all begun something, have you? And when was it begun? Now in my books and when I speak to you, I use simple words, usually. And the people sometimes write asking why I do not give proper methods—that is, more and more instructions as to how to do this and that. So when I say to you, let your classes thrill with quality, it is up to you to discover what quality means to you. And when I say to each of you, classes or no, that your lives be lives of quality, of beauty and truth, I am not about to define beauty or truth for you. That is your challenge.

Seth withdrew; after relating his remarks to Jane, we got into a discussion of recent world events, which included the November [1978] mass suicide of the People's Temple group in Jonestown, Guyana; and of the conflicts between gays and heterosexuals stirred up in Florida in the wake of singer Anita Bryant's anti-gay campaign. Someone remarked that television coverage of her speeches was responsible for making her viewpoint more credible to a mass audience. At this point, Seth re-entered the conversation:

Now, subject: Anita Bryant. Subject: Jonestown. Subject: Communication of the official consciousness and what it has wrought.

If it were not for television, you would not know much about Anita Bryant; you would not know much about the Reverend Jones [*who led the People's Temple to its death in Guyana*], who believed he was God and "led his followers into folly." If it were not for television and technology and the official line of consciousness, you would not know of the fanaticism of Anita Bryant, American apple pie, good religion, and all the rest.

Now Anita Bryant serves a purpose, for all of her distortions. She makes each person question the nature of their own beliefs concerning sexuality. And sexuality is not only a personal question. It is not only a question of when to do it, with whom, and how. Sexuality in your time means: What is American? Is it American to be a football hero and a gung-ho male? Is it American to be a homosexual and love poetry or dancing or music or children? Is it a cliché to think that all homosexuals are sensitive and love music? Are there no violent homosexuals, and no bastards? Are all stereotyped "masculine" men that way because they want to be that way? Are they forced to hide certain feelings? What are women? How do men consider them?

Now Anita Bryant with orange blossoms [*referring to Miss Bryant's television commercial appearances for Florida citrus juices*] presents you with all of those questions. And each person who views her on television must look into their own beliefs. And the same applies to our Reverend Jones, and to any fanatic. For the fanatic speaks in exaggerated terms, but he or she speaks beliefs that to some extent each of you hold — but to what degree? And so they are teachers in their way. You may hate them or deride them. And you may say they are fanatics, which they are. But they frighten you, because you know that in your hearts some of their beliefs exist, in weaker terms, and where do you draw the line?

So even the fanatic serves good purposes. And I will tell you that no one and no fanatic leads masses of people. People follow because they want to and no one leads them. And if you think you are a leader, you misunderstand the people, for they are taking you where they want to go. Only you are taking the responsibility and not they. You form your own reality. All of this, you see, is much trickier than appears at the 100th or second 100th or 1,000th glance.

Vic related Seth's comments to Jane, but was interrupted halfway through by Seth's sudden return:

Now, I wouldn't drink her god-damned orange juice either!

"Good for you," Vic said.

Now, I love all of you, and I know that you love me. And I hope that that love is somehow distantly able, distantly, distantly, to contain some — some — some — [*whispers*] *some* kindly feeling for people like Anita Bryant . . . Remember, and I do not expect any of you practically in daily life to hold this as a rule, but remember, it is because you expect so much from people that Anita Bryant and fanatics fall so short. And that is why you are angry at them. Your love for humanity holds . . . You do not hate anyone that you are not capable of loving. Remember that.

I do not expect any of you to be saints. For if you were saints, you would not be here. And if I were a saint, I would not be here either. But in the vast range of your emotions, leave room for loves that are very distant, so distant and so alien that you do not recognize them. And hold room for the feelings of loss and bitterness and anger that are behind Anita Bryant's statements. And the feelings of lack of worth that power her statements and feelings. It is as if she were a meadow upon which no rain had fallen. Then certainly she would be bitter and cry.

We told Jane what Seth had said.

Humorously: You forgot the part about trying to love Anita Bryant, significantly.

"We were about to say it," Rudy said hastily.

"It's on the tip of our tongues," Vic assured him.

Just a tiny, tiny, distant love.

Now, Sue is greatness. Richie is greatness. Joseph [*Rob*] is greatness. Rudy is greatness. Roni is greatness. You are all greatness. To know you are greatness is quality.

Then your expressions are true expressions of quality, and they are not marred. Whatever they are, they are not marred. You recognize quality. Instinctively, whether or not you can say what it is. It inspires you. You run away from things that are not of quality, whether you can say why they are or not. Your dreams are quality. *Your dreams are quality!* No one need tell you how to dream. You dream instinctively, automatically, and beautifully. You commit a beautiful dream each time you dream. And each dream is a dream of quality.

Each breath you take is a breath of quality. All you have to do is realize that each breath you take ultimately reaches to the ends of the universe and helps your world. You are alone and not alone.

Now, that statement is far more important than it sounds. For in your aloneness, and in your togetherness, and between the two, there is the meaning of your humanity. And there is the meaning of your life and your death. You cannot be completely together. You cannot be completely alone. Yet always must your existence flit between the two. Between the desire and the ideal, between the dream and its execution, between your love and your expression of it. There dwells your reality and your meaning, and therein lies the validity of your soul.

Now, if you believed what I said, then you would bank upon yourselves. You would really trust yourselves. You would really know that you are an intimate part of the fabric of the universe; you would trust your abilities and bet upon yourselves. You would, without repressing anything, experience you own reality without impediments. You have a way to go!

But you have support. You have biological support. For your atoms and molecules are not imbeciles. You could learn from them! The pupils of your eyes see far more than you see visually. As Ruburt said earlier [*that evening*] I am not telling you that you can have heaven upon earth. For one thing, there is no such thing as heaven, and for another, if there were, you would be bored. You need a challenge. Any flower uses it. And I am not talking about problems and challenges being the same thing. I am speaking of initiative, and desire and accomplishment; the need to use your abilities. They need to be used as a stem needs to grow. That is what I am speaking of.

Now all of you this evening, tell yourselves you will have a True Dream from the Gates of Horn, and we do have a city building. A city. Highly impractical, it seems, at this time. A city that does indeed exist mentally. But all things exist mentally first, or they will never be materialized. And someday, that city might exist physically. But it will not be when you are here. Yet your memories will be in it and your desires. And to that extent, you will be founders.

And you forge such dreams in your sleep and in your private imaginings, and in your inspirations. For when one member of a species dreams such dreams, those dreams are transmitted to all other members. They do not die. When a runner at the Olympics does better than the runner before, then all the sportscasters say, "How grand! We did not know man could run so fast!" And so now records are being broken all the time. And mentally, the same thing applies.

Dream a grand dream. For when one member of the species dreams, all members, to some extent, participate. And the psyche, and the soul, and the heart of man take new leaps, in your terms, not taken before. So trust yourselves, and trust your love and your dreams. [*To Rudy, and Charlene, and Vic, looking at Rudy:*] And tell your students I say [*shouts*] R-A-YYYY!!!! Which means hooray. [*Shouts*] HOOORAAAYYY!!!!

EXCERPT FROM AN "INFORMAL" CLASS
HELD SEPTEMBER 29, 1979

The autumn night was magic again, and former class members met at Jane and Rob's house for some reminiscing and conversation. Again, many of the people drove up from New York City. Gary and

*Rhoda were there with Samantha, their five-month-old daughter,
who cooed and gurgled, wide-eyed, throughout the evening. At one
point, Jane posed the following question: "We form our own reality,
and we do it according to our beliefs, but what help do we have in
doing it, or what do we have to help us out? What do you think con-
nects you to the inner self?" Several people offered some ideas, and a
rambunctious debate began, just like old times. Seth came through
at this point, carefully handing Jane's glasses to Rob, who sat across
from Jane at her cluttered worktable.*

Now. We have a very young baby in this house [*Samantha*] and that baby does not know my name. The baby has not read
The Seth Material. That baby knows how to grow. That child trusts
its impulses.

It is one thing to imagine a spontaneous self or an inner
self or an inner entity to whom you must, then, it seems, somehow
relate. But you were born with true impulses and they are always
with you, even though you have been taught not to trust them. So
you must ask, is this impulse from my creative self, or shall I follow
this impulse, or shall I not? And so you have forgotten the language
of impulses.

Now, impulses are meant to help you create your reality.
They are meant to help you move through belief systems. They are
meant to help you find your best fulfillment and not only your private best fulfillment; but you are, through your impulses, led to situations where your best improvement also aids the species and all
species—when you listen, when you trust your impulses. And I am
talking about your private, innocuous, everyday impulses, also.

Now, in Framework Two,[3] there is no time, and from
that vantage point you form the events that you know; and so your
impulses fit in with all of the impulses of all of the other individuals
in time as you think of it, throughout the planet. But when you do
not trust yourselves, you do not trust your impulses. It does not do to
say, "I trust my inner self, but I do not trust my impulses." Now, impulses are meant to help you move. You are born with the impulse to
be, as this young child in the house is. That child follows its impulses. *It knows how to grow.* It plays by following its impulses. I
want you to think of that and I will return—it is good to physically
see you all again!

*The group got into a lively discussion about impulses and
what to do when you have contradictory impulses. "What do you do
when you have the impulse to take two different directions at once?"
one of us wailed. "What if I had the impulse to run away with the*

neighbor's husband? What if I had the impulse to set fire to your house?"

"Well, you might try just running away with the neighbor's husband for one night," Jane suggested humorously. "See, there's the idea put on top of an impulse that sex, for example, is so destructive that you have to squash every tiny impulse you get, until it grows into some act larger than you originally meant."

"So how do you know which impulses are really coming from your inner self?" Richie asked.

"Well, Seth said that he thought we forgot the real nature of impulses because we can't tell the difference anymore," Rudy replied. But before we could go on, Jane's glasses were on the table-top.

I am saying that *all* of your impulses come from the inner self. I am saying that despite your experience with impulses in your culture, despite their contradictory nature as you know of them, that your lives have that impulsive shape. I am saying that spontaneity knows its own order and that your impulses, when you allow them to do so, would ideally, spontaneously, work not only to your advantage, but to the advantage of the entire world.

When you are afraid of impulses, you are afraid of them because you think that basically you are murderous creatures, that you come from the animals—and you think of them in those terms, then, as beasts. It seems to you that your beastly nature will betray itself in your impulses. But your impulses come from that natural impulse *to be*. And your natural impulses, left alone, are those of cooperation and joy.

"How do you know when they're left alone?" Kurt asked.

When you have distrusted your selves as a species for centuries, when you begin teaching your children that impulses are wrong, that spontaneity is bad, then you begin at a very early age to misread and distort your impulses. . . . If you are angry at your new wife [*to Kurt, who had recently married Charlene*], and you want to say "Shut up, bitch," and do not do so and hold it back, and think, "That is wrong, I will not do it," then you can come up with the situation where you have the impulse to hit her or she to hit you. If you realize that your impulses are meant to tell you something, then you can use your conscious minds to distinguish what courses of action you want to take. Remember what I have said about probabilities. When you cut down your impulses, you cut down the roads of probable action, and whenever you do so, you cut down creativity.

Seth departed, and, hardly stopping to repeat his words to

Jane, everybody jumped into another debate on contradictory impulses. What about the man who impulsively molests children? Who impulsively shoots people? Do you just lock these people up for now, and hope that an upcoming, aware generation learns to deal with impulses before they go that far? "Seth seemed to be saying this time that if you really trust your impulses, even all of them for a change, that they would start clearing up, so to speak," Rudy proposed.

You [*Rudy*] do a good job of spooking the universe! What I am saying: learn to trust the selves *that you know.* Learn to trust the selves that you know and you will discover the inner selves. But you will not discover the inner selves if you do not trust the selves that you know. Do not imagine a distance between yourselves. You are *one.* And your impulses, when you learn to understand them, will be your best contact with the inner self.

Now, I have spoken about a city. A dream city that you do not see now, Sue. It is not before your eyes. But this world as you know it came from some un-where. It came from a mental dimension and was then materialized. And so our city that is not manifest now, is a reality of the mind. And since it is a reality of the mind, it will somehow be a reality in physical fact. And it will be a realm, however small, however large, in whatever probability, and you will be a part of it. And it will be a realm in which men and women know themselves and walk in honor, and in freedom. And it will be a realm, however small, however large, in which there is indeed an infinite creativity, and it can be a creativity that seeds worlds.

Your thoughts now seed worlds. It is only because you do not know that, that what I say sounds strange. You are here because your thoughts before your birth seeded this world into which you would grow. You did not come here strangers. There is still, you see, much to learn . . .

Now, the creative abilities do not just help you write books, paint pictures, play the piano, compose. The creative abilities are largely responsible for keeping you alive. Your selves are created. You are alive because you wanted to create. Every act that you perform is creative. Your creative self, your spontaneous creative self, the self that speaks through your impulses, keeps you alive . . . It keeps your heart beating and [*to Kurt*] your mustache quivering now. It helps Eddie yawn and Elaine bake pies and Harold run his [shopping] mall . . .

Rob asked, "What do you think of all the faces around here, now that you haven't seen them for a while?"

Humorously:

574 / Class and Un-Class Ever Since

I am afraid to make even the simplest comments! Here, when I am faced with such a rambunctious group, I am sometimes tempted to say, *"Don't be so spontaneous!"*

Thunderous applause and whistles.

Seth withdrew, and Jane and Rob explained some of the current theories of the origins and development of life on the Earth. Rob compared the theory of evolution [as originally posed by Charles Darwin]⁴ to the Scientific Creationist theory that claims the Earth to be only 10,000 years old. Rob noted that the Darwinist idea is the one taught almost exclusively in this country's school systems, "with no serious consideration given to the fact that the Theory of Evolution as it's understood is full of contradictions, and often uses the Theory of Evolution to prove the Theory of Evolution!⁵*

"The thing is," Rob said, *his voice filled with anger,* "the notion that our existence is based on a series of accidents is passed on as absolute fact to each succeeding generation of children without question!"* At this point, Seth appeared.*

Now, Creationists, Scientific Creationists, believe that an objective god created the world 10,000 years ago, and all the species thereof that you know of now, were created then. There was a perfect world according to this theory.

Now, Evolution believes that the world becomes more complex with time. That there is "evolution." The Creationists believe that the Lord in His holy wisdom created a perfect world which then promptly began to decay. They also believe that the good Lord in His holy wisdom set upon this world a catastrophe so that all of the organisms were greatly set upon. The species almost vanished. The species of man was separated, and therefore began the growth of various languages. They believe that the original language was given to man by God.

This god, then, the scientists—the Creationists—say, set this catastrophe. They do not say, because they are scientists, that God *punished* man by the catastrophe, but that is, of course, what they believe. That was not in the book, however [*the book on Scientific Creationism Jane and Rob were referring to*].⁶ [They believe] the world was created by an objectified god who then set it into being with all of the basic laws of nature that you know. These are called laws of conservation. So that with time, the world must disintegrate. The evolutionists believe that the world instead was created simply through chance.

Now, I am, in very important ways, no longer a member of your species. You *are* a member of your species, and you were brought up with an odd mixture of both of those belief systems, so that you still are not aware of the weight of those beliefs upon your mind.

Whispers, very intensely: I would dearly love you to imagine the magical changes in your personal realities that could occur if suddenly, for a moment, you freed your minds from the weight of those beliefs; if you could look upon your reality as [Gary and Rhoda's] baby does now, with new eyes not so ready to thrust beliefs upon this world, *but to perceive it with the freshness and originality that is a part of your heritage.* And to throw aside from your thoughts and minds and beings all thoughts of belonging to a blighted species, whether it be a spiritual or a physical one.

And if I could force you to accept a gift from me that were mine to give, I would, for a moment at least, give you that gift of pure vision and pure perception that is within your reach if you but understand that it is.

I bid you all a fond good-night, and where you are I am, because I represent the part of you that you know you are. And I am nothing that you are not. I am nothing that you are not, in true fact, in the true meaning of the word. So any wisdom or power or energy that you assign to me, you cannot do rightfully, unless you assign that power to yourselves. I am in your dreams because I am the self that you know you are. And you are in my dreams for the same reasons.

There is room in our system of beliefs for different tastes. For those who have a love of terms and those who do not; for those who have different styles of being. I bid you, then, the joy and energy that you recognize and acknowledge as your own. Let it always be a support and mental and spiritual couch to each of you.

NOTES FOR CHAPTER TWENTY-ONE

1. A house that Jane and Rob considered buying at one point. See Sessions 737, 738, and 739, plus Rob's notes in Volume 2 of *The "Unknown" Reality* on Jane and Rob's house-hunting and the probabilities, symbols, and needs called up by such activities.

2. According to medical knowledge, aspirin can cause severe internal bleeding, as the drug inhibits the body's natural blood-clotting ability.

3. A reference to Framework 1 and Framework 2, which are discussed in detail in Seth's *The Individual and the Nature of Mass Events*

and in Jane Robert's own *The God of Jane: A Psychic Manifesto*, both published in 1981.

     4. In his *Origin of Species,* published in 1859, Charles Darwin (1809–1881) presented the idea of natural selection. His thinking was also drawn from some of the work done by nineteenth-century English naturalist Alfred Wallace.

     5. For more information on Rob's thoughts and research on evolution, plus some of Seth's comments along these lines, see Appendix 12 for Session 705 in Volume 2 of *The "Unknown" Reality.*

     6. *Scientific Creationism,* the public school edition, edited by Henry M. Morris, Ph.D., Creation-Life Publishers, San Diego, Ca.

Will Ives

EPILOGUE

THE WAY OF FRISBEE
(for Will Ives, 1944-1976)

Soaring flight, wingless,
unpiloted, unplanned,
yet guided
by winds and lifts unseen,
unpredicted
in nuances of
slight-of-hand—

Willy,
the Way of Frisbee
was
Cosmic indeed:
Purpose spinning in
its round, round ways.

         —*SMW*

Warren: "Seth?"
Seth: "My dear friend—one more time!"
Warren: "All-That-Is knows of the portion of
      himself that is us. Is there . . . "
Seth: "All-That-Is does indeed know himself,
      or itself, and wakens to itself as you."
Warren: "Is there a part that sent us out,
      similar to All-That-Is, that knows each
      part of us that is?"
Seth: "There is indeed."
Warren: "Is there any way that we can make
      ourselves aware of the portion that sent
      us?"
Seth: "There is indeed."
Warren: "What is it?"
Seth: "Know yourself."

APPENDIX
FIVE

A Waking Dream:
The Probability of Eyau

"There are species of consciousness with which you have not been in-volved," Seth told us during a probability discussion in 1974. "Your race has embarked upon many experiments of animal/man and man/animal that have progressed in other probabilities not your own . . . There is no one-line development. There is no evolution in one-line terms as you have been told. There are parallel lines of development, and there always were, even as now in your present there are probable lines of development."

I had been sitting up in bed that cold December night in 1974, re-reading this class session and thinking again about the fascinating implication of probabilities on history. What worlds exist around us, intersecting with ours in a continuous undercurrent, ex-changing "facts" and fictions across an open board of time and space? How else, I wondered, the Coelacanthus,[1] the Loch Ness monster, the tonsil? What "dreams," I mused, that go on beneath the waking state—what flashes of "illogical" thought—represent glimpses into these co-existent, parallel worlds? My head buzzed with this swarm of ideas, but I felt sleepy nonetheless. Soon I began to drift off into that pre-sleep twilight where scenes and events often seem to flash past on journeys of their own, with no impetus from the sleeper at all.

Suddenly, I realized that I was looking down upon a bril-liantly clear scene, and that I had been staring at it for several seconds. A group of beings was standing in a peculiarly random, and yet orderly, fashion around an entrance to a mine or cave of some sort. These beings, I could see, were humanoid in appear-ance but not *Homo sapiens*—or anything else out of our physio-logical "history." The one closest to my field of vision was standing in profile, staring off in the distance to my left, as though he were day-dreaming. He, like all the others that I could see there, had a face that consisted mostly of an enormous ridge of bone around ap-parently lidless eyes. This facial ridge swept up into the area that on a human face would have been the scalp. The eyes themselves were round and dark, and either lashless or with extremely thin lashes. This whole bone structure gave the face an open, surprised look; nostrils seemed to be flat openings on the face, without a nose; the ears were hidden in a fine, tightly compacted fur. A clot of stringy, matted-looking hair hung down from the top of the head. The mouth seemed to be fixed in an open grin—but it was the eye struc-ture that was by far the most arresting feature of these beings.

The one closest to me, as well as the dozen or so others, was wearing a uniform of some sort—a dark green material with dark blue trim, a belt around the waist, a dark blue collar that came up around his thin neck, and blue trim down the sleeves and criss-crossed on the body of the suit. His hands and the lower part of his body were hidden by his position behind a large rock. There were many boulders spaced around the mine or cave entrance, all part of a desolate and harsh landscape. I would say that these beings were almost feline; yet not because they looked particularly like cats, but because their precise, calculated stance suggested the pose of an alert, watchful, yet relaxed, cat. My point of view was from slightly above their heads, looking down.

All of this landscape, plus the pose of the beings there, seemed at once random and also filled with a purpose that defied my normal logic. At the same time, while the scene was in stop-action, it was so suggestive of motion that I could almost *feel* them moving: it was as though I had cut across a second of their time in a sideways slice, like putting one's finger in a glass of water and perceiving only the portion of the finger touched by the water's surface. I wondered if the creatures were guards for mine workers, or for some kind of archeological expedition.

Then, suddenly, I realized that a "side" view had appeared in my field of vision, adjacent to this scene, showing a large map of the Florida Keys (which I first visited three years after this experience). A loud voice, speaking close to my ear, said, "Florida opens up inwardly as a gateway to other universes." At that, the side-view map opened, like a door, into the adjacent scene, where the strange beings were still standing in their moment—and immediately, I was so close to the character in the foreground that his face was enormous, filling the sky. Again the voice spoke in my ear, this time in a melodious singsong: "And Eyau's eyes opened for him to see what lay beyond them."

Instantly, I knew that "Eyau" was the name of this being closest to me, and that the sentence was from writings of his own—that it was my *interpretation* of a sentence of his; and that in some way, this "Eyau" and I had communicated, and that he was daydreaming of a slice of *my* world and of a whisper of *my* mind's musings—and that somehow, the Florida Keys had served, symbolically, to "open up" each world to the other.

With that, I jolted awake. The light was still on, and only five minutes had passed. As I wrote this experience down, I thought of the stop-action scenes that Rob Butts had perceived of his counterpart history. Had I been doing the same? Had I tuned in on a probable system of development, as Seth had been discussing in the class session? Was all of it a pretty fantasy, brought on by my pre-sleep reading? Or—once again, this last choice gnawed at me—was it *all* of that, and something more that I didn't understand? Whatever it was, the clarity and immediacy of that strange scene stayed with me for a long time. Would I ever meet up with him again, this Eyau, somewhere in a mutual dream state?

NOTES

1. The Coelacanthus is the famous "extinct" fish that turned up in a fisherman's net off Madagascar in 1938. The typical deep-bodied, lobate-finned coelacanth was common in the Mesozoic period, and was known by fossil form only—and therefore thought to be extinct—as one of the genera of "lungfish," or fish capable of breathing out of water.

APPENDIX
SIX

Comments on the Christ Consciousness:
A Spontaneous Seth Session,
August 5, 1977

Brian Kent is a staff scientist in the Stanford Research Institute of Menlo Park, California. In August of 1977, he visited Jane and Rob to discuss with them some of his latest projects, which included the testing of conscious control of ovulation, technological approaches to earthquake prediction, and development of a self-repairing computer for commercial aircraft. His group was also doing a study of "psychic" answers to scientific questions—in other words, a study of different individuals who, according to Brian's own project description, "can enter at will a dissociated mental state, somewhat like hypnosis, from which they answer in detail questions on virtually any topic." Brian's research team had been working with a group of ten such individuals, "perhaps half of whom have proven to be quite accurate and versatile," his report stated.

That Friday night, I joined Jane, Rob, and Brian for an evening of conversation. Brian had spent the afternoon with Jane and Rob and was talking enthusiastically about Seth's ideas. At one point, Brian raised a question regarding the Christ story as related by Seth in The Seth Material *and* Seth Speaks. *He remarked that Seth's account of the three-person embodiment of the Christ personality and his version of the Crucifixion was a stumbling block for many who have found Seth's philosophy otherwise acceptable and helpful.*

At this point, Jane's glasses were whipped off and Seth's voice boomed out unexpectedly, startling Brian into frantic fumbling with the tape recorder he'd brought along.

Now. Brian Kent: What's in a name? But what Brian Kent is, is not altogether contained by a person called Brian Kent. The greater self that you are is within Brian Kent, but not contained in Brian Kent. Moreover, Christ could not be contained in one historical person either. And without casting any great aspersions against Brian Kent, Christ *did* have a great historical import!

The person that Napoleon is thought to be had great historical import. The greater Napoleon, having many other abilities, could not be expressed through that one person. No one person can contain [all of his] psychological reality.

Two or three sentences were lost in the noise of adjusting the recorder.

The great truths of Christianity do not involve murder and sacrifice. The great truths of reality do not include the fact that God sacrificed His only son, either. The Christ story was much more than that.

Another portion lost here to background noise.

You can, most comfortably, look at other people's gods and the gods of the past, as you know the past, and smile. You can look at the animal gods; the gods of Olympus; buried and forgotten and forsaken gods whose names exist only in footnotes in history books. And you can smile.

You can look at other people's religions and other people's folktales. But you cannot look at your own god, or gods, in the same manner. For it seems that the folktales involving Christianity are not folktales, but truths, and surely Christ is more real than Zeus! Zeus is a legend! There was no voice that roared like thunder! (*Very loud*:) There was no Mount Olympus! There were no gods who danced with human maidens on the hillsides! Superstitious nonsense!

Your own stories, however, are "truth." There was a God, invisible; a God the Father, who sent down His only son to be crucified, born of a virgin; a miracle worker who changed history. For is not your civilization a result of that God's work?

Many civilizations believed that they were born with the birth of gods. This does not mean that beneath those myths there are not truths. This does not mean that there is no meaning to the progression of the gods — there is. They are not apart from your consciousness, but born from it; and yet independent. In one way, the civilization took a great road toward progress when your fine Egyptian said, "There are not many gods, but only One." [*Earlier, we had been discussing Egyptian philosophies.*] And in another way, [civilization] took a step backward, for your Christian concept of God disinherited the animals, disinherited the women, disinherited nature. You did not have a united concept in which the frog had a god, or the toad or the snake or the baby or the cat. You had no room for such nonsense.

Now, the old gods, in their way, combined the best and the worst of human qualities, but man could relate to those gods. There were indeed homosexual gods. There were animal gods. There was a great mixture between existences that combined divinity and humanity in every species. And in those terms, each species was divine. Now you have lost that. Christianity could have represented a great progress in a different way, but those aspects were not stressed. Those aspects fell by the wayside, so to speak.

There is a reality behind the idea of Christ as you know it. But that Christ is not, and never was, any *more real* than Zeus. And Zeus was, and is, real — and so is Christ.

Break; discussion.

Ruburt said [all of this] in *Oversoul 7* and he did not want to hurt people's feelings. So I will say it . . . and then I will take the blame!

You do not really understand what I mean when I say that the inner world is the source of the objective one. The churches have believed that if they could prove that the historical Christ was crucified and then raised from the dead, that the religion itself would become more valid. It would satisfy your love of details!

If, however, Christ were one historical person, in the way that you have been taught, his reality would not have been nearly as vast. You do not understand as yet that your creativity and energy and being and reality come from an inner source. When I say, therefore, that the gods, or the divine sources of being, move through your world but do not come from it, I am saying that they are indeed the source of your own reality from which you spring; and therefore, in those terms, they are more fully [dimensional].

In certain terms, Christ was a myth who did not exist in the terms that you believe. Indeed there was a man called Christ. *There were thousands of men called Christ!* There were miracle-workers all over the place! There were politics involved — and the Romans and the Jews and the Essenes and a thousand different Jewish groups. That part of the world was seething emotionally. They were searching, and from their desire and from the state of their consciousness, then, emerged the story.

There *is* a Christ consciousness. That consciousness existed before the story. But it has little to do with the tale. And it did not involve a crucifixion. The Jews wanted a man crucified. Certain members of Jewish political groups wanted to see the idea of a Messiah ended, for all intents and purposes, in those times. Other groups wanted a Messiah to rise from the dead. They wanted a crucifixion and they wanted a martyr — a Jewish martyr.

The great drama that formed the Christian civilization was indeed like the great drama behind the Greek civilization. It was an emotional and spiritual drama that men acted out. It did come from another source, and you may call that source divine, for there is a Super-Nature, as there is a nature. But that Super-Nature works *through* nature, and forms it.

That is my bit on Christianity for now.

"Thank you," Brian said. There was a short discussion and Seth appeared again:

There is a Christ consciousness, in those terms, that existed first, but the *name* is meaningless. And when you attach the name to the pseudo-historical fact, then you end up with legends.

Now, legends are all right, and for a while they serve a purpose. But people grow out of their legends, and if they believe that their legends are Truth, there are psychic growing pains indeed! If they realize that their legends are symbols, then they can move more readily.

More discussion, leading into Brian's explanation of the possible use of animals to predict earthquakes, and whether people should feel the need to run away from earthquakes.

Very loud: The animals leave! That sounds like good sense to me! Think about it!

Much laughter. "All right," Brian agreed.

Amid the mad scramble, you *do* make your own reality. I admit that this sounds too simple, but you will not be caught in an earthquake if you do not want to be; and no one dies who has not decided to do so. You make your own reality — or you do not. And if you do not, then you are everywhere a victim, and the universe must be an accidental mechanism appearing with no reason. So that the miraculous picture you have seen of your body came accidentally into creation, and out of some cosmic accident attained its miraculous complexity. And that body was formed so beautifully for no reason except to be a victim.

That is the only other alternative to forming your own reality. You cannot have a universe in between. You have a universe formed *with* a reason, or a universe formed *without* a reason. And in a universe of reason, there are no victims. Everything has a reason, or nothing has a reason.

So — choose your side!

APPENDIX
SEVEN

On Time in No Time:
The Incident of the Train

Perhaps the most peculiar waking experience I've ever been involved in happened to my longtime friend Bernice Zale and me in the old Penn Central railway station at Syracuse, New York—in which we seemed literally to jump the tracks of linear time. I include it here because, for one thing, I've often wondered since that afternoon if all of us are *constantly* leaping the physically defined boundaries of time without acknowledging that we do. Is time naturally just a product of our individual conscious intentions, flying by or slowing down according to how we choose to make use of it?

Bernice had been visiting me in Elmira for a week that July of 1971; she'd come from Albany by train to Syracuse, which was about two hours by car from my house. We drove back up to the East Syracuse depot on July 19: here, I'll quote from my notes, made later that evening:

"Bernice and I left for Syracuse at 2 P.M. to be at the station in plenty of time, since her train left at 4:15 P.M. We made good time, got mixed up on the exit once, but when we got in the train station, the clock in the main terminal room said 3:25. That was way too early—we'd made *too* good time. We checked the clock in the ticket office. Sure enough, there it was: 3:25. Also, the schedule on the wall announced that the eastbound train would be thirty minutes late. I looked at the clock again; so did Bernice. It all meant that we had more than an hour to wait.

"We sat down in the main room across from the clock. Bernice jokingly suggested that we 'go into Alpha and make the clock jump ahead.' We laughed about this and recalled an earlier conversation about 'mashing' time up—that the past week seemed smashed between Bernice arriving and Bernice leaving.

"Then we got up and walked outside onto the plaform. I noticed a large wooden wagon shining in the sun near the right wing of the platform roof. It had wooden and metal trunks on it, and for some reason its presence reminded me of the train stations I'd seen in Europe. The two of us stood on the edge of the platform—no one else was around—and I recalled the train station in Innsbruck, Austria: especially the brilliant blue skies and looming mountains there. I gazed up the tracks, and briefly, one of those extremely vivid sense-memories came over me—the kind where smells, emotional impressions, even tactile sensations, rush over you—and it seemed that I was re-living Europe; that I was standing once again on that station platform in Innsbruck, where my twenty-year-old self had once stood, trying to sort out a million impressions and ghostly memories that could not rationally exist.

"At that moment, Bernice turned to me and said, 'You know, I've never been to Europe, but now this train station reminds me of Europe.'

"I laughed. 'Well, that's funny, because I've been standing here imagining that I'm in Europe,' I said. It was the kind of little ESP-communication we often experience between us. All of this took no more than ten minutes, if that.

"We turned to go back into the station — but we turned to face a crowd. All of the people were now outside on the platform! We walked past them, puzzled. As we got to the door, a uniformed man opened it up for us. 'About five minutes now,' he said, speaking directly to me. I had the weird momentary feeling that he was answering a question that I'd posed to him years before.

" 'Five minutes?' Bernice repeated, scowling. 'Five minutes to *what?*' I shrugged — another train, most likely. We went into the main terminal room and looked at the clock.

"*To our complete shock, it was quarter to five!*

"We stared at the clock, our mouths hanging open, stared at each other, and back at the clock. Numbly, without saying a word, we walked back onto the platform. I noticed then that the shadows from the right wing of the roof now covered the wooden trunk-wagon — which a few minutes before (by *my* reckoning) had been in total sunlight. In that minute, the eastbound train rumbled into view down the tracks.

"Everyone picked up their bags and filed on the train. Bernice and I just stared at each other, unable to articulate what we were feeling. Slowly, she let herself get caught up with the boarding passengers, and disappeared onto the train among them — all the while staring back at me. We didn't even exchange good-byes.

"Oddly, I'd recorded a dream on the night before this incident, in which I was supposed to meet a friend in Syracuse at 3:30, but overslept until 5:00. In the dream, the difference in time took on an almost *living* emphasis. Was this a hint of this weird 'lost' hour to come?"

The day after this incident was class night, and we spent the better part of the evening doing some alteration-of-consciousness experiments and a little table-tipping. I'd spent a few minutes describing the incident in the Syracuse train station, and when Seth appeared during a later conversation, I was secretly hoping that I'd have a chance to ask about it.

"Now, I am glad that you have all had such a jolly evening," Seth began. "In the table's energy, I hope that you saw a reflection of your own . . . Beneath the fun and games, feel your own vitality and get to know it. Enjoy its sensation."

With that, Seth turned to stare at me. "Let it bring you, as it did this week, to escape from ordinary ideas of time and limitations."

"Oh, wow," I responded, "then we *did* jump ahead in time—the train incident was valid?"

"It was indeed," Seth said, "and it was intended to lift you—as it did you [*to another student*] in your dreams—from the ordinary world that you know.

"Let it enable you to understand yourself better as you are [*to Marjorie*]. Let it show you portions of your own identity as it has [*to Bette*] with our cousin of Richelieu and our secretary over here [*to Natalie, who was recording the session*]. Let it lead into other aspects of consciousness and vitality, as it has with our friend over here [*to Helen*], and to open doors of feeling as it has with you [*to Alison*]. Let it bring families closer together as it has in your case [*to Janice*]. And let it above all also arouse questions, as it has with you [*to Arnold*] and with you [*to Joel*]; but realize again that this vitality that rings through this voice rings through your own identity: that the power beneath this voice is but a shadow of the vitality that is within each of you.

"Let it then give you confidence in your own identity and in your own reality. Move yourselves, and tables will take care of themselves."

This was not the only incident of "collapsible" time reported by class members, as I learned after I'd already drafted this Appendix. One hot summer Tuesday night, Matt Adams had agreed to drive Richie Kendall back to New York after class.

"But first," Matt recalls, "Richie and several others drove off for a dip in Florence MacIntyre's swimming pool. I was sitting behind the wheel of my car, in the bumpy driveway of Jane and Rob's apartment building, pointing head out and ready to go, wishing that Richie would get the hell back so I could start the journey home. But if we create our own reality, why couldn't I create that one? So I idly closed my eyes for a moment and concentrated on choosing the reality in which that station wagon would drive up, with Richie in it. And when I opened my eyes again, there it was, its side door opening to let out Richie and the others!

"Had I fallen asleep? I'm sure not, because I was particularly keyed up and impatient for the drive home. To my best estimate, my eyes weren't shut more than fifteen seconds—which hardly allowed Richie enough time to go to Florence's, take a swim, and be pulling back up on West Water Street."

APPENDIX EIGHT

Natal Therapy and the Joy of
Becoming: Seth in Class,
February 26, 1974

Born in Essen, Germany, in 1920, Elizabeth Fehr came to this country fleeing the Nazis. Later, she studied psychiatry on her own and was granted a license to practice psychology. In the 1960's, she established a live-in therapy center in New York City for homosexuals wanting to be "cured" of their gay orientation. Much of Elizabeth's work at this center involved her own Natal Therapy, a framework where patients were supposed to relive their birth experience—from which, Elizabeth believed, adult traumas sprang. Participants would crawl (laboriously!) down a long padded mat, ending the journey by being bathed in a tub of warm water. During this birth re-creation, many of Elizabeth's patients would regress to a psychological babyhood, recall the circumstances of their actual births (with many of these unknown details later confirmed by the patients' mothers), and experience a kind of rebirth—including, for some, a "new" heterosexuality.

By the time she visited Jane's class in February of 1974, Elizabeth's therapy work had attracted national attention among psychiatrists and psychologists. R. D. Laing and others in the self-awareness movement were observing her techniques and incorporating Natal Therapy into their own methods. Yet in spite of Elizabeth's achievements, her longtime friend George Rhoads notes that she was "insecure, hyperactive, in a panic about something at all times."

Attending class at George's urging, Elizabeth's explanation of her work inspired one of Seth's most unforgettable deliveries on the nature of physical existence. But pale and exhausted from the effects of a variety of lung ailments, Elizabeth would not live to see her group project through: three months after this class, she died in her sleep.

Class had been discussing dreams, out-of-bodies, and probabilities, when Elizabeth Fehr explained her Natal Therapy sessions and how these seemed to give almost instant help to her patients. Warren Atkinson then read from the last part of Chapter 10 in The Nature of Personal Reality.* *Seth interrupted, speaking primarily to Elizabeth:*

Now, excuse me. I have a few remarks to make, and this is the time to make them, for they are in reference to what you [*Warren*] have just read [*concerning natural therapies and the nature of beliefs*].

*Unpublished at the time of this class.

My dear friend [*to Elizabeth*], you are providing people with a framework in which you tell them that it is all right to feel the feelings that they have. You are dealing, then, with a group of beliefs. The people that come to you believe deeply that the reasons for their difficulties are beyond them, and that they cannot solve them for themselves. They have been stripped of a sense of their own integrity, for they do not believe in their own power.

Now, you provide them with your birth sequence; with a framework in which they can safely express feelings that they have. They do not feel that it is safe to do so otherwise. But you must also look beyond the beliefs and realize that you are indeed using a framework—a framework that they do indeed need; but then you must go beyond that for yourself, and for others. For you already suspect—and I know that you do—the initial belief in guilt that is behind your patients' difficulties. And it is that belief that you must, and will indeed, tackle.

Seth withdrew. Elizabeth started to tell Jane what had been said when Seth suddenly interrupted again:

Elizabeth, you are using a framework of belief, and in a creative manner. Now understand that I am saying that clearly. Beneath the framework of the belief, however, there is nothing "wrong" with birth. It is a joyful, aggressive experience. People accept the idea that their problems originate from birth because it is a belief system in which you and they agree. You use that belief system, then, and they need that system because they believe in it.

But you, for yourself and for them, must move also beyond it, and through it, where you realize that the idea is not valid in basic terms; that nature comes out of itself with great glory and validity and exuberance; and that that exuberance can be re-created, and is, whether they know it or not; and that your very therapy is filled with creativity and joy that itself comes from the energy of your own physical birth.

Now, I return you to the class, and to a little bit more at least of the [book] chapter.

Interpretation of Seth's remarks followed. Seth returned to comment:

Now, I enjoy the interpretation. In the vernacular, however, you [*Elizabeth*] are still hung up on a particular belief, and you do not understand your own magic. Your belief works, my dear lady, because you believe in it so thoroughly. But you are also a highly creative, imaginative person; so do not be hampered by the nature of your own beliefs, but go beyond them, and then you will find what *I* know you are after.

But I tell you now, there is nothing destructive in birth. When you have patients, however, who need to hang their guilt on something, and you give them birth to hang their guilt upon, then you can indeed help them, and relieve them, and provide a system for them. But you must, for yourself, feel free of the framework in which you find yourself, and allow your own joyous creativity to go beyond it; and not be so cowed by respectable psychiatrists or psychologists who now say, "Aha, yes, her methods work." But go beyond, for yourself and your patients, and enjoy your own creativity.

But here [*to the class*] you see someone [*Elizabeth*] who did indeed dare to take chances on her own beliefs. The only danger is that you [*Elizabeth*] allow those beliefs to blind you, become limiting, or that you accept the respectability that they can now afford you, and therefore feel too frightened to go beyond [your beliefs], and follow through in your own way.

The conscious mind has been given for a reason, and it holds the answers more clearly than you recognize. You [*Elizabeth*] have been taught and brainwashed to believe that the ideas are hidden; and so, out of the great compassion of your heart, you find frameworks through which patients can work, and without humiliation feel the natural feelings of their creaturehood. But *you* do not need the framework, and you can indeed work through it. Use it—use it, but work beyond it, and in doing so, you will understand your own joy and vitality.

Now, let an old ghost tell you that I have, again, been born in more times and places than Ruburt, at least, would like to admit. And let me tell you that birth is indeed an aggressive act; a joyfully aggressive act, and an intrusion into a new dimension; but it is one filled with the exhilaration of new existence . . . And if you are terrified of one birth, then how can I explain probabilities to you? How am I going to explain to you that you die and are reborn in every instant, and that you form the joyful reality of your own being out of the integrity of your intent, your spirit, and your flesh? The energy of my voice is nothing compared to the squalling exaltation of one child that travels from one dimension to another, and emerges victorious and yelling at the top of its lungs through the multidimensional channels of the womb!

Class started to relate Seth's words to Jane, when he abruptly returned:

Now, excuse me — I have a point I forgot to make.

Richie: "You forgot??"

I forgot! Now my dear friend . . . I never made any pretense at infallibility, and were it not for my quite fallible emotional reality, you would not relate to me at all!

Now, after that preamble: The danger, my dear lady [*Elizabeth*], is this. If your patients then do believe that birth is an unfortunate and dangerous experience, they will pass that idea on to their children, and it will therefore be perpetuated. You must see to it that that does not happen!

Now, infallible Seth, very fallibly, will return you to your fallible selves — if I have your permission, Dickie.

Class discussed Seth's remarks, and again he returned:

I do come back, because I want to untangle your own ideas [*to Elizabeth*] and your own feelings from what you have been taught. Now it is a universal idea on the part of psychiatrists and psychologists that birth is a terrifying experience, but any other human being knows better! You are indeed a creative and an intelligent and a beautiful mind and woman, but you have fallen for precepts that are unfortunate.

Now, listen to me, oh, lovely woman, for the men who threw these precepts upon you never gave birth. They were wrong. They did not give birth.

They interpreted their own experience for themselves, but not for humanity. And those ideas, and any ideas, have validity for individuals, but not generally for masses. Many individuals have had terrifying births. There have been many conditions where the infants have great difficulty being born, but that is not a universal condition — it cannot be generalized on the part of *each* individual child born.

Birth is itself a joyfully aggressive experience. You have been brainwashed — and you know it. But, even being brainwashed, you have creatively used what you have learned. I merely challenge you to listen to your own experience, and to forget what you have been told.

Already you have initiated new advances on the basis of precepts that do not hold water! Therefore, when you accept precepts that *do* hold water, what can you not do? Your own vitality is the only thing that gives success to your therapy. Therefore, be free enough to examine the nature of your beliefs and to accept your own creativity, and throw aside the ancient ideas upon which you have still managed to form creative therapies. Free yourself and your patients and your own creativity and forget the dusty theologies perpetuated upon you in the name of psychology and science. They are as dogmatic as any most fundamental religion against which you would stand and raise your voice in protest.

Listen to me! Because I recognize your creativity and energy, then realize what I am saying to you! You are cheating them when you give them your energy. You must teach them to feel instead the vast energy that was, in your terms, available to them at the time of their birth. You must allow them to leave you behind, lovely lady, and feel instead the fantastic charge of creative energy that *was* at the birth of the universe, and *is* now, and *was* at their own birth. You must lead them to feel that virgin—if you will forgive the term—that virgin and initial creative energy that would, then, in your terms, form being into new being in this system of reality.

You must teach them to feel the innate wisdom and knowledge of the fetus that grew without knowing how it grew; the innate wisdom that brought them from a fetus to a fully grown adult; the innate wisdom that allowed them to grow through the nights and the days, and to emerge from a seed into the blossom of adulthood; to sense within themselves that innate wisdom and energy that *was* at their birth, and *is* now—but they have been taught to forget it.

Put them in touch with the reality of the energy of their birth, and they shall indeed be freed, and they shall be freed to their own unique individuality and strength. That is what you must learn to do, and in so doing, because of your own beliefs, must you also put yourself in touch with the great joy and vitality of the fetus from which you yourself sprang, and identify with that triumph and that joy, and feel that energy still surging through the cells and atoms and the molecules of your being, leading you on to further creativity and strength and knowledge; and that is the direction that I hope you will follow and the direction that you feel.

After relating Seth's words to Jane, Warren continued to read Chapter 11 from the Personal Reality *manuscript. Seth again interrupted, turning to Elizabeth:*

Now, excuse me, and again, a P.S. to [my] last sentence. What is ignored in birth therapy is the sense of power on the part of the fetus that emerges into a new dimension of reality; that kicks and cries and though puny in physical terms, manages to travel through unknown dimensions into physical reality, and triumphs.

The birth experience is indeed an experience of power, and not of powerlessness. It is the emergence of consciousness into new, inviolate form. Only because you have been taught that a physical life is a time of trial and disaster and guilt does the framework that you are using work—and it *does work*. I am not denying the validity of the results, you see. If you were not so creative, you could be quite content with that framework, and you could indeed continue to do [your patients] good. But you are creative, and so you must not allow the framework to entrap you. You must rise beyond it, and become in touch with, at that moment of birth, the feeling of joyful aggression and great triumph with which the fetus so joyfully finds himself in the reality for which he was meant.

Through what dimensions of un-being, in your terms, has that fetus swum? Through what realities has he struggled to emerge, finally, victoriously, in your time and place, through the unique validity of the womb?

Then, let your patients feel that triumph, and through the birth experience, feel their own joy and uniqueness, and you will indeed triumph for yourself. And you will lead the field of psychiatry into new understanding, for you will have the credentials that they recognize.

Therefore, be not intimidated by those who know less than you do! Do not allow them to hamper your creativity because they say you are doing well now. Do not be afraid to go beyond that point.

Now, I return you all to your own grown fetuses, and I would like each of you to feel in touch indeed with your own birth, and realize that that birth was never finished with your physical birth, but is in each moment of your existence always re-enacted; and that you have now at your fingertips the same energy and the same joy that once drove you through unknown dimensions into this system of probabilities. You have within you now the same wisdom that grew you from a fetus to [an adult]. Know thyself, and do yourselves just honor.

I return you then to the true infallibility, which is the infallibility of your beings; and infallibility of your strength; the infallibility of your inner knowledge. You sit before me, and your energy is unassailable, and it is indeed infallible, and it is your right. Let yourselves not be robbed of it through beliefs.

Warren continued to read from Chapter 11. The sentence he read was, "You can learn more from watching the animals *than you can from a guru, or a minister, or from reading my book."* Seth interrupted:*

    —or from reading my book, or from listening to me. Therefore, always do I return you to the wisdom and spontaneity of yourself. My voice is a distorted echo of the sound of the leaves at eventime in April. I merely translate their meaning to you. I translate to you the rustling of the cells within your own bodies, to whom you do not listen. Therefore am I at the service of the universe, and I am a humble servant, translating the nature of the Earth, and your own natures, because you are too hasty to listen.

    You look for superior selves. You hope for senior selves; for spirits that know what you do not know; and yet I speak for the humblest cell within your body, to whom you do not listen. If you listened to the smallest leaf that falls upon an autumn walk, then you would know what I am saying; so I speak for the leaves, and the wind, and the cells within your body. I speak for the knowledge that you have! I speak for the strata of your own psyches. *You* are the superior selves toward which you struggle with such great seriousness, and you cannot understand that it is precisely that seriousness that cuts you off from the intimate knowledge of the playfulness of your own being.

    When my voice is needed no longer; when you realize my voice is unnecessary; when you realize that gurus have no truths that the leaves do not possess—then will you accept and experience the spirituality of your creaturehood; will you hear the voices of the god-hood through the falling rain; and will you listen to the echoes that speak within the strata of your being and the fossils of your knowledge.

    Therefore, though the words, in English, that I speak, even were they meaningless, so would the very spirituality within yourselves rouse to them and be lifted as the leaves in the autumn wind; and so would you emotionally understand, though the words I spoke were gibberish (as, indeed, in many cases they are, for they are couched along the lines of your own beliefs—but within those beliefs are the realities of your being!).

    Why do you think [*to Ira*] that you must go to a guru and be whipped; or that you [*to Elizabeth*] must lead your patients to a disastrous birth encounter in order that joy be encountered; or that any of you must encounter trials before you can become enlightened; or that you [*to George*] must struggle through the

*Page 237, *The Nature of Personal Reality*.

worlds of art to find your being; or that you [*to a visitor*] must come here feeling left out and alone . . . And our Lady of Florence also, who must, it seems, for now, be caught in a dilemma of beliefs, daring to believe and yet frightened to believe.

But each of you has, within yourselves, the vitality and the joy that came, in your terms now, consciously knowing—puny—into this world through the womb of a mother. And despite any difficulties that you encountered, [you] grew yourselves like any wise flower into grown adults.

Trust that spontaneous direction. Thank whatever gods you know that when you were two feet, five inches tall, you did not say, "What guru must I go to, to find out how to grow another inch?" You knew, and that knowing is joyfully within you now, and you do not need any old ghost to tell you. You only think that you do!

My purpose is to remind you of your own being; to put you in touch with what you have been taught to forget. It is, shortly, spring—and stupid flowers will be growing all over the Earth! They do not need to go to gurus or psychiatrists or priests or teachers or me to say, "How will I manage to get one poor, puny leaf out?" And you have within yourselves that same joyful knowledge.

I am simply a touchstone for you; a point of energy and focus in the universe that reminds you of your own reality. I return you, then, to that vitality, to that wisdom. I feel your breath [*to Rudy, who was sitting on the floor by Jane's chair*] against Ruburt's arm, and when you breathe spontaneously, without your conscious calculation, you preserve your life, your being, and your knowledge. *Trust the breath of your being.*

Shortly after Elizabeth's death in May of that year, George Rhoads asked Seth in class why she had chosen to leave physical reality. Seth answered: "She feared, in the framework in which she was existing, the integrity of her own being. She felt that what she was, was wrong. In her own way, she was a perfectionist, and she could not bear to be that which was wrong. Neither could she see her way out of her career beliefs.

"She'd received acclaim for ideas that she realized basically were leading her only further into a maelstrom. She felt therefore that it was easier, under those conditions, to leave and to begin again.

"And she is doing all right!"

APPENDIX
NINE

Counterparts Who Dream:
Libraries of Probability

The notion of counterparts hadn't entered our conscious awareness in the fall of 1971, but my dreams of the York Beach couple (as related in Chapter 16) had fired up my interest in probabilities: It seemed that all I had to do to spark vivid dream adventures was to suggest a "York Beach experience" before falling asleep—and I'd soon find myself fully alert, in some probability excursion that I'd remember well enough to record in detail upon waking.

It was an exciting time in my dream life; my consciousness thrilled with daring, joy, and uninhibited fascination. And one of the intriguing dream series of that time involved "the library." This library was always situated in the little wooded area behind my parents' house that we called "the Lower Garden," and I always got there in a fully awake, out-of-body state. After drifting off toward sleep, I'd quite consciously decide to leave my body and float down the Lower Garden path to the place where this library existed. I'd turn around a "corner" in the air, and the landscape would simply open up, like a cubistic door, and reveal the library's interior, with groups of people within going about their work. As I've stated in previous pages, I didn't relate any of these library dreams to Jane at the time.

Much later, in late 1974, Jane started receiving information from a library that "opened up" in a corner of her living room. Her experiences there led to her *Psychic Politics*, much as my dream experiences would lead me to my own contemplation of identity—and this book. But aside from my feeling that these charged "corners" represent the coordinate-point phenomena discussed in *Seth Speaks*, I think it's fascinating to compare the inner experiences of those involved in counterpart relationships—as Seth asserts of Jane and me.

Do our experiences simply reflect the symbolism dear to the hearts of two writers, and nothing more? My feeling is that by virtue of the fact that both Jane and I *used* these inner events as springboards for creative work in the physical world, more than daydream symbols was automatically involved—if "use" is indeed a yardstick for validity, in those terms. In other ways, the attention and exploration such events inspire as to the nature of personality—what is it that counterparts *actually mean* in daily terms, for example—brings out the new order of logic in these experiences all over again. Like Jane's "Sue Watkins" character in *The Chestnut Beads*, one's dreams and psychic events pose all kinds of questions. What *are* the boundaries of coincidence? How much information *do* we possess about our existence? How is it that we process this information into the results we call daily life?

From my notes of September 26, 1971, I'll relate the first of this library-dream series; it's interesting to compare it with Jane's library-visions as recorded in *Psychic Politics:*

"I floated down the Lower Garden path, knowing that I was projecting. The bend in the path opened up in front of me, and I could see a huge library beyond. This didn't surprise me at all—it seemed very logical and appropriate. I knew, looking inside that place, that the word 'dream' was a misnomer. This was a 'real' place that had been somehow going on for years beneath my sensual awareness. I tried to recall my waking days in a logical sequence, but there didn't seem to be one—or if there were, it was hidden beneath another kind of sequence that swirled in and around itself, having nothing to do with the march of days and weeks; and yet, this was the stuff I built my notion of time upon.

"I walked into the library. The main room was large, lined with tiers of bookshelves, and divided up into sections by more bookshelves that came out from the walls. It was a warm and secure-feeling place, filled with book-nooks and tables piled with lovely old leather and gilt-leaf volumes. But the room also had a peculiar quality of largeness and smallness all at once—vast and high-ceilinged, but small and cozy and warm, too. The knowledge that this place was infinite—that I might even be able to directly perceive infinity through it—frightened me a little, and probably accounted for the cozy book-nooks that fell neatly into place as I looked around. A woman smiled at me from her position behind a card-covered desk.

"I could see that the library was filled with people going about bookish business, doing research, writing, copying things. I walked down one aisle of books, trying to memorize their titles, and saw Linda B., an old friend from high school days. I hadn't seen her in several years, but she often appeared in my dreams—and always seemed to know what was going on in them when I didn't.

"'Hi,' she said, 'how have you been?'

"'Just fine,' I answered. 'Uh—I guess you know that this is a dream?'

"She laughed, as though I had said something that was really funny, and shook her head. 'Of *course* it is,' she said. 'Or at least that word will do for now, won't it?'

"'Who are these others?' I asked, indicating the people wandering around the book stacks.

"'The Outer Circle and the Inner Circle,' Linda said, watching me closely.

"'Outer and Inner Circles, huh?' I teased, a little annoyed. 'That sounds kind of exclusive, doesn't it?'

"'Words,' she said. 'Just words. Go find your friends. Your classmates are here too.'

"'What are you working on?' I asked.

"Linda gestured at one of the books on the table. I saw that one was open to a page which was either hand-printed in beautiful blue and golds, or else had been made on an extraordinary printing press. The first letter of the first word was elaborately drawn, with tiny animals and gnomes sitting on it, something like the ancient illuminated manuscripts. 'That's beautiful,' I said, 'what are you doing with it?'

"'Translation,' Linda grinned. 'I think your interest is more in the lines of travel, isn't it?'

"'Well, we all got here somehow,' I joked, but at that moment, my interest was drawn away, as though some crazy magnet were tugging on my skull, toward a door that opened in the wall to my left. I walked through it.

"The door opened out onto a street, and I stepped into a warm, sunny day, the street of worn and yellowed cobblestone. Directly across from me was a huge, round building with an enormous domed roof. I knew immediately that I was in Florence, Italy. I had seen this building during a brief tour I'd taken of Florence in the summer of 1965: the Duomo.[1] I remembered standing in front of the physical Duomo, wondering, for some reason, if you could ride a bicycle around the top of its fluted dome. Well, maybe now, in this state, I mused, I could try it out.

"As I stood there gazing at the building, a young boy, perhaps fourteen, walked up to me. He was dressed in brightly colored clothes: a brilliant lavender silk tunic-top that came to his mid-thigh, with slightly puffed sleeves and a waist belt; dark blue leggings; soft brown shoes. He was small and thin, but obviously healthy and well taken care of. His light brown hair was cut squarely around his angular face, and his hands were long and delicate. I wondered if this were my idea of the young Michelangelo character from *The Agony and the Ecstasy*.

"'Greetings,' he said cheerfully.

"'Hi,' I said, feeling a little wary of him.

"'You know where you are?' he asked.

"'It looks like the city of Florence. Who are you?'

"'Petro,' he said. 'I know who *you* are.'

"'Oh, really?' There I was, once again, in the middle of people who knew what was going on in my dreams! 'What century is this?' I asked him, indicating the Duomo, which, I noticed, had a suspiciously brand-new look about it.

"'The fifteenth, approximately, in your reckoning,' he said, 'although it's really quite unrecognizable to your historians now.'

"The fifteenth century? The library door had led me back in time also, then. I looked back. The door was still there, in the wall of a rough wooden house, people inside, wandering through the books on their own business.

"'Do you go in there?' I asked Petro, indicating the library.

"'Oh, yes,' he said, 'but half the time I forget what I'm doing. Want to look around?'

"'You don't talk like a fifteenth-century person,' I pointed out.

"'Well, you're not familiar with how a fifteenth-century person *would* talk,' Petro answered. 'This is *your* conversation, after all.'

"'My conversation?'

"'Sure. From my side of the fence, it's completely different. You should hear it.'

"We walked around the big round building. Two large, thick doors were open behind it. I expected to find the same interior as I'd seen in my physical world's Duomo, but as we walked inside, I saw that it was cut up into tiny, windowless rooms, all turned in on themselves like a giant rat-maze. Somewhere up above us, a chorus of voices was singing a medley of weird arias.

"'This doesn't look like any building I'd expect to find in Florence,' I grumbled to Petro.

"'This isn't the Florence *you* would expect to find.' he said. 'This Florence didn't go the way your Florence did. The Renaissance here took an entirely different direction. You can see the results all around you.'

"'What direction did it take?' I said, feeling the implications of his words rumble through me. Somehow, I was catching the thread of this Florence and its environment—whatever its exact material appearance, I could sense a world that had escaped, in my terms, the great religious emphasis of the Renaissance. 'It would go along with my personality to find myself here,' I stated smugly.

"'But it also goes along with your personality that you should be alive in a history that includes the "Florence" as you think of it,' Petro countered, smiling at me.

"'Let's go outside,' I said. 'I want to see more—I want to see the art, especially the paintings.'

"We walked together down a little corridor, out the door

and back into the sunny street. I checked the library door—it was still there. I must need that reassurance, I thought; I've never done this kind of thing before. I wondered if I could get back to my physical body, lying in its bed back there someplace, if I lost the door to that library. Suddenly, the possibility of this happening became too great a worry. I stopped.

"'What's the matter?' Petro asked.

"'I'm sorry,' I said, 'I think I have to wake up now. I don't want to get too far away from that doorway.'

"Petro shrugged. 'I should probably wake up myself,' he said.

"'You mean you're asleep too?' I asked, suddenly knowing it. 'You're from the history with this other Florence behind it, aren't you?'

"Petro laughed 'But we still have things in common obviously.'

"Something was pulling at me, and I was giving in. 'I'll be back,' I said to him, 'will you?'

"'If not here, then maybe we can find another place,' he said. With that, I floated away from him, back into the library, past the bookshelves and the smiling librarian (who waved at me as I went by), back out the Lower Garden 'door,' up the path, and into my bedroom, where I woke with a jolt to find strange furniture—velvet-covered and beautifully carved straight-backed chairs—sitting in my room.

"I sat up and stared at the chairs. I was wide awake, but these chairs were not mine. All at once, a voice came down out of the ceiling, saying, in an amused tone, 'You were so energetic that you pulled a few symbols back with you.' An odd tingle went through me, and the chairs vanished, Cheshire-Cat-like, from the room.

"I lay back down and fell into a light sleep, waking a few minutes later, light-headed, excited, and utterly entranced."

NOTES FOR APPENDIX NINE
   1. The Duomo, or the Cathedral of Santa Maria del Fiore, is one of the most prominent buildings in the city of Florence. Designed by the architect Filippo Brunelleschi, the Duomo was begun in 1296 and finally consecrated in 1436—a fact of the fifteenth century that I didn't know until I looked up the above information for this footnote.

INDEX

NOTE: All references below page 291 pertain to Volume One of *Conversations With Seth.*